Keep the Faith

Keep the Faith

A Memoir

FAITH EVANS

with ALIYA S. KING

GC

GRAND CENTRAL
PUBLISHING

NEW YORK   BOSTON

Grand Central Publishing
Hachette Book Group USA
237 Park Avenue
New York, NY 10017

Printed in the United States of America

Grand Central Publishing is a division of
Hachette Book Group USA, Inc.
The Grand Central Publishing name and logo
is a trademark of Hachette Book Group USA, Inc.

ISBN: 978-0-446-19950-6

Contents

Keep the Faith

Prologue

$\mathcal{I}$ thought I had more time. And it was already too late.

On a late night in March 1997, I was in a car with my girlfriends, climbing up the Hollywood Hills on the way to a party.

"You gon' call Big and let him know you coming?" my friend Toni asked.

"I'll see him when we get there," I said, trying my best to look unconcerned.

Toni just rolled her eyes. "Whatever. You know you can't wait to see him. What if he's acting funny?"

I smiled. "He better speak to me. He knows what's up."

We joked and laughed as we parked the car and made our way up the private driveway of a house that music executive Andre Harrell had rented for an event. Before I could get very close, a car driving away from the property stopped next to me. Inside was rapper Heavy D.

"Faith," he said to me. "You need to get to the hospital."

I didn't immediately think about the shots I'd heard earlier. "The hospital... for what? What's wrong?"

"Faith. Get back in the car. You need to get to the hospital."

Heavy's face was serious, and I felt my throat tighten and my heart start to race.

Heavy D answered my question before I could ask it.

"I think something happened to Big."

Sometimes, it seems like Los Angeles is some kind of magical land where nothing can go wrong. I'm from Newark, New Jersey—a place where there are four seasons. Some days are bright and sunny; some are dark, rainy, and cold. There can be two feet of snow piled at your front door, waiting to be shoveled. Or you can be stuck in a heat wave with no air-conditioning, struggling to stay dry.

But the City of Angels is different. The constant sunshine and ocean views can make me feel like anything is possible. When I arrived, one week before the party in the Hollywood Hills, it felt like the kind of day when nothing could go wrong.

I was in town for a week of parties and events surrounding the Soul Train Music Awards. I flew out with my infant son, CJ, planning to make the usual music industry rounds while doing a bit of publicity on local radio and television stations.

But I had more on my mind than just work.

The Notorious B.I.G.—CJ's father and my estranged husband, the man I called Big—would also be in town. His sophomore album, *Life After Death*, would be released in three weeks, and he was in town to present at the awards and promote his new CD.

Big and I weren't together. And we hadn't been for some time. In fact, I knew that he was dating someone new. We were still married but we were moving on. I'd met this great guy named Todd whom I was really feeling. We planned to go out while I was in LA. And yet, Big and I had been through so much together. We'd fallen in love fast and hard. He loved my daughter like he loved his own. And I'd given birth to our son just four months before. We had a bond that could not be ignored—no matter how hard either of us tried.

I was so young. And in a lot of ways, even though I'd lived enough for two women, I was still a bit immature. I remember on that night, my plan was to run into Big and let him see that I was doing fine without him. I knew we'd cross paths at a few of the parties. And I wanted to make sure he saw me looking cute and having a great time. As a matter of fact, I felt like I needed the entire music industry to see that. With all the whispering being done behind my back for a number of reasons, I wanted people to know that I wasn't hiding, I wasn't afraid, I wasn't heartbroken, and I was still having the time of my life.

The official afterparty for the Soul Train Awards, sponsored by *Vibe* magazine, was held in the Petersen Automotive Museum. Earlier that day, I'd gone to a celebrity basketball game with a few of my girlfriends; after dropping off my son at the home of my girlfriend's mother, we were off to the museum.

During the ride, we smoked a blunt and I began to relax and let my mind wander. I thought about how my friends would make sure to let me know exactly when Big walked into the room. Or perhaps the DJ would announce his arrival by playing "One More Chance," one of his biggest hits and a song I sang background vocals on. I also thought about Todd. I knew he'd be there. We'd been seeing each other whenever we could. And we'd planned to go hang out that weekend while I was in town.

For some reason, I wasn't dressed up at all that night. I'd always taken pride in my appearance—especially at industry events. But that night, I wore a sweat suit in a fatigue pattern and a pair of Timberland construction boots. Looking back, I know I probably dressed that way because I was on high alert.

There were so many misconceptions circulating about me at the time. And everyone thought they knew the real story about my relationship with Big; my rumored relationship with his sworn enemy Tupac; my son with Big; my beef with Lil' Kim—I had taken a beating in the court of public opinion.

And honestly, I was ready to fight the first person who said the wrong thing to me. I wasn't looking over my shoulder that night. But I was ready for whatever.

We got to the party early, and Big wasn't there. I kept to my friends as we drank and smoked, trying to look like we were paying no attention to whoever came in. But of course, we all had our eyes peeled. By the time Big came in with his entourage, the place was crowded enough that we couldn't see each other.

Before long, a friend of Big's came up to me, asking me if I'd seen Big. I knew instantly that he'd been sent to scout me out. He smoked with us for a little while and then slipped back into the crowd. From where I stood, I watched him walk toward a doorway leading to a larger room with more guests. I knew Big was in there, and I thought about going over to him.

Through the years, I've thought a lot about why I didn't go over and speak to Big that night. Part of it had to be pride—I've got a lot of it. And I wasn't about to look like I was playing myself out. *Please.* Walking through a crowded party to see *him*? I don't think so. I needed him to see *me*. I never actually decided I wasn't going to talk to Big. I just figured I'd have all night to run into him and say a few words.

And then I saw Todd and started talking to him and his friends when they came by to say hello. But it was hard to forget Big's presence. Especially since the DJ played Big's new single, "Hypnotize," on repeat for the entire night.

There was talk of an after-afterparty in the Hollywood Hills, and I needed no convincing. As I headed to the car with my friends, we heard some commotion coming from the exit to the museum. I thought I heard someone say something about shots ringing out, but we were able to get into our car and out of the lot with no problem, so we didn't think twice about it. Our driver had followed a long line of cars up La Cienega Boulevard and into the Hollywood Hills.

Oh God…oh God…oh God…oh…God. Please let him be okay. Please please let him be okay…

I barely remember the ride from the Hollywood Hills to the hospital. I just remember rocking back and forth and mumbling and praying to myself. I was trying to think positive. Just because Big was shot didn't mean that the worst had happened. He could just be wounded. Could be sitting right there in the waiting room with his arm bandaged up. And then I could just run up to him and throw my arms around him and give him a hug and a kiss.

The car drove right up to the front entrance to the emergency room, where a small crowd had formed. I spotted some random faces that looked familiar, but I didn't see the main people I needed to see: Puff, Lil' Cease, D-Roc—the people who could tell me what was going on.

There were police officers and security guards keeping people from coming into the hospital. And then I saw an old friend of mine, DJ Rogers, standing near the front door.

"That's his wife," he said, walking over toward me and leading me to one of the officers standing guard. "She needs to go inside."

I was ushered through the emergency room and into a smaller waiting room. Inside was Sean "Puffy" Combs, the head of my record label. Mark Pitts, Big's manager, was sitting next to him. There was also Stevie J, one of Bad Boy's producers; Paul, the security guard who traveled with Bad Boy; and Damion "D-Roc" Butler, one of Big's best friends. They were all sitting there with blank faces. And they all had their heads down, looking at the floor.

Oh God…please…please let him be okay. I will stay with him tonight. I will. Forget all this arguing. I'll go get CJ. We can go out for breakfast or something…

Puffy was the first person to come over to me. He was walking so slowly and his lips were pursed so tight that it looked like he was physically in a lot of pain.

"Puff, what happened? What's going on? Where's Big? Is he okay?"

Puff looked up at me. "Faith…" His voice trailed off and he closed his eyes.

"I'm gonna let the doctor talk to you."

Puff left the room and came back with a tall, older white man.

"This is his wife," Puff said to the doctor. Then he returned to his seat.

"Mrs. Wallace," the doctor said. "We tried to revive your husband. We massaged his heart several times to get it beating again but we were unsuccessful."

"What are you saying?" I asked him.

"The bullets ricocheted through his body. We could not revive him."

"You're not going to try again? You have to try again!"

"Mrs. Wallace, we can't."

The doctor never used the word *dead*. But it hit me. Big was gone. The enormity of what had happened started to slip over me and I began to shake uncontrollably. For some reason, I didn't cry, I just panicked. I was wearing several rings at the time and I just started yanking them off and dropping them on the floor.

Someone led me to a chair. I sat down. And I wept quietly for twenty minutes. My husband and the father of my newborn son was dead. All the tension that had been building over the past year had reached a cataclysmic end. In that moment I felt like I'd known all along that something tragic was bound to happen.

It's been over ten years since Big was killed. I grieved for a very long time. And then, as time passed, the icy wall of grief surrounding my heart began to thaw and I began to heal.

I remarried, had more children, and continued to record and release more music. I continued to live my life. And while I can never discount the time I spent with Big, I've never felt the need to live in the past.

But sometimes, I still find myself thinking about Big being rushed into that hospital, and I break down in tears.

It's not just because we hung up on each other during what would be our last telephone conversation. And it's not because the last time I saw him, I barely glanced his way. And it's not even because I am raising our son, a young man who has never known his father.

It's partly all of those things. But mainly, it's because he wasn't ready to go. His debut album was called *Ready to Die*. But in the end, he wasn't.

Big never got a chance to tell his story. It's been left to others to tell it for him.

In making the decision to tell my own story, it means that I've become one of those who can give insight to who Big really was. But I can only speak on what he meant to me.

Yet I also want people to understand that although he was a large part of my life, my story doesn't actually begin or end with Big's death. My journey has been complicated on many levels. And since I am always linked to Big, there are a lot of misconceptions about who I really am.

I hope that in reading my words, there is inspiration to be found. Perhaps you can duplicate my success or achieve where I have failed. Maybe you can skip over the mistakes I've made. Use my life as an example — of what to do and in some cases, what *not* to do.

It's not easy putting your life out there for the masses. But I've decided I'll tell my own story. For Big. For my children. And for myself.

CHAPTER ONE

Let the Sun Shine In

I stood straight ahead, facing the back of Emanuel Baptist Church. My hands were at my sides, and my whole body was stiff. I stared at a spot on the back wall and sang out as loud as I could.

"Sing it girl!" someone said. I saw some random hands flying up in the air.

"Go on, girl! Sing that song!"

More arms were raised, and I saw folks looking at me with bright smiles and wide eyes. I took in a sharp breath to belt out the chorus to my favorite song.

I was three years old, performing for the first time for the congregation at Emanuel Baptist Church. After seeing the reaction of my first audience, I knew I would be a singer. I wasn't sure how it was going to happen. But I knew I'd found my calling.

Since that day, I've performed around the world, earning critical acclaim, platinum record sales, and legions of loyal fans. But no matter how far I travel or how large my audience becomes, so much of what makes me who I am begins with the city where I made my debut performance.

I'm from Newark, New Jersey. It's nicknamed the Brick City because of the housing projects that were erected in the 1930s and '40s. Although many of the projects have been replaced by condominiums and single-family homes, the nickname remains. It fits: Bricks are tough and unforgiving. And they are building blocks. It's an accurate way to describe the city—and the people—that raised me.

I can't remember coming into Newark for the first time. I was less than a year old. I was born in Lakeland, Florida. My mom, Helene, was only eighteen years old and barely out of high school when I was born. At the time, she was living in nearby Dade City, Florida, with her mother; her twin sister, Hope; and her younger siblings, Missy and Morgan.

From what I hear, my mom and her twin sister were something to behold down in Dade City, a very poor area with a large concentrations of black folks. The nearest major city is Tampa, nearly an hour away.

My mom and her twin sister were very popular with everyone, black and white. They were personable, outgoing, and musically talented.

All I know about my father is that his name is Richard Swain. And that he was from the area and dabbled in music like my mom, who was a singer. I've heard people mumble something about him being Italian but I don't know for sure. I do know that he was white. I remember hearing my aunts talking about me, thinking that I couldn't hear them. They'd say stuff like, "You see how light she is. It's 'cause her daddy's a white man." Or I might be dancing at someone's house and I'd hear someone say, "Poor girl. Can't dance for nothing. Guess that's 'cause of that white daddy she got. Gave her that flat butt, too."

I don't know what happened with his relationship with my mom. All I know is that I've never met him. A few years ago, I looked up the name *Richard Swain* and found several listings in the St. Petersburg area. My mom seemed to think it could be him, so I sent letters to the addresses. But they all came back to me with an ADDRESSEE UNKNOWN stamp.

So I don't know where he is. I think he knows who I am. If he still lives in Florida, where I have tons of family members, it would be pretty hard not to know. It ain't too many towns he could be living in and escape running into *someone* from my family.

I haven't really talked to my mom to get the real deal on what happened in that relationship or to get any details about my father. I've never really lacked a father figure. So perhaps that's why I've never been too stressed about finding him.

I think it's pretty interesting that he's never popped up. Lots of times, when someone experiences some degree of fame, all kinds of family members start coming out of the woodwork. But so far, Richard Swain is still a mystery.

Being biracial was never really an issue with me. I was raised 100 percent black and have always considered myself a black woman. Because I am very light in complexion, I've often been asked if I'm mixed. So it has always been something I'm conscious of. But it never really affected me in any significant way. Ironically, I even have Irish and Puerto Rican branches in my family tree, spread out through Brooklyn. My uncle Dock married an Irish woman and their children intermarried in the Latino community.

My mom's an interesting character. I've learned so much from her, and we have a lot in common. She's always been willing to go it alone and give a big F-you to anyone who tried to stop her or criticize her. And she's never let anything said about her deter her from what she needed to do. In many ways I've adopted that same stance, and it's served me well.

I look like my mom in some ways. We both have one small mole in the same place. And I definitely inherited her wide hips and her sharply defined full lips. For years, she wore a short Afro and then began to let it grow, allowing it to frame her caramel complexion like a halo.

Most importantly, I inherited her love for music. My career in music is definitely a by-product of being Helene Evans's daughter. My mom performed in a few bands when I was growing up. I didn't hang out with her too much when she was performing, so I didn't catch the bug from actually seeing her perform. Although my gift ultimately comes from God, I know it was sent through my mom.

Helene Evans was a bit of a hippie back in the day. She hung with a multiracial crowd and loved rock and folk music. And she didn't let my birth stop her from continuing to try to pursue her music career. When I was a newborn, we lived with my maternal grandmother, Helen Arnold. I don't remember too much about my grandmother. She died when I was very young. I do remember that her house in Dade City always smelled like Pine-Sol. Aunt Hope had cats, so my grandmother was a bit of a fanatic about keeping the house clean.

From what I hear, my grandma Helen was a real spitfire. She worked in a numbers house and had a very fiery and feisty personality. I do know she was beautiful. I have a painting of her that one of her brothers did. And she was very fly. I'm not sure if I have much in common with Grandma Helen. But I do know we may have had the same taste in men. One of my aunts recently told me that Grandma Helen once dated a man everyone called Uncle Biggie.

Grandma Helen told all her children that once she was done raising kids, she was done for good. And that she would not help out any of her children who decided to have babies before they were ready. She wasn't doing no babysitting. And she wasn't going to let her kids live up in her house with their babies, either.

After my birth, I think there was a lot of pressure on my mom to get her act together. She didn't have a career, but she always worked two or three jobs.

My mom was still a teenager when she had me. And she had this passion to sing and to perform. So being a single mom was tough. Lucky for me, she met Bob and Mae Kennedy, the couple who would end up raising me.

Now, I've always called Bob and Mae Kennedy my grandparents when I'm doing interviews because it's just easier that way. But they're not my grandparents. It's just so difficult to explain how exactly we're related. To make a very long story short, my great-uncle married Mae's aunt. So Mae and Bob Kennedy are really my cousins.

After moving up north in the '60s, Mae and Bob often drove down to Dade City to visit family. In December 1973, they came down to visit and ended up at my aunt's house. My cousin Pee Wee, whom I call my aunt Pee Wee, was watching me for the day and, as the story goes, Mae Kennedy took one look at me in Pee Wee's arms and fell in love.

Mae held me in her arms and told Pee Wee what a pretty baby I was. Mae and Pee Wee got to talking about how my mom was so busy working and trying to get on her feet. I'm not sure how the whole discussion went down. But somehow, after a few conversations back and forth between Mae, Pee Wee, and my mom, Mae offered to take care of me until my mom got on her feet with her own apartment and a better job. My mom agreed. And Mae and Bob brought me to Newark, New Jersey, at the end of 1973.

In the mid-'70s, Newark was still sliding into the decline that began with the riots in 1967. Throughout my childhood there, the population would continue to decrease as white families made a beeline to the suburbs. The closing of factories in Newark would lead to a loss of jobs, bringing in larger numbers of poor folks. But for the most part, I was insulated from the changes that were taking place in the neighborhood. My entire universe centered on the white, single-family house near the end of Grumman Avenue in the Weequahic section of Newark.

My earliest memories are at the Emanuel Baptist Church, a

few blocks away from Grumman, over on Chancellor Avenue. My grandparents had been members for many years and I was quickly enrolled in many church activities, including Vacation Bible School and, of course, services every Sunday.

When I was three, my favorite television show was *The Flintstones*. And there was this episode where Pebbles and Bamm-Bamm performed "Let the Sun Shine In." I would go around the house singing that song all the time. By the tender age of three, I already had an anthem. And then, at preschool, my teacher Miss Henry heard me singing and encouraged me to learn all the words to the song.

And that's how I ended up singing for the first time in church.

But before I could even get my first solo, I got a taste of the music business. After my first performance, there was some talk of putting me in the children's choir. I was only three years old. And the minimum age was five. But I was entered into the choir anyway. Immediately, there were grumbled complaints from other members in the church. I was too young for anyone to have said anything to me directly. But I heard my grandparents talking about it.

"Should we still let her join? Some folks are saying she should have to wait," Mae said to my mom.

By this time, my mother had moved to New Jersey from Florida and was staying at my grandparents' house while she looked for a place to live.

"If they want her to be in the children's choir, why shouldn't she be?" my mom asked.

"I don't know, Helene," Mae said. "I just don't want folks to be upset."

My mom sucked her teeth and rolled her eyes. "If she's good enough to be in the choir and they *want* her to be in it, then that's that. Whoever don't like it—fuck 'em."

It may not have been a very church-like attitude, but my mom was keeping it real. Her abrasive and direct approach to life was a sharp contrast with Mae and Bob, who were very laid-back and easygoing and didn't like to make waves. Over the years, I'd learn to incorporate both of their ways into my own lifestyle.

For the first few years on Grumman Avenue, it was just me, Mae and Bob, their son Ronnie, and my aunt Pee Wee. Later their son Fred and an adopted daughter, Rhonda, would join them.

I still went down to visit my mom occasionally in Florida. At one point, before she came to New Jersey for good, she was living in a house in Santa Ana, Florida, with a few white folks she was cool with. I vaguely remember the house; there were goats on the property. I can remember my mom giving me goat's milk to drink, still warm and fresh from the udder.

My peoples in Dade City were straight-up unapologetic country folk. I came down to visit my mom when I was about six years old and ended up at the home of one of my aunts. It was either Sylvia or her sister Nita. I'm standing out on the porch when I look into the house and see her son and my uncle wrestling with a burlap sack.

"Kill that possum!" I remember Aunt Sylvia telling the boys.

The possum got out of the sack and started running around the house. I watched—in horror—as the guys chased the possum around with a hoe in their hands.

"Get 'im now!" Aunt Sylvia said. "That's good meat right there! Don't let him get away!"

They cornered the possum and then beat the animal to death with a hoe. I was so scared. I watched as they burned the hair off the animal and then prepared to skin it. I didn't watch that part. Dinner that night was a stew with hunks of meat inside.

"Faye," my Aunt Sylvia said. "You not having no stew? It's good!"

"No thank you," I said. "I'm not hungry."

To this day, my aunt Sylvia will pull over if she's driving and sees a turtle—dead or alive—on the side of the road. And dinner will be turtle soup.

Obviously, Dade City was a completely different atmosphere from Newark. Dade City was laid-back, Newark was bustling. Dade City was country while Newark was the very definition of urban. In Florida, I would run around outside barefoot and explore on my own. In Newark, I was always supervised and never left the house without an adult chaperone.

But the house on Grumman Avenue was my home base. And while I was doted on by Mae and Bob, I was by no means the only child there. That house would continue to fill up with random folks for the entire time I lived there. Mae and Bob would eventually take in over one hundred foster children. There were *at least* four children and teenagers living there all the time. Some, like me, were family members. Others were official foster children placed by the Department of Youth and Family Services. And others were unofficial foster children.

And on top of running a large household and working at a factory, Mae also babysat various neighborhood children while their parents were at work — or just out and about. I noticed early on that Mae's kindness was often taken for weakness. She is such a good-hearted person. She's always trying to do the right thing and help people out. I love that about her. But at the same time, I hated watching her being taken advantage of. After a week of watching someone's badass kids, I'd see the parent pick them up at the end of the week and no money would change hands.

My grandmother wasn't the type to set an amount, charge someone, and be sure to collect. She was just doing things out of the kindness of her heart. But we didn't have money like that. She definitely could have used the extra. There was always something in the house that needed fixing. For the entire twenty years that I lived in that house, the shower on the second floor didn't work. And Bob was constantly adding on bedrooms in the basement to accommodate the growing household.

I watched her being used by people who should have known better and made a mental note at a very young age not to do that to her or to let that ever happen to me.

My grandparents kept me very sheltered in my early years. There were three places you could find Faith Renée Evans: Louise A. Spencer Elementary School over on Muhammad Ali Avenue in the Central Ward, Emanuel Baptist Church, and the house on Grumman Avenue. If you saw me anywhere else, it was probably church- or school-related. Socially, they would let me go to my friend Courtney Terry's house. They liked her parents and knew she was a good girl.

My grandparents were very, very strict. Particularly my grandmother. There was no secular music in the house. And because there were so many foster children in and out of the house, there were a lot of household rules so that they could try to keep some kind of order.

The one place where it was incredibly hard to shield me from drama was the apartment building on the corner of Grumman and Elizabeth Avenue.

My grandmother's best friend, Mrs. Hayes, lived in that building on the third floor. She had eleven kids, and some of the younger ones were my friends. Although my grandmother was okay with me befriending Mrs. Hayes's children, I was not supposed to be in that building. Now, I was a good girl, and for the most part I did what I was told. But there is something very alluring about an apartment building where it seems like the families are just a little bit more lax.

Mae and Bob did not spare the rod. And just about every spanking I did get as a young girl was because of something that went on in or around that apartment building. I'd get on my bike to go for a ride with Shonda and Penny, two of Mrs. Hayes's kids, and somehow end up three towns over in Roselle. My granddad might get out the thick alligator belt for a stunt like that. Or perhaps I'd end up playing Spin the Bottle or Truth or Dare with some neighborhood boys. If word got out about something like that, my grandmother would get a switch from a tree and wear me out. And my mother would too.

It didn't matter. I still found myself spending lots of time with my folks in that building. They were all a little faster than me—they had lots of siblings, lots of exposure to pop culture, and spent a lot more time on their own. So being over at that apartment was always a real education, and it helped me to grow up a bit faster. At home, it was Sunday-morning prayer circles and gospel music. But just a few feet away, there was hip-hop, little boys trying to play Catch-a-Girl, Get-a-Girl, and old-school soul music, from the Delphonics and Blue Magic to the house music that had trickled down from Chicago to Newark. My grandmother would warn me that most of the kids in the building were troublemakers. (Which I knew—that's why it was so fun to be there.)

My mother would also warn me that some of the kids I wanted to hang out with seemed cool, but weren't really my friends.

She had a point. I noticed early on that the people who were supposed to be my friends would always show their true colors at some point.

Folks who seem like they want to befriend you may have ulterior motives. They might want to be close to you just to use you. Or they may be jealous of you and want to keep you nearby to demean you. I experienced all of that—and more.

(When I got into the music industry, I would again experience this several times, with both famous and not-so-famous people.)

A lot of times, someone would want me to sing for their friends. And then they would immediately start hating on me. *She think she cute 'cause she can sing.* If I had a nickel for every time I heard *that.*

Thankfully, I was never in that building in any sort of unlimited way. I had pageant rehearsals, choir practice, and other activities. So although I was in the mix over there sometimes, I still maintained the lifestyle my grandparents and my mother wanted for me.

Although Mae and Bob were strict when I was young, it became harder to enforce their rules as I got older because they worked so much. By the time I was in middle school, Mae was working the night shift at a wire factory called Elrob. I'm not even sure what she did there. But I know she would come home at two in the morning with pinpricks in her fingers that matched the patterns on the inside of a wire cable. And Bob was working during the day at the Drake's bakery in Wayne, New Jersey. He always brought me goodies from work. I was never without a Devil Dog or a Funny Bone to snack on.

And though I was expected to be in the house pretty much all the time, I started trying to find small ways to escape. We had a washing machine but no dryer, so on Saturdays me and my cousins Candy and Gaye and our foster sisters would drag huge bags of wet clothes up to Maple Avenue to the Laundromat. It was annoying—but we were out of the house!

I'd look for any reason to walk up to Bailey Avenue to visit the Shambergers—I was out of the house! But mostly, we couldn't leave the block. And on some days, we might not be allowed to leave the front porch.

I'm sure my grandparents were trying to protect me. But keeping me in the house didn't protect me from drama—it mainly just exposed me to different drama. I lived in a home with foster children moving in and out, which brought its own share of problems—there were children with different issues, plus parents drifting in and out to pick them up and drop them off. So downstairs there might be some random guy picking up a daughter whose mom was just killed in a bar fight. And upstairs there might be a woman dropping off a son, saying she'll pick him up in two days—but she won't be back for months. There was a steady stream of random folks in and out of the house, which is why we had a lock on the phone, the pantry, *and* the extra refrigerator in the basement.

It was all very unpredictable and, unfortunately, some of the characters in and out of the house were just as suspicious as the people my grandparents were trying to protect me from on the street.

My grandparents wanted me to be a mannered young lady whose spiritual development was intact. And my mom wanted to make sure I was respectful, respectable, and exposed to the arts. When I was six, she took me to see *The Wiz* and I was transfixed throughout the performance. (Although I was petrified when the Cowardly Lion came dancing down the aisle.)

I continued to be nurtured in the arts by my family and my community. One of my neighbors, Mrs. Malachi, worked in the control room at the Newark Airport. She knew that I was a talented singer, and she would bring me to her job to sing for her co-workers. In a room circled by wide windows, I'd belt out songs while watching air-traffic controllers lead planes onto the runway. I'd always score a nice little bit of money in the form of tips from her co-workers, most of which I turned over to my grandparents. It was really about getting experience. Even from a young age, I loved to perform, whether I was in church or in an unconventional place like the airport.

To continue my exposure in the arts, my mother entered me into a local pageant, Miss Fashion Teen, when I was eight. My godparents Wayne and Dorothy were friendly with Sharon Carswell, the person who put the pageant together each year. The contestants had to model outfits in different categories, including sportswear and evening wear. You had to submit a written essay and perform a talent.

The prize was a savings bond, a trophy, and a trip to Florida to perform with other winners from different areas. I won the pageant. I was the youngest contestant—and technically, I wasn't a teen. But

I won. And the runner-up, a thirteen-year old who happened to be the oldest contestant, looked at me with pure hatred as we stood together for the crowning ceremony.

I wasn't tripping. I knew I'd won because I deserved it. And although she made me nervous with her attitude, I knew I hadn't done anything to earn it so I tried my best to dismiss it.

I knew I had something special from a very young age. When I was barely six years old, I sang at my maternal grandmother's funeral down in Florida. My mother tells me that when the organist began to play, I made a face and signaled to my mom to make the woman stop playing so I could sing a cappella. I vaguely remember that the older woman was playing the organ in an old-school fashion, and it wouldn't work with how I was planning to perform. I had some nerve! And my mom actually asked the woman to stop playing—and she did!

When I was thirteen, my mother had another daughter, my sister Janeal. Since we were so far apart in age, we didn't end up hanging together a lot. But I did spend some time with her. Now that she's older, she's one of my best friends.

When I was about fourteen, I ended up in a gospel group called the Spiritual Uplifters. It was formed by Mrs. Wilson, an evangelist from our church. We called her Sister Wilson; she had a daughter, Tammy, who put the group together, and a son, Kenny, who I called my godfather.

Sister Wilson was best known for putting on local plays, including the one in which I made my theatrical debut. It was called *The Devil Used My Children!*

Even though Sister Wilson's plays weren't big-budget theater, they did give her some cachet in the hood. When I joined the cast, I was surprised at how serious everyone took the production. Whether there were twenty people in the audience or two hundred, Mrs. Wilson expected us to give 110 percent.

I joined the cast in the role of Wendy, an alcoholic, who ends up singing a duet with the devil about the temptation of alcohol.

Okay, it might sound funny. But I'm telling you, I really feel like I have theater experience because of that play. You can't front on how you get your first start. And I learned that no matter how small the audience, you should always take each performance very seriously.

It was also said that Sister Wilson had real Hollywood acting experience. Everyone talked about her role in the 1984 movie *Brother from Another Planet.* Now, in reality, she was an extra in a train scene. But still. That was kind of a big deal around the way.

She even ended up getting me a role as an extra in a video. Rapper KRS-One had a song called "You Must Learn," and because of some connections Mrs. Wilson had, you can see me and my friend Courtney in the video, sitting at desks, playing students.

I liked and respected Sister Wilson. But even though I didn't think I was really interested in being in a gospel group, rehearsing and performing meant I was out of the house! We even traveled to places like Harlem, Philly, and Connecticut. I really appreciated that.

After months of singing together and performing at different churches and other venues, I started to try to put together my own songs. I'd write rudimentary lyrics and melodies and teach them to the girls just to hear how they'd sound outside my own head. I liked the feeling of putting songs together and performing them. But I knew that a gospel quartet wasn't going to be my opportunity to showcase what I could do musically.

I felt a pull toward popular music although my grandparents' house was strictly gospel. Like so many singers who are raised in religious households, I loved gospel music—but I also felt stifled by it. Whenever I visited my mother's apartment, I would spend hours going through her vinyl collection, staring at Donna Summer's album with the foldout cover and Anita Ward with baby's breath behind her ear on the cover for her hit single, "Ring My Bell." My mom was also a really big fan of Earth, Wind & Fire. My aunt Hope always told me about how they went to see them in concert at a place called the Cow Palace, down in Lakeland, Florida. And somehow, one of the members ended up grabbing Aunt Hope's hand and singing to her. So they *loved* some Earth, Wind & Fire.

When Aunt Hope moved to Linden, New Jersey, I'd go over there and listen to Rick James. She tried to teach me how to do "the hustle," and we'd spend the whole afternoon dancing with her son Isaac, who would also teach me how to beatbox.

During this time, I started obsessively reading album credits and liner notes. I loved seeing all the people who came together to create a song. And I noticed when the performer was also listed as the songwriter for a particular song. I could pore over George Benson's albums for hours. This was before videos were really big; if you liked a song or an artist, the only way you could really connect was with that album cover.

I was entranced by the music I heard, and between my mom and my aunt Hope, I was put on to everything from the Mamas and the Papas to Joan Baez, Joni Mitchell, and Jimi Hendrix. And of course, New Jersey has a long history of club and house music, from Gwen Guthrie, Loleatta Holloway, and Colonel Abrams to Jocelyn Brown, CeCe Rogers, and Marshall Jefferson. I soaked it all in. And that exposure, plus the steady diet of gospel music I got at home, helped inform my style.

My mom noticed that I'd been messing around with writing songs and bought me a Casio keyboard. I couldn't play, but I could read and write music. I knew what the notes were on paper, so I'd sit up in my room and plink out melodies that would become little songs. I'd hook up the outgoing message on my answering machine with my own personalized message, complete with my own voice in four-part harmonies.

Most of the stuff I was doing then was just experimentation. I knew

I had a gift. Even though my songs weren't on the radio and I wasn't performing for crowds, I knew — even then — that I had *something*.

Writing and singing my own songs felt natural. Much more natural than singing "John 3:16" at a church in Philadelphia.

Occasionally, Sister Wilson would give us some money for performances. We even recorded an album, which gave me lots of experience. So there were certain things that helped me. I was doing *something*. But I also knew I would be moving on at some point.

Part of the issue with being in the group was the style of singing. It was a traditional gospel quartet. Gospel quartets have a definite place in the history of Southern gospel music. Groups like the Gospel Highlights and the Mighty Clouds of Joy were the epitome of a gospel quartet. The singers use a lot of vibrato and falsetto and take it back to the old school.

There are lots of popular singers today who got their start in gospel quartets. K-Ci and JoJo, from the group Jodeci, were well known in the South as part of a traveling gospel quartet. This style of music is a little world unto itself. These gospel quartets travel the country, visiting churches, competing in small contests, and maybe — if they're lucky — recording an album or a single for a local gospel label.

I have a great respect for gospel tradition. But I knew that was not going to be my path in the music industry. I liked the more modern sounds of gospel, particularly the Clark Sisters. The Clark Sisters are *bad*. They are four sisters: Twinkie, Jacky, Dorinda, and Karen. They kept the elements of gospel music, but it wasn't as staid and regimented. They knew how to throw in a riff to give their performances an extra punch. And they were particularly good at making their music very melismatic. Better known as vocal runs, or just runs, melisma is when a singer takes a note and bends and stretches it through several notes. (Think of an artist like Mariah Carey, who's known for having a very melismatic sound.)

I loved the Clark Sisters. Their renditions of gospel standards thrilled me. And they even crossed gospel music to a pop audience with their song "You Brought the Sunshine." It was played in churches and on the dance floor at nightclubs. I loved that they were able to appeal to a wide swath of folks who just loved good music.

I tried teaching some of my favorite Clark Sisters songs like "Name It Claim It" and "Is My Living in Vain" to the girls in the gospel group. Saying that it didn't sound the same would be a huge understatement.

I told my grandmother that I wasn't really feeling the group, but she brushed me off. I could have been more forceful about what I wanted, but I just didn't know how to plead my case.

Sometimes I have gone along with things I didn't agree with in order to keep the peace. It would take many years before I would be strong enough to speak up for myself.

One great thing that came out of working with the group was my introduction to Tyrone Holmes. Tyrone was related to the woman who started the gospel group. He had a tiny home studio out in the Bronx, and we went out there occasionally to work on music. I learned a lot from Tyrone about how music is produced. I had already figured out how to write a song. But at Tyrone's house, I learned some of the technical aspects of recording. He had a mini version of everything I would later use in a traditional studio. He had an eight-track tape that he could use to record onto a cassette. He had keyboards and a guitar or two. And of course a drum machine to make beats.

Although I didn't learn to use all the equipment, I learned how to record and then equalize my vocals. When you equalize your vocals, you're making sure the bass and treble are where they need to be and that the sound is smooth. If you are layering vocals to make harmonies, you also want to make sure the sounds are even and balanced.

During this time, I was really into stacking my harmonies. It started with the outgoing voice mails on my answering machine. I'd sing the parts over and over to make it sound like I had a whole group performing. I wanted it to have the lush, rich sound that the Clark Sisters had. But I didn't have three sisters to fill out my vocals. So I'd stack my own vocals on top of each other. I'd sing a chorus or a hook three times in a contralto. Then I'd sing it three more times in a mezzo-soprano, and then three *more* times in a soprano. Then I'd stack all nine versions together and blend them to make a full Faith Evans choir.

I would try this kind of stuff out at Tyrone's house. And I even let him listen to some of my first attempts at songwriting. He was very encouraging and urged me to continue writing and recording. I started feeling again that it was time to move on from Mrs. Wilson's gospel group.

I prepared to tell my grandmother once more that I wanted to quit the group. This time, I wrote her a letter. In the letter, I told her that I was leaving the group — permanently. And that I wasn't entertaining any ideas about staying. I had the nerve to get all dramatic in my letter, too. The first line was: *As of this day, I renounce my standing in this group.*

My grandmother was upset. But she saw that I was serious and told me I was free to make my own decisions. I didn't hesitate to quit the group, and I never looked back. I would dabble in groups here and there a few more times. But I knew that ultimately I would be a solo act.

It was one of the first times that I successfully asserted my independence. But as time went on, I'd have to speak louder and louder in order to be heard.

CHAPTER TWO

Dangerously in Love

*B*y high school, I had a bit more freedom. And the more freedom I had, the more my lifestyle changed, depending on where I was. At home, I was still Faye: sweet and well behaved. I attended University High School, one of the top-ranked public schools in the area at the time. They had a special program for academically gifted students; if you had the grades and passed certain tests, you could attend the school beginning in seventh grade. In addition to being in this gifted and talented program, I was also an honor student in advanced placement classes. I had classes with some of my friends from elementary school, including Sampson Davis, George Jenkins, and Rameck Hunt. They were cool; we took physics and pre-calculus together and helped each other study for exams.

By the late 1980s, Newark had been crushed by the crack cocaine epidemic. And students who were focused on education and who had bright academic futures were rare.

I knew far too many people who were dropping out of school and having babies. Sampson, George, and Rameck had a plan—they made a pact while we were in high school that has now become legendary. They vowed to support each other through high school, college, and medical school. The three of them wanted to become doctors, and they did it—they are now nationally recognized as the Three Doctors. Their inspiring story began at my high school, in the classes we shared.

(Years later, I'd have the honor of presenting my good friends with an Essence Award for their accomplishments. We'd come a long way, and I remain very proud of them.)

I was staying on point with my schoolwork. But I was beginning to stray farther and farther from the house on Grumman Avenue—not just physically but mentally as well.

Once I discovered boys, it was on. And because of the insular, tight-knit environment of my grandparents' home, I went right for the bad boys. There had been small crushes in elementary and middle school. The first boy I really liked was a quiet, polite young man named Reggie who was the brother of my good friend Roz from school. But once I started to really date, I went for the boys with swagger and a cocky attitude.

In high school, it was someone I'll call JT. I met him at McDonald's right in downtown Newark. I had just ordered my food when he walked up and paid for it before I could. He wasn't super-handsome. (But then again, I would never really go for the super-handsome type.) He was brown-skinned, medium build, and not much taller than me, but he carried himself well. He was dressed nicely and I could tell that he was older and had a little something going on. It turned out that he was a small-time drug dealer. That didn't faze me at all. I thought I was grown, and we started dating right away. He had his own apartment near downtown Newark, and everything we did together was new and exciting.

We went on real dates. We would take the train into Manhattan to his favorite Italian restaurant near Central Park and we'd walk around the city afterward. I would tag along with him when he went to the diamond district to buy his little gold rope chains and 3-D rings from Mannie's jewelry store.

Things got serious pretty quickly. I started going to JT's apartment after school—I even had my own key—and hanging out for as long as I could.

I kept it all from my grandparents for quite some time. I told them I was studying with a friend, or singing here or there, to keep them from finding out. But a friend's mother learned of the relationship and told my grandparents.

My grandparents didn't like it one bit. They came down to JT's apartment looking for me a few times. I stayed one step ahead of them, avoiding them.

I stayed at JT's place for a few days, refusing to go home. Finally, he took me home and met my grandparents for the first time. I have to give JT credit—he made me go home and told me it was wrong to disrespect my grandparents.

I'd made a point. I didn't want to be sheltered and treated like a child anymore. I wanted to come and go as I pleased. Although my grandparents still worried a lot, I started hanging out pretty much whenever I wanted to.

But things with JT quickly took a turn for the worse. I was in love with him, and the feelings were mutual. But he had a mean streak and could be very jealous. If he even heard that I was talking to another guy—any guy—he would grill me about it for hours.

It would drive me crazy and we'd end up arguing and pushing each other around. But soon, it became much deeper.

One afternoon, as I was on my way home from school, I ran into a male friend I'd known for years. We chatted briefly and exchanged numbers so we could stay in touch. JT found out about it and was pissed off.

"Where were you today?" he asked. I could tell immediately that he was angry.

"I went to school and then I came home."

"I need to talk to you. Come to my house. Now."

"Why?" I asked. "What is your problem?"

"What's my problem? You always walking around talking to other niggas—that's my problem!"

I rolled my eyes at the phone and took a deep breath. "Are you talking about Jonathan?" I asked. "You know we're just friends."

"You need to come down here. Take a cab."

"I don't have no money for a cab."

"Just call the cab, Faith. I'll pay for it when you get here."

JT hung up. I called a cab and told my grandparents I would be back soon. During the ride to downtown Newark, I went over in my mind how I was going to get JT to calm down. Sometimes I was able to talk him down from being angry. But something in the pit of my stomach told me this time would be different.

JT lived in the heart of downtown Newark, directly across the street from City Hall in a high-rise called Hallmark Towers. As the cab drove down Broad Street, I could see the building growing larger. There was a circular driveway that spanned the front of the building, and the entrance was directly in the middle. As the taxi turned into the driveway, I looked toward the front door to see if JT was waiting in the lobby for me. But he was actually even closer. As soon as the cab pulled in, before we could even pull up to the front door, JT was standing right there. He stopped the driver on the spot, instead of letting him pull up to the front door, where there was a security guard sitting in a vestibule. I knew I was in trouble right then.

"That's nine dollars," the cabdriver said.

"Wait one second," I said, as I opened my door. "I'm going to get the money right now."

JT had these big wide eyes that would pop out when he was angry. And as I soon as I started climbing out of the backseat, the first thing that I noticed was that his eyes were bulging and his mouth was tight.

"What the fuck is wrong with you?" he screamed, grabbing my arm and yanking me the rest of the way out of the car.

"JT! Get off of me!" I screamed.

The cabdriver leaned over to the window on the passenger's side. "*Yo!* I need my nine dollars!" he said.

"Pay him, JT!" I said.

"Bitch, I ain't paying nobody *shit*," JT said.

I struggled to get JT to stop pulling my arm, and then I saw him clench his fist and pull his arm back. I felt like his arm moved in slow motion. It was so wrong and out of place. I was standing right in front of his building in broad daylight on a busy street. I was little more than a child. And there I was, with a grown man's fist heading straight for my face.

On his pointer finger, JT was wearing a thick gold ring with 3-D detailing. The band of the ring was so wide that it reached from the bottom of his finger to his knuckle. JT punched me in the face like I was a grown man. I fell back and hit the gate that circled the driveway.

As soon as he hit me, the cabdriver sped off. I was stunned and in pain. I stood there bent over from the waist and held my nose. There was blood pouring through my fingers.

"What the fuck is *wrong* with you?" I cried out.

"Why the fuck was you talking to that nigga?" he screamed as he pulled me up to a full standing position.

"He's just a friend of mine," I said. Now I was sobbing. "That's all. I swear."

JT's eyes were still bulging, and his nostrils were flaring in and out.

"Let's go," he said, pulling me into the building.

He half dragged me through the lobby, onto the elevator, and then down the corridor to his apartment, cursing me out the whole time.

"Think I'm playing with you...talking to every fucking nigga you see...trying to play me out..."

But by the time we got inside his studio apartment, his demeanor had softened. He sat me down on his sofa and went into the bathroom to get tissues for my nose. I sat there, tears streaming down my face, blood pouring from my nose, and just stared out the large floor-to-ceiling windows that faced Broad Street. The apartment had a wide view of the city, and sometimes looking at Newark's skyline could be mesmerizing.

"You know I love you," JT said, as he dabbed my face with hydrogen peroxide.

"Yeah. I know."

He sat down next to me on the sofa, put his arm around my shoulder, and pulled me closer.

"I am so sorry. I will never put my hands on you again," he said, a line I would hear many times.

And of course, I took him back, the way many women in abusive relationships do. But it didn't stop. He'd hear something about me talking to some guy. And then he'd smack, kick, or punch me. And he had the nerve to cheat on me continually while flipping out on me because he *thought* I was cheating.

There was a Puerto Rican girl in Harlem whom I heard had been taking the train to Newark to come see him. One of my friends spotted her going into his building and told me all about it. There was a girl from Newark he was messing with who actually came up to my school looking for me. And then there was some older woman named Terry he was flat-out dating, not just messing around with.

I heard this Terry chick had been spending a lot of time in his apartment. So I went there one day after school to see if I could catch her there. I still had the key, so I let myself in.

And there they were, sitting on the couch watching television. I jumped in the girl's face and we both started screaming at each other.

"Bitch," she said. "If you don't get your young ass out of here…"

I looked at the girl closely and then cocked my head to one side. "Yo. You got a dead eye or something? Get the fuck outta here with your ugly ass."

That really set Terry off and she lunged at me. We both threw a few punches while JT tried to get in the middle to break it up. At one point, I went into the bathroom to find some cologne so I could pour it in her eye. I'd heard that was a good way to disable someone in a fight. I got the cologne but JT tackled me before I could reach Terry with it.

She ended up leaving. JT and I continued arguing over why she was even there.

"You always accusing me of shit and *you're* the one doing dirty!" I yelled.

"Who the fuck do you think you're talking to like that!"

"I'm talking to *you*…," I said, putting my finger in his face.

JT froze and his eyes got really wide. I knew I'd gone too far. But it was too late. He charged at me, and I turned to run away but he grabbed me by my waist, lifted me off the floor, and started walking over to the windows overlooking Broad Street.

The window right in the middle was wide open with a screen in it. I was kicking my legs and screaming while JT pulled the screen out of the window and then pushed my head and shoulders out of the window.

"NOoooooooooooo," I screamed out. "Pleeeease, JT—STOP IT!"

"You wanna talk shit, Faye? Huh?" He said, pushing the top half of my body farther and farther out the window.

We were on the eleventh floor, and I could see the cars parked around the circular driveway below me. If he pushed me any farther, even by mistake, I knew I'd be dead.

"You got anything else to say?" he yelled.

"No. No, JT. Please just pull me up. Please!"

Eventually, he brought me in and then smacked me hard in the face for getting smart with him. And as always, minutes later, he was apologizing to me and begging me not to leave.

I was growing up fast — too fast. And I was allowing my personal life to cloud my goals for the future. I knew I didn't want to just be a typical girl. I didn't want to end up having a baby by JT and then being tied to him for the rest of my life. But he provided a certain level of independence and freedom I'd never had before.

I wanted something different out of my life. And true to my very name, I had to have faith that God would provide a path for me to take.

CHAPTER THREE

Faith Is Just To Fly

Many times, before things can get better, they have to get worse. Before you fully learn a lesson, sometimes it has to really bring you to a point where you can sit back and reflect on it. Making positive changes in your life doesn't happen quickly.

One of my major weaknesses has always been that I tend to move a little too fast, especially when it comes to relationships. I fall in love quickly and I fall in love hard. And then it dawns on me that I should have given things a little more thought. If I'd kept just a bit of distance from JT in the very beginning, I would have seen his temper issues and perhaps avoided the physical abuse. But by the time he showed me his true colors, I was already in too deep.

When it came to having sex, JT and I were very irresponsible. And soon after he tried to throw me out his living room window, I found out I was pregnant. It wasn't the first time I'd gotten pregnant, either. I'd gotten an abortion after an unplanned pregnancy in an earlier relationship.

I had no intentions of telling anyone that I was pregnant by JT. But I confided in one of my foster sisters, and it eventually it got back to my mom.

I came home from school one afternoon and saw my mother sitting at the kitchen table in my grandparents' house. I knew by the look on her face that she was upset.

"Hey, Ma," I said, taking off my book bag and draping it over the back of the chair.

"Have a seat, Faith."

Even though my period was only a few days late, I suddenly felt like my flat stomach was bulging and she'd be able to tell I was pregnant just by looking at me. I pulled my jacket closer around me and then sat down at the Formica table.

"What is this I hear that you're pregnant?"

I looked away and thought about denying it. But my mom's eyes were burning a hole into me and I couldn't do it.

"I am."

My mom rolled her eyes. "What is *wrong* with you, Faith? You are only fifteen years old!"

"I know that, Ma."

"I thought you were on the pill to regulate your period anyway?"

"I am. I mean I was. I forgot like, twice."

"I've already made you an appointment at the doctor. You're not going to school tomorrow."

The next day, my mom drove me to a doctor's office in South Orange. The building was tiny but clean. And they had an assembly-line method of dealing with all the young girls in there, most of whom were speaking softly to each other. They would call you up, have you fill out paperwork, and then move you to another room, where they would take a blood sample and then send you into *another* room, where they gave you a brief counseling session, on and on, until you were with a doctor wearing a thin robe. After the procedure, I rested there for an hour while my mom waited for me, and then we went back home.

"I hope you've learned a lesson from this, Faye," my mom said.

I nodded.

"I'm serious," she said. "You can't be doing this shit to your body."

"I know."

"And I expect more of you than this. This is not the plan for you, getting knocked up by worthless niggas who are not even worthy of your time. Remember that."

Unfortunately, that incident didn't automatically teach me a lesson. My relationship with JT was so rocky and emotional that I continued having unprotected sex with him even though I knew better.

It's hard for me to go back to that place—in such a dead-end relationship and making such foolish choices. But I know there are young girls out there who are going through the same crap right now. And I want them to know how important it is to respect their bodies. I didn't really have anyone to talk about this stuff with when I was a teenager. I couldn't even dream of talking about sex with my grandmother. She would have insisted that I wait until I was married, which was not realistic. And I was too afraid of how my mom might react to keep it completely real with her.

My grandparents did end up accepting JT. They even allowed him to go with us on their annual bus ride to Florida the summer that I turned sixteen. My grandmother always sponsored these bus rides to Florida. We would stay for a week and go to Disney and Epcot and all the parks. It was always a lot of fun. JT had his own room, of course. One night, one of my cousins told me that he had another chick in his hotel room. I marched over there with Candy and Gaye and a few other girls and tried to get into his room, but he wouldn't open the door. The rumor was that he'd had a local prostitute in there. But I never really knew for sure what happened.

I do know that soon after we came back home, JT ended up infecting me with a venereal disease. And I always wondered if it was related to whoever had been in his room in Florida. I ended up in the hospital for a week with complications from the disease. I was embarrassed and afraid. Especially when the doctor told me that I would have a difficult time getting pregnant because of the intensity of the illness.

I remember my mother walking into my hospital room and shaking her head.

"Here you go again," she said flatly. "I really thought you had more sense than this. You can be so *stupid* sometimes, Faye."

I couldn't even speak. I knew she was right. But at that moment, I needed a hug, some warm words of encouragement. I knew she was upset. But I was scared and already upset with myself.

I still didn't break it off with JT, and the mental and physical abuse continued. In many ways, I was in a very dark place. The only thing that kept me going was music and my focus on school.

Even when things were really bad with JT, I managed to keep my grades up in school and perform here and there. I would sing "You and I" or "The Lord's Prayer" at the occasional wedding. Although I'd stopped performing with the group, I stayed in touch with Tyrone, the producer we'd worked with. And I was going up to Tyrone's home studio in the Bronx two or three times a week to record the songs I wrote in my room.

Although I had begun to rebel against all of my grandparents' rules when I started dating JT, they were still trying to keep me on a pretty tight leash with a firm curfew. And there's no way they would have allowed me to go to the Bronx to record secular music—love songs at that! So I had to sneak out my bedroom window and take the PATH train from Newark to New York's Penn Station and then take the subway to the Bronx—alone. Sometimes, I'd have to get money from Tyrone to get back home.

Even though I knew it was extremely risky, I felt like I had to do it. It wasn't a part of any grand plan. I still didn't know how I was going to make my living. But it was just a calling. I was a singer and a songwriter. So I needed to do it. The same way a kid who loves basketball will constantly shoot around, I needed to be surrounded by music and hone my craft. Looking back, it was all a great education and preparation for my career.

But I really wasn't conscious of it at the time. One of my teachers had once told me that writers who wrote commercial jingles made good money, so I'd even thought of doing that. I thought maybe I'd be a lounge singer. I had nothing firm in mind. I just wanted to record my songs and practice stacking my vocals. Whatever came out of it, as far as I was concerned, was beyond my control.

Tyrone had been talking to a friend about me, telling him about my voice and the songs I'd written. The friend was a small-time drug dealer from Harlem, and he happened to be good friends with music producer Teddy Riley.

One afternoon, Tyrone told me that Teddy Riley was going to be in the New York City area—and that I was going to sing for him. I was really excited and of course very nervous. I think some of the songs I'd been working on with Tyrone had found their way to Teddy's ear, and the producer had decided he wanted to hear me sing.

At this time, Teddy Riley was the most influential producer in hip-hop and R&B. He'd worked with everyone from Michael Jackson to Aretha Franklin. And he'd put together his own groups, Guy and BLACKstreet, which both released multiplatinum albums.

He's credited with ushering in the entire era of New Jack Swing music after producing Bobby Brown's smash hit *Don't Be Cruel,* which sold seven million copies and had been the best-selling album of the year just two years earlier. I didn't know much about the inner workings of the music industry. Back then, the producer wasn't necessarily well known. (That would come later, when my future boss, Sean "Puffy" Combs, would come on the scene.) I still knew that performing for Teddy Riley was a big deal.

I was only sixteen at the time and I had no idea where this could lead — if anywhere. I just wanted to do my best.

I went out there dressed to impress. Growing up, I had consistently worn church clothes — dresses, stockings, and low heels. But by the time I got into my teens, I had started to switch up my style and sometimes I would rock more ghetto-fabulous gear.

That night, I had on a fur coat, red knee-high Gucci boots, and my favorite gold earrings: huge gold hoops in the shape of an apple with the New York skyline across the top. Through the middle were the words FAYE IS JUST TO FLY. (The Chinese people at the jewelry store in downtown Newark forgot the extra *o* in the word *too* on my earrings, and I was so pissed. Of course I wore them anyway).

I had my hair very similar to the style that female rappers Salt-N-Pepa made popular: a fluffy asymmetrical bobbed cut dyed in a honey-blond color. With all that and my fuchsia lipstick, I really thought I was at least looking the part.

I sang something for Teddy in the lobby of his hotel. Unfortunately, I don't remember what it was. He was really quiet and didn't say much when I was done.

"You have a nice voice...," he said.

"Thank you."

"I'm working with a female singer right now named Tammy Lucas..."

His voice trailed off, and I just nodded. We made a bit more small talk, and the visit was over. I'm not sure what I expected to happen. But nothing came out of that impromptu audition. I met him years later, when I had a record deal. And he said that he remembered hearing me sing for him but I don't know if he truly remembers. I would imagine he had lots of people singing for him at that time.

Anyway, I wasn't stressing it. I had a lot going on. I was trying to finish high school, applying to college, and trying to get my personal life straight.

I was occasionally performing in various gospel concerts with a group of seasoned singers from the area. I think they were called Revelations or something like that. One of the musicians was a man named William who played the organs and keyboards. Sometimes the group would practice at his house in Irvington. William was an older married guy. He was brown-skinned and had an average build. He kind of looked like Jeffrey Osbourne.

Sometimes I would work on my vocals with William. Back then, I didn't have a lot of control over what my voice could do. Like with riffs—those melodic bits of melody within a song. I'm known for my riffs now. But when I first started out, I was nervous about singing that way because if you don't have control of your voice, you can end up not hitting the notes and sounding flat.

Being able to control your voice is the difference between sounding good in the studio and sounding good live—which was important to me. William and I would practice running the scales, and he would encourage me to listen to music by Vanessa Bell Armstrong and BeBe and CeCe Winans. He would listen and guide me, showing me how to control the notes instead of letting them control me.

I was still dating JT, and occasionally William would give me a ride downtown to JT's apartment after our rehearsals. William was a nice enough guy. But he was much older than me and I was still dealing with all the JT drama. Once, he took me to JT's apartment so that I could attend a concert with him.

"So who are y'all going to see?" William asked.

"We're going to see the Yellowjackets and Steely Dan." I could see he was impressed that I had somewhat mature musical tastes.

"That's cool," he said. And then he pointed to my arm, which was bruised. "But why would you be with someone who hits you?"

"It's not really like that," I said. "I mean, yeah, we fight sometimes..."

"That nigga should not be putting his hands on you," William said.

As I continued to rehearse with the group, William and I became cool. He was relatively well known in the local gospel music world. He played the organ and was sometimes hired by different church choirs if they wanted to record a gospel album. And I was honored to develop my sound with the group he rehearsed with. I knew I could sing. But I didn't always have great control of my voice at that time. The voice is an instrument, just like a guitar or a piano. You have to learn how to rein in the notes and make them work properly. There's always the danger—particularly in gospel music, which can be very emotional—of oversinging and ruining your voice. I learned that being a good singer was more than just being able to manipulate the notes and make them shake and vibrate in my throat. When I was younger, I thought anyone who had a strong vibrato was a good singer. But as I worked with these accomplished singers, I began to learn how to hold back on a note instead of always belting it out.

Me and my friend Lorne Rawls, whose family had a gospel group in Newark, started calling it "the goo-goos." We would laugh and roll our eyes at some of the church choirs whose members screamed and manipulated their voices, stretching out one note for a full minute. Although I was brought up revering that style, once I started being exposed to other performers who were a bit more restrained, I began to enjoy singing with people who were not just all about the goo-goo sound.

I began seeing more and more of William as we worked together, and our professional relationship turned into a personal relationship. I was seventeen. William was thirty-five. And he was married.

William had continually urged me to leave JT alone. Which I did. But I traded JT's drama for William's. Before long, I was in *way* over my head. I was dating William, a married man. And I would have to go to his basement studio for rehearsals—while his wife was upstairs.

Eventually, other members of the group found out what was going on. But I thought I was grown. I knew what I was doing was very wrong. But I didn't try to stop it, either. In my own immature way, I felt like William's wife was not my problem. I was not trying to be the catalyst for breaking up a marriage and I definitely didn't want him to leave her for me or anything like that.

In my mind, I knew that dating someone who'd taken marriage vows would come back to haunt me at some other time. I didn't take it that seriously. But I knew I would have to pay the price for that indiscretion.

A few times, William and I teamed up to perform for weddings—I would sing "You and I" or "The Lord's Prayer" while he played the music for the processional and the recessional. I had already started singing at weddings, funerals, and the occasional retirement party.

William was a professional musician, and I believe he thought that with my songwriting and vocal talents, we could be some sort of a team. I was willing to try it out. But I continued to write and produce with Tyrone as well.

At one point, William told me I should meet with Stuart Levy, an entertainment attorney who was well known in the music industry.

William and I drove into Manhattan one day after school, and Stuart Levy welcomed us into his office. He was very warm and friendly. He was a big guy, really tall. He had a wide smile and over-size eyeglasses.

"What do you see for yourself, Faith?" he asked.

"I'm not sure," I said. "I want to sing for a living. But I don't really know how it's gonna happen."

Stuart leaned back in his chair and nodded. "You know, a lot of very talented people are not able to support themselves in the music business. Everyone doesn't get a record deal with a major label."

I thought about my mom and how hard she'd worked on her music when I was a little girl. "I know," I said.

"I like your demo," he said. "It sounds really good. I can't promise you anything. But I'll definitely keep you in mind if projects cross my desk."

Stuart called me a few weeks later.

"Would you like to sing background vocals for a record?" he asked.

"Absolutely," I said, grabbing a notepad and a pencil.

"There's a group on Jive Records called Hi-Five. They need a vocalist to do some backing vocals. Can you be at the studio tomorrow at eight?"

"I'm there."

"Great. Tell the producer who you are and they'll tell you what to do."

It's a testament to my personality that I went alone into Manhattan to the studio for my very first music industry assignment. I may have told folks that I was going into the studio. But I didn't tell them that it was an official music industry thing. I may have told my girlfriend Roz. Roz was the sister of Reggie, my first real boyfriend. She and I were always together, and I told her everything. But I didn't ask her to come with me. And even though I was excited, I didn't tell anyone about the potential that this opportunity could bring.

Honestly, I didn't think it was going to lead to any kind of big break. Just like singing for Teddy Riley, I figured it would be a good way to learn something else about the industry. I didn't expect anyone to sign me to a record label after I sang a few backing vocals, though. I wasn't even looking for that. I knew I was going to be a performer—there was no doubt in my mind about that. I didn't necessarily know if I would be an artist on a major record label. But whether I was a lounge singer or sang commercial jingles, I knew I'd make my living with my voice. So when things like singing backup for an artist on a major label came up, I just accepted it and tried to do my best. But I expected nothing.

I don't even remember much about my first session. I know I

wasn't intimidated, because being in the studio wasn't new for me. There were a few other session singers I recorded with. I met the producer, listened to the track they wanted me to contribute vocals to, and that was it. Not a big deal at all.

I was in the middle of my senior year and besides music, my thoughts were preoccupied with SATs, college applications, prom, and graduation. Toward the end of my senior year, I got a check from AFTRA for six hundred dollars for the work I'd done on the Hi-Five record. I was thrilled. It was my first time being officially paid for my singing talents. And I was still in high school. I did make a little money at the time. I set up a salon in my grandmother's kitchen. I would hook up the weaves and acrylic nails of the girls in my 'hood.

I still wanted to go to college as a backup plan. I didn't feel like the music industry was secure enough that I could just dive in and try to make it work without an education. I also wanted to make my mom and my grandparents proud. I felt a bit of pressure from my community. I was a "good girl," someone whom people had a lot of hope for. I knew they expected me to go to school, and I understood that.

I graduated with a 3.8 grade point average and had applied to a number of top-ranked schools in the area, including Princeton, Fordham, St. John's, and Syracuse. Initially, I thought I wanted to attend the famed Oberlin Conservatory of Music in Oberlin, Ohio. But by senior year, I'd realized I was not trying to be a conductor or a music teacher.

I was accepted into Fordham University, which had everything I wanted. It was close to home (I had no desire to live on campus, because I feared being broke). It had a good reputation, and it was in New York City. But it was also expensive, over twenty-five thousand a year, and I had no idea how I was going to pay for it. I'm sure I would have qualified for some kind of financial aid, but I didn't know much about how to go about applying for it.

In June 1991, I graduated from University High School. And during the ceremony, I got the shock of my life. The principal called my name, and I walked up to receive my diploma. As I made my way to the stage, he made an announcement to the audience.

"Ladies and gentleman. We've been recently notified that Miss Faith Evans will be receiving a full academic scholarship to Fordham University!"

The audience erupted in applause. I was shocked. I'd had no idea that I was receiving a scholarship.

As I prepared for a new phase of my life, I was hopeful and looking forward to making my family proud at Fordham. I was still dealing with William. And JT was still in and out of my life. But knowing that I had this opportunity made me feel like I could get past the messy situations I'd been in with men. I was being given a concrete path, a road that could help me achieve whatever I wanted out of life. That summer was full of hope and excitement.

I had already defied so many of the odds. I was a young black girl in Brick City, New Jersey. I had been raised by pseudo-grandparents in a poor household. There were so many girls just like me who had not made it as far as I had. I had graduated from high school at the top of my class. I could see my life unfolding before me, and my future was a lot brighter than a lot of the girls I grew up with.

I was blessed.

But that summer, as I prepared for school and hung out with my friends, I had no idea that in the very next year, I would slide dangerously close to becoming a statistic. I was seventeen years old. And I was still a bit immature when it came to men. I still fell in love too hard and too fast. And I often leapt into situations before really thinking about them. All these facets of my personality would blow up in my face when I crossed paths with a mysterious young man who had a lot of secrets.

CHAPTER FOUR

A Teenage Love

I was proud that I made it to college. I never really got into the whole college-life scene, though. It was okay. But I was way too ambitious and driven for college parties and pillow fights. I had so many dreams about what would happen *after* college. It was hard for me to focus on the day-to-day grind of being on campus. I had practically lived with my boyfriend for a short time when I was in high school. I had traveled into Manhattan on my own for years. College just felt like something I had to do. It wasn't necessarily a journey I was going to enjoy along the way.

Beginning in the fall of 1991, my routine was simple: I'd take the #59 bus from the corner of Elizabeth and Grumman to the corner of Broad and Market, the busiest intersection in downtown Newark. I liked walking down to Penn Station from there because usually I'd run into someone I knew—like my ex-boyfriend JT—and I liked for people to see me on my hustle.

After I got to Penn Station in Newark, I'd take the PATH train to 33rd Street in Manhattan and then take the D train up to the Bronx to Fordham's campus.

I had a full schedule of classes, and my days were consumed with getting out to the Bronx for class, studying, writing papers, practicing with the gospel group that my then-boyfriend produced for, and hanging out with my friends. I was also working on my music with Tyrone Holmes, who still lived in the Bronx. So some days, I would dip over to his home studio before or after class.

One afternoon, I was on my way to Penn Station to catch the train to Fordham. It was the spring semester, near the end of my first year in school. I was wearing one of my infamous Champion fleece sweat suits that I wore all the time back then. I ran into someone who looked familiar—a fellow musician named Kiyamma Griffin. I didn't know him well, but I knew his name and that most people called him Kiy. I knew that he'd played keyboard in the jazz band at Weequahic High School, which was near my house. I sang with the jazz band at University High School, and our high schools had performed together a time or two. I also knew that he had a bit of a connection to the music industry. He was a part of a production crew called Three Boys from Newark. They'd become local celebrities due to their work with an R&B singer named Christopher Williams, who'd had some success in the early '90s.

At Penn Station, Kiy and I exchanged a bit of small talk. He had a very round face and dark brown skin; he wore oval-shaped wire-rimmed glasses.

He asked me where I was going, and I told him about Fordham. He told me he was coming back from a recording session with Christopher Williams at a Manhattan studio.

"What do you usually do after you get out of class?" he asked me.

"Nothing really," I said. "Just take the train back home."

Kiy nodded. "Are you still singing?"

"Here and there," I said.

"You know what? You should come by the studio tomorrow after you get out of class."

The next day, I couldn't wait for my last class to end. When I left my writing class, I went to a pay phone to get directions to the studio.

When I got to the building, I had to look on a board in the lobby to find out what floor the studio was on. I went up to the fourth floor. There was a reception area right in front of me.

"Can I help you?" the woman at the desk asked.

"I'm here for the Christopher Williams session."

She pointed to the doors on either side of the desk. "He's using both studios. You can go in either one."

I pushed on the heavy glass doors and found myself in a hallway with two or three doors on either side. A young man who looked about my age walked briskly past me. He was carrying what looked like a guitar in a case on his shoulder.

"Excuse me, I'm looking for Kiy?"

"Oh, he's not here," he said. "But when he comes back, he'll probably be back there in that room." He pointed to a door at the end of the hallway.

I went down the hallway and opened the door. Inside, there were three or four young guys laughing and talking. I recognized Floyd Howard, a brown-skinned brother with curly hair who had gone to Weequahic High School with Kiy.

"Hey, Faith," he said. "Kiy told me you were coming through." Floyd introduced me to a few of the other people in the room, including Ike Lee, a pretty boy from Queens who made the beats for the tracks they produced. The guys were sitting around a mixing board, pushing buttons, playing a track over and over, and trying to come up with lyrics to go with the sound.

"I think it needs a heavier bass line," Floyd said. He fiddled with some of the knobs on the massive boards in front of him and then replayed the track. "See, it should have that funky sound. Like this…"

Everyone started nodding to the beat. They had thoughtful

looks on their faces as they tried to envision where the song should go next.

"Sounds like a love song to me...," Ike said.

"For a guy or a girl?" said one guy I didn't know, who was strumming on a guitar.

"I think a girl. Something where she's begging a guy to take her back." The door opened and a young girl came in. The guys greeted her. She walked behind where they sat at the mixing board and went into a little small enclosure near the boards. Inside there was a glass panel, so that we could all see her from where we sat. There was a microphone set up and a chair. She sat down, put on a pair of headphones, and then punched a few buttons.

"Aiight, fellas, what we working on today," she said into the microphone.

"We're writing a song about heartache," Floyd said.

The girl sucked her teeth. "I can do a whole album about that," she said.

"Just sing whatever for now...," someone said.

The girl cleared her throat and started to sing.

One guy who was sitting in the corner of the room near an electric keyboard started playing a melody that matched what she was singing. The guys began to ad-lib along with the girl and then fed her new lyrics to try out.

I just sat back and watched. Even though I hadn't been in a professional studio since recording with Sister Wilson's group, I knew the lingo. The girl in the booth sang a line and her voice cracked, and she laughed and asked if she could "punch in." I knew that meant that she wanted the engineer to cue up the song to where she left off so she could sing just the part that she'd messed up on. And when the guys told the engineer to "double" certain parts, I knew they wanted her vocals to be fuller and layered.

But the atmosphere was a lot different from what I was used to. When I was in Tyrone's studio, it was just the two of us. And that was a blessing. I had one-on-one studio time — something a lot of people would have loved. So seeing a group of people working together and sharing time was different.

I was there for over an hour, waiting for Kiy. And I had no idea when he was going to arrive. I wasn't even sure what I was supposed to be doing there. Was I going to sing for Christopher Williams? Listen to Kiy's music? Help write a song? I had no idea. But I did know one thing: I wasn't going to hang out indefinitely waiting for him to show up.

Some people who are trying to get into the music industry work as studio rats. They'll spend the night there, eat all their meals there, just to be close to the scene and perhaps have a chance to get on. I was never like that. I wasn't famous or well known by any means. But I wasn't tripping off being in a studio. It was cool. And if something was meant to come out of it, I'd be pleased. But I wasn't going to play myself out, hanging around musicians and hoping they'd give me a shot. I had way too much confidence in myself for that.

Eventually, Kiy did show up that night. And he and the rest of his production crew played a few tracks they were working on at the time. I continued to sit back and watch as they played tracks and people floated in and out of the studio.

The guys were listening to one track over and over. It was a ballad that would be sung by a male and female duet. They had vocals on it for the guy's verse, but they still hadn't found anyone to sing the female's part.

"Do you sing?" asked one of the guys that I didn't know.

"Yeah, I do…"

"Can you do me a favor and just sing this verse so we can hear what it sounds like?"

"No problem," I said.

As I approached the booth, the guy gave me a sheet of paper with the lyrics on it.

"That's okay, I don't need that." I told him.

I'd heard them singing the song over and over for the whole evening and had learned the lyrics just from sitting there watching.

I remember going into the booth, chuckling to myself. Back then, people who didn't know me always tended to underestimate what I was capable of once I hit the booth. It's like I become another person entirely. I may look unassuming in person—but then I get in the booth, take a verse and melody, and completely blow people away with my voice and my vocal arrangement. On more than one occasion, I'd been in this situation, only for people to say afterward, *I didn't know you could sing like* that.

After I finished my vocals, there was dead silence. I looked out into the mixing room and I saw that everyone was smiling. But it was quiet. I knew they were very impressed.

Over the next few months, I continued to come by the studio on the weekends and when I wasn't in class. I helped write tracks they were working on and occasionally tried out different vocal arrangements for songs. I eventually met Christopher Williams, who was at the height of his success with his appearance in the movie *New Jack City*. In the movie, there was this really funny line when a character refers to someone as "Grandpa." So I jokingly called him Grandpa, and we always laughed about it.

I thought Grandpa and his girlfriend Natalie were very warm and sweet. Although he was popular, he was very cool and down to earth. The studio was becoming like a second home.

Kiy, Floyd, and Ike were on the cusp of having some success in the music business. There was talk that they were going to get a record deal as a group and also going to be signed as producers, along with Christopher Williams. They were closing a deal and moving out to Los Angeles to begin recording.

I continued to help out, but I didn't expect to be a part of their equation. I felt like we were family, but I didn't feel like they owed me anything. I just came to the studio to learn, observe, and absorb what I could. I knew that once they moved out to LA, I might not have the opportunity to be in an official recording studio again. So I wanted to learn. And for me, it was also just something interesting to do.

And then there was William and JT. I had been trying to break things off permanently with both of them, but they still liked to pop up at my house or at my school unannounced. (Once they both showed up on campus at the same time.) So being in the studio was a welcome escape, although I knew it was temporary.

Floyd and Ike would occasionally make comments about Kiy having a crush on me. I didn't see it. He never tried to approach me. I didn't think he liked me at all. We'd take the PATH train home from the studio together some nights. But the conversation was essentially just small talk.

There was something very intriguing about Kiy. I couldn't figure him out. I would hear that he liked me. But when I saw him, he'd barely speak to me. He'd ask me to come to the studio and then not show up. We'd take the train together and not talk much. Even his smile seemed reserved.

But of course, being around someone every day can lead to things happening. And even though we hadn't declared any romantic attraction for each other, we ended up having sex one day. It happened in the studio, in the recording booth. It wasn't romantic. It was just something that happened. It was the kind of situation that's supposed to happen once or twice and then never again. And then you grow up and laugh about it together.

But instead, after the second or third time we messed around, I noticed that my period was late.

I really didn't think I could be pregnant. I'd been irresponsible in other sexual relationships and hadn't gotten pregnant. I assumed that I wouldn't be able to get pregnant because of the complications from the sexually transmitted disease I'd contracted from JT. The doctor told me I probably wouldn't be able to get pregnant. And indeed, in the time that had passed since JT, I'd never gotten pregnant in other relationships.

So when I took a home pregnancy test in the bathroom at my grandmother's house, I was completely freaked out when it came back positive. I went to the doctor and it was confirmed. I was pregnant.

This was a problem. We weren't in love. He was cool. And we hung out in the studio together. But that was the extent of our relationship. There were no movies and Italian dinners like with JT. And there was no performing together at weddings like when I was with William.

I mean, I liked Kiy. But it was more the mystique that drew me in. I *wanted* to like him and I wanted to get to know him. I just went a little too far in my quest to feel him out. I ended up pregnant when I really just wanted to get to know him a little better.

I wasn't sure what I was going to do. But terminating the pregnancy was pretty much at the top of my list of options.

One of the first people I told was my foster sister Malika.

"You pregnant?" she asked, her eyes wide.

"Yeah," I said. "This is not good."

"What are you going to do about it?" Malika asked.

"Get an abortion, I guess," I said.

"You better figure something out quick."

"I know," I said. "Just don't say anything to anybody."

"I ain't saying nothing," Malika said.

And of course as soon as we were done with that conversation, Malika went and told my grandmother that I was pregnant. And she was so upset.

"I just don't understand why you would not be more careful," my grandmother said.

I had a hard time even looking at her in the face. She had so much invested in me and she thought I was special and different.

"I know," I said. "I made a mistake."

"And whose is it?" she said, wrinkling up her nose. "That married man?" My grandmother had never met Kiy so she assumed I was pregnant by William, whom she disliked because she knew he was married.

"I'm not pregnant by him!" I said. "It's. . ." I looked down at my hands.

"It's somebody else."

My grandmother just shook her head. Here I was, eighteen years old, in my first year of college on an academic scholarship, and pregnant by someone she hadn't even met. She had bigger and better expectations for me, and I knew that.

For that matter, I had better expectations for myself. If it had been JT's baby, someone I loved and had dated for a while, that would have been one thing. But I didn't even know Kiy well. I really planned to be married before I had a baby. And at the very least, I thought I should have been in a serious relationship with someone my family knew and accepted.

I decided I would tell Kiy about the pregnancy and let him know that I was planning to terminate.

I was at my grandmother's house when I called the apartment he shared with his mother in the Brick Towers housing projects.

"You don't have to worry about it," I told him. "I'm getting an abortion."

"No, you're not," Kiy said.

I was speechless for a second and then collected myself.

"What do you mean?" I asked. "Me and you are not really like that. It don't make sense for me to be having no baby by you."

"It does make sense," he said. "You're not getting an abortion. We're moving to California. You're having my baby. And I'm going to marry you."

I wasn't sure what to make of what he was saying. But he sounded like he was dead serious. By this time, Kiy and his crew had solidified their deal. As producers they were now called CK Blunt Productions and had a deal with Warner Bros. Records to produce tracks. At the same time, Kiy and Ike had also formed a singing group called 1-2-3. Their third member was a young man from the West Coast named Curtis Baldwin, who had enjoyed a taste of celebrity from his role as Calvin on NBC's television series *227*. Curtis was married to Carolyn Griffey, whose dad, Dick, was well known as the founder of Solar Records.

While things were picking up for Kiy and he was making plans to relocate to the West Coast, we'd never even discussed whether or not we were in a relationship. In all honesty, we *weren't* in a relationship. And I knew that I wasn't a part of any plans to move to California. But now I was pregnant. And Kiy wanted me to come with him? The whole thing was bizarre. And the very idea made my head swim. Would I even consider dropping out of college, moving to Los Angeles, and having a baby? It seemed like such a leap from what my life was like at that point. And the more I thought about it, the more tempting it sounded.

I wasn't thrilled with college. I was working my ass off and my grades were decent. (Although I got a D on a paper in a religion class and it pissed me off 'cause I felt like I was being graded on my opinion as opposed to my ability to present my argument.)

But I just wasn't into school. I think part of it was because I didn't live on campus. So I wasn't getting the full experience. I just went to class and then came right back home to Newark. I could have lived on campus, but I was worried about being broke. I knew I could always hustle my way into a few dollars if I stayed close to home. I was still singing at weddings, and other opportunities came about occasionally. Being up in the Bronx with no way to make some paper was not going to work. By this point, I was used to keeping my hair and nails done, rocking my cute little outfits; I wasn't prepared to be a really broke college student.

And as much as I felt like I didn't belong at Fordham, I felt like I didn't belong at the house on Grumman Avenue, either.

I had gotten to the point where I was ready to see how the world worked for myself.

It was right around the time that Kiy offered a new way of life that I had been having these thoughts. Which made it even more tempting to accept his offer and move to Los Angeles.

It wasn't just my thoughts that seemed to outgrow my grandparents' house. Physically, I felt like the house was crowding me, too. With so many people in and out, it was harder and harder for me to carve out my own space. Now that I was in college, I wanted more privacy. And that just wasn't happening in a place like my grandparents' house. I knew that, ultimately, my family would always be there for me. But in that moment, I was ready to see what else was out there.

My whole reason for going to college was so that I could get a decent job and then get my own place. But now Kiy was offering a shortcut to my original plan. And the idea of being on my own was very appealing. The more he asked me, the more I started to think about it seriously.

I spent the summer hanging out with my friends. And I was still going into the studio with Kiy and Christopher Williams and the crew as they prepared to relocate. I earned the nickname Mama partly because I was always putting people in their place. And partly because I became the one to order lunch for the guys or host their girlfriends who come by to check up on them.

Occasionally, Christopher Williams would ask for Mama to come lay down vocals on a track.

The plan was that Kiy and the crew would go out to Los Angeles first, set up house and get everything arranged, and then send for me to follow.

In the meantime, I had to swallow my pride and apply for welfare.

I had no job and no health insurance. I needed to get prenatal care so I went down to the welfare office on Broad Street in Newark and began receiving benefits. I hated it. But I knew it was just temporary. I didn't have a plan mapped out; I just felt like it would somehow all work itself out.

Before I went out to LA, there was one bump in the road that disappointed me but didn't deter me. I'd gone to see Kiy's mother, who lived in Newark with his brother Wendell. We were talking about the baby, and I told her about how her son said he wanted to marry me. She just chuckled and said something about Kiy being three years younger than me.

I was stunned. I was nineteen. Kiy was sixteen.

At that point, when I was nineteen, three years younger was worlds away. The guy I dated before him had been thirty-seven! I couldn't believe I had been so hasty in the relationship that I didn't know these key facts until it was too late.

I asked Kiy about it. But he couldn't give me an explanation that made sense, and I told him I needed a minute to think.

At that point, the plans to move to Los Angeles had already been made. I had to decide whether I was still going to go out there with him or break it off completely and stay at home.

At this stage in my life, I was all about trying to figure out if a guy liked me. If he did, and I was sure that he did, *then* I would figure out if I liked him. It was a completely ass-backward way of approaching relationships. You should figure out how you feel about a person, not just hang around whoever is showing you some attention.

Kiy had convinced me that he really did like me. And I was still figuring out how I felt about him. In the process, I decided I would still continue with our original plan.

I flew out to Los Angeles that fall. When I should have been starting my sophomore year at Fordham, I was instead relocating to California three months' pregnant.

Kiy was staying at the Oakwood Apartments, a well-known spot for corporate housing. A lot of artists, actors, and other would-be celebrities and executives would live in the Oakwood until their deals were solidified and they could move on.

The Oakwood is right near Universal Studios. It's a huge complex with twenty-six buildings, labeled A–Z, and each one has three to four levels with several apartments on each floor. It was huge. And when I arrived, it all seemed a little overwhelming. It wasn't super-luxurious. But it sure wasn't anything like back home.

The three-bedroom apartment was furnished. I settled in when I arrived, meeting all the other bandmates and their girlfriends who shared the place with Kiy.

It was all kind of weird. We were a couple at that point, I guess. But it was sort of strange because before I had gotten pregnant, I can't say there was anything official about our status. And now I was not only having his baby but living with him as well. I think I mentioned earlier that I've been known to be a bit hasty in relationships. Here was a great example of that.

It only took forty-eight hours of being in Los Angeles to realize that things were a little bit off. On my second day at the Oakwood, I was home alone while the guys were working in the studio. While I was unpacking, I heard a knock at the front door.

There was a young woman standing there. She was pretty — kind of short with brown skin and long hair. She talked very proper.

"Hello there," she said. "I'm looking for Kiy. Is he here?"

I looked her up and down. I was instantly suspicious. "Nah," I said. "He ain't here."

"Oh, okay," she said, smiling. "I'll come back later to see him."

Oh really? I'm thinking to myself.

Before she left, she said, "And you must be the vocal coach, right?"

Is that what Kiy had been telling people? That he flew me out to LA to move in and be the vocal coach?

"No," I told the woman. "I'm out here because I'm Kiy's girl-friend and I'm having his baby."

She looked like she wanted to say more. So I added a little something about fucking her up if she had a problem and that was the end of that.

That whole interaction threw me off. The woman obviously didn't know that Kiy and I were supposed to be a couple. I hadn't asked to come out to LA. Why would Kiy send for me if he was doing his thing out here? Why would he tell me to have the baby if he was going to try to play me out?

I thought maybe the girl popping up was an isolated incident. But I quickly learned that now that Kiy had a record deal, he was feeling himself—a lot. We barely spoke. He was in and out of the apartment at all hours. I never knew where he was or what he was doing. It was obvious that I had made a big mistake by coming out to LA.

His group, 1-2-3, was recording and preparing to release an album. Since I lived there, I heard the music all the time. Kiy was a good key-boardist and a decent vocalist. The ballads were hot but I didn't see them being the next Boyz II Men, who were huge at the time.

Christopher Williams, who was an established artist, was supportive. But it just didn't seem that great to me. And although I kept it to myself, I thought they were all overestimating their future music careers. But what did I know? I was pregnant, flat broke, and living with them on the money they were earning from a recording contract.

Luckily, even though Kiy was acting out, I'd made some new friends in LA that would last a lifetime. I met Toni, a young lady who was from Compton and dating one of the members of the crew. Toni was cute, a light-brown-skinned girl with long legs, a slim frame, and sleepy eyes that always made her seem like she was high. At the time that I met her, all I knew about Compton was the gang violence portrayed in the movies *American Me* and *Colors*. So I assumed Toni was going to be some kind of hard-core gangbanger.

The first day I met her, when she came by the Oakwood to visit, I noticed she had a small letter т tattooed on her hand. I assumed it was some kind of gang sign. I was so naive that I didn't think it could just be a simple tattoo, which it was. Toni turned out to be really fun. I liked hanging out with her.

I was miserable at the Oakwood but my new friends made it a little better. We hung out a lot, going to the studio, grabbing a bite to eat from Del Taco, or just chilling inside the apartment. Toni loved to laugh at my Jersey girl accent, especially when I said words like *car* and *water* so much different from the way LA folks say them. Many times she would beg me to say stuff over and over because it sounded so different.

Richard was another person I met in Los Angeles who would become a very close friend. At the time, he was working as a stylist for an R&B group named Jade. We formed a very deep bond and when I became an artist, he would end up working with me as my stylist and become a very trusted part of my inner circle.

About a month after I arrived, Kiy started getting really bold when it came to dating other women.

It was early November, and it was strange to me that the weather was so warm. It was Los Angeles, so people had Thanksgiving dinner barbecues and walked around in shorts all year 'round.

I was sitting in the living room with Toni one night, talking and hanging out. I happened to be looking out the window, watching people park their cars and come into the building, when I saw Kiy pull up to our building in the passenger's seat of some chick's car.

"Oh no, this nigga is not trying to play me out like this!" I said to Toni. I didn't know it at the time but she had been going through some similar stuff with her boyfriend, so we had bonded in the few weeks I'd been there.

"Who is that girl?" Toni asked, coming over to the window to take a peek.

"I don't know," I said, moving toward the door. "But I'm 'bout to find out."

I dashed out of the front door of the apartment, down the stairs, and out into the parking lot. It was pitch black outside, and I knew Kiy couldn't see me walking up to the car.

And there he was, sitting in the passenger's side of a silver Toyota Celica. As I marched over, I could see that he had his head turned to the side, facing the girl. She had one hand on the steering wheel and she was looking over at Kiy with a flirtatious smile on her face. She had a slim face that was nondescript. She wasn't unattractive. But she wasn't cute, either. Kiy said something to her and she threw her head back and laughed. This was obviously not a platonic friend.

I think she saw me first, because she said something and then Kiy turned in my direction, but by then I had already passed the front of the car and come around to the driver's side.

"Who the fuck is this?" I screamed.

I motioned for the girl to roll down the window. She rolled the window down and before she could say one word, I punched her right in her face.

"Get out the car, bitch!" I yelled.

The girl's hand went up to her face in shock. "Roll the window up!" Kiy said to her. "Come on, let's go."

I continued cursing them both out as the girl threw the car in drive and peeled out of the parking lot.

I could hear Toni and the rest of them screaming and laughing out of the window. Toni later told me that when she saw me pop that girl, she knew we were gonna be friends from that moment on.

They drove off. And I walked all the way across the development, through the mountains, in the dark, looking for that car, with Toni and a few other people following me.

After that incident, I wanted to go home. I had already gone back and forth a few times to collect my monthly welfare benefits and see my obstetrician. And every time I came back to LA, Kiy's behavior was more erratic.

One day, I came home to find that Kiy had flown out to Arizona. I had no idea why and didn't really care. But I just realized that we were on two very different pages. When he returned, I didn't ask any questions and he didn't offer any answers. We just communicated on the very basic level—no more and no less.

I was getting larger and more uncomfortable, and living at the Oakwood was becoming more and more depressing. I didn't have a job. I had no money. It was hot. I was pregnant. And I was away from my family.

The only way I could relax would be to lie in the tub and let the shower rain on me. I'd been told that hot baths were dangerous when you were pregnant. So I'd climb into the tub and turn on the shower instead. I spent many evenings this way, listening to Brian McKnight and wondering how the hell I'd let this happen. I was mad at Kiy and I was mad at myself. I had never given any thought to who he really was. I was being hasty and not looking at the big picture. But I knew I had to deal with the consequences. I had to deal with the situation that I'd gotten myself into and do the best that I could.

I prayed a lot for guidance on what my next move should be. I was about to be someone's mother. And it looked like I was going to be a single mother. I was going to have to grow up fast. The first step was going to be to get the hell out of LA and get back to the Brick City to rebuild.

But before that could happen, I'd have to find the money to get there on my own. 'Cause I wasn't asking Kiy for shit.

Chapter Five

Mama

"*M*ama! You need to come down to the studio. Now."

It was Ike Lee. I was at the apartment, trying to figure out how the hell I was going to get back to New Jersey, when he called.

"Why?" I asked. "What's going on?"

"We got Puff Daddy here," he said. "We're trying to play him this track we're working on but we need a female to sing the part."

"You need me to come down there now?" I asked. I was about six months' pregnant and not capable of rushing around too much.

"Yes. *Now.*"

I could tell from the sound of his voice that it was urgent. So I got dressed as quickly as I could and drove down to the Larrabee Studios in West Hollywood.

Just like singing for Teddy Riley two years before, I didn't really think of it as a big deal. Even though by this time, Sean "Puffy" Combs was on his ascent to the Next Big Thing in the music industry.

It was 1992, and Puffy was best known for his work with Mary J. Blige. That summer, she'd released her seminal debut album, *What's the 411?* Hip-hop and soul music had never really been combined in a way that appealed to such a large audience before; what Mary accomplished on that first album was groundbreaking.

Puffy had been an intern at Uptown Records, which was distributed by MCA. He later became an A&R executive, under the direction of Andre Harrell, the president of Uptown. One of his first assignments was to oversee Mary's album. He didn't actually produce that many tracks. But he was instrumental in developing her style, both musically and otherwise.

Everything about Mary was just the bomb. She really represented the streets. You have to understand: Successful female R&B singers at this time were mostly still throwbacks to an earlier age. You had Anita Baker, one of my absolute favorites, who was on her fourth album by the early '90s. And then even the younger women, like the ladies in En Vogue, were patterned on girl groups from the 1960s like the Supremes. Mary's sound was new and fresh and exciting—hard-core hip-hop beats with singing instead of rapping. It was a novel concept, and it caught on quickly.

When I first got to the Oakwood, I heard Kiy and his people playing her music around the apartment before it was released. She didn't have that classic gospel vibrato that I was used to so I didn't understand what all the buzz was about. But after her album dropped, I understood immediately. It was more than just her voice. It was the style—the hat cocked to the side, the combat boots, the hair over one eye. It was all about the swagger. And she had it.

Puff had also worked his magic on R&B group Jodeci, who released their classic debut album *Forever My Lady* in May 1991. Again, they were a new take on the whole boy-group concept. Unlike Boyz II Men, who came out around the same time, Jodeci was raw and street. And Puff's touch made them white-hot.

Just based on his work with Mary J. Blige and Jodeci, I knew it was huge that Kiy and the guys were working with him, although I didn't know that much about Puffy himself. I just waddled my pregnant self down to the studio and went straight into the vocal booth. Puff didn't really notice me. I don't even think we were formally introduced. I was simply Kiy's pregnant girlfriend helping out in a pinch.

I don't remember anything about the song—or if it even appeared on Christopher Williams's album. I was just doing my job—as a friend to the crew. I sang the chorus they wanted me to sing and that was it. I went right back up to the Oakwood. I never even gave any thought to how performing for someone like Puffy could help me out. At that moment, I didn't think of myself as a singer with a future in the music industry.

The only thing I knew for sure was that it was time for me to go home. But I was flat broke and I was not about to ask Kiy for plane fare. I didn't even want him to know I was ready to leave. I called my friend Roz back in Newark and told her what was going on. Her brother Reggie, the sweet and shy eleventh-grader I'd once dated, had by this time become Redman, a rapper signed to Def Jam Records. Roz told me that Red was on tour in San Diego and that if I could get there, he could probably give me some money to get home.

"Kiy, give me your car keys," I told him one night when he came back from the studio.

"Why?" he asked. "Where you going?"

"I'll be right back. Just going to the store right quick."

Kiy gave me his keys and I left. I got behind the wheel of his Bronco and headed straight for the 405 freeway. I didn't know anything about driving in LA. I'd only had my driver's license for a year or so. And up until that point, the only driving I'd done in LA was from the Oakwood to the studio and maybe over to Del Taco for a burrito.

It was almost ten o'clock at night when I left. The car had no gas when I got in. And I knew I'd have to fill up at some point. But it was late at night and I wanted to get on the road as quickly as possible.

As I drove down the freeway, I looked at the different signs, trying to figure out the best place to pull off and get gas. I didn't recognize any of the names. I didn't know which places were safe and which to avoid.

The road was nearly empty, and it was pitch black outside. I kept the windows slightly cracked so that I could get some fresh air in the car and stay alert and awake, although I was incredibly tired. The gas gauge continued to dip lower and lower until a light turned on, warning me that the car would shut off soon.

I read a sign that said LONG BEACH and thought that would be a good place to stop. I'd never heard of it, but it had *beach* in the name so I expected a sleepy little beach town. I got off at the exit for Long Beach and drove about half a mile in to the first gas station. I thanked God that I'd made it and then climbed out of the car.

The gas station had six pumps in the center of the lot. And there was no one parked at any of the pumps besides me. I got out of the car, looked around the vacant lot, and peered into the storefront to see if it was open. I saw one older man standing behind the counter so I went inside. There was a slight chill in the air, but it was extremely quiet. There were no sounds at all, not even wind or crickets or other cars. I paid the eight dollars — half of it in change I scrounged up — and told him which pump I was using.

I looked around on my walk back to the car, slightly concerned that it was so deserted in the area. I picked up the gas pump and slipped it into the car and stood there, one hand on the pump, the other resting on top of the car.

Suddenly I heard a loud *pop* and then a whizzing sound close to my ear. At the same time, I felt something sting my arm and I jumped.

I looked over at my upper arm and there was a quarter-size hole in the gray cotton sweater I was wearing. And whatever hit my arm had it stinging like hell. I was petrified. I knew I needed my gas. I stood there, jiggling the pump to make the gas come out faster and holding on to my arm with my free hand. As soon as I had all eight dollars' worth of gas in my car, I jumped in, slammed the door, and pulled off, one hand on my arm the entire time.

I had never heard a gunshot before, but I immediately assumed that's what it was.

I was shot. I couldn't believe it. I sped down the freeway for ten minutes, driving with one hand, too scared even to look at my arm. Finally my heart started to slow down, and I pulled over to the shoulder.

I shrugged out of my sweater and pulled up the sleeve of my T-shirt. The skin there was red and swollen and there was a small mark—but no blood. I breathed a sigh of relief.

I was so scared I didn't even want to go to the hospital. I just wanted out of Long Beach and out of Los Angeles. I still have the scar on my tricep. I think that it was just a BB gun. But at the time, I wasn't sure and I was petrified.

I drove straight to San Diego, stopping just twice to get gas and use the pay phone to make sure Red was still waiting for me. I was running out of what little money I did have and I was scared that I'd get to San Diego with no money left, only to find that Red and his crew had moved on to the next spot on their tour.

Thankfully, I caught up with Red.

"Yo, Faye. You aiight?" Red asked when I got to his hotel.

"I'm okay. I just need to go home."

"Here," he said, handing me a wad of cash, about five hundred dollars. "You need more? 'Cause I can probably get it from somewhere."

"Nah, I'm good," I said. "Thanks, Red."

He gave me a long look. "You need me to fuck somebody up? 'Cause I'll fuck a nigga up for you. You know that."

I smiled. It felt good to be around someone from home who had my back.

"Nah, you ain't gotta beat nobody up," I said. "I'm just getting the hell off the West Coast."

On my way back, I called the apartment. Curtis, one of Kiy's roommates, told me that Kiy was worried.

"Whatever," I said. "He's just worried about getting his car back."

I got back to the Oakwood and told Kiy I'd be leaving as soon as I could get a flight out.

By February 1993, I was back in Newark. Back in my room on Grumman Avenue. I had learned a valuable lesson — no matter what, I would always be able to return to my family. Even today, I know that if it really came down to it, I could go right back to my grandparents' home. Back with Roz and my friends Dena and Ticia and my cousins.

I was also hanging out with my good friend Donovan, a preacher's kid who played the organ with Hezekiah Walker's choir out in Brooklyn. Donovan and I went to Je's, my favorite soul food restaurant in downtown Newark, almost every day. I'd have the Salisbury steak, sautéed spinach, and macaroni and cheese. I was back in my comfort zone, but I was also without a game plan.

I was seven months' pregnant and trying to prepare for motherhood. I was happy to be out of LA and away from Kiy. But I knew I wasn't ready for motherhood. I was still receiving welfare benefits and getting prenatal care at Beth Israel, the hospital closest to my house. Beth Israel was far from a high-ranked hospital. But anyone who was receiving health benefits through public assistance had no other choice. It was bare-bones health care: I got one quick ultrasound throughout the entire pregnancy.

I wasn't sure what the future would hold with Kiy. I just knew I needed to be back in familiar surroundings. I didn't feel like I knew him any better than I had that day in the studio when I first sang for the whole crew.

We didn't communicate once I returned home. I just told him to send me some money so that I could buy a car before the baby came. He did, and I bought a used 1988 black-and-gray Ford Bronco just before my due date. We'd never had a serious relationship. But now, as far as I was concerned, Kiy and I didn't have any kind of relationship.

My due date came and went. And my baby wasn't interested in showing up. I was getting bigger and bigger and not liking it. I was normally a size ten, a little thick but perfectly normal. A size twelve for me was kinda chunky. By the time I was nine months' pregnant, I was straight-up fat.

One night, I lay next to my grandfather feeling just awful. Couldn't quite put my finger on what was wrong but I just didn't feel good. I didn't think I was in labor. But my grandfather got tired of hearing me moaning and groaning and drove me over to Beth Israel. They decided it wasn't time yet and sent me back home, instructing me to walk around the neighborhood to get things started.

Within several hours, I was fatigued and crampy and I knew it was time. My grandfather took me to the emergency room entrance. I held on to his arm as he walked me inside, moaning the entire way.

"This girl's in labor," my grandfather told the woman sitting at the information desk. "And this is my second time bringing her here tonight. Y'all got to keep her 'cause she is ready to have this baby."

The woman barely looked up at us. "Who's her doctor?" she asked.

I told her, and she pushed some buttons on her telephone keypad.

"From the clinic?" she asked. "Have a seat over there."

In a few minutes, someone from the labor and delivery ward came down to get me and took me upstairs. They put me on a gurney and checked to see if I was dilated.

"You're four centimeters dilated," the nurse said to me. "You'll be able to start pushing soon."

My grandfather had gone to make phone calls so that my family could come. All I could think about was the powerful cramps that were so painful I felt like they were blinding me.

"I need...something," I told the nurse. "Something for the pain. I can't take it."

The nurse looked at my chart and made a face. "I'm not sure if there's an anesthesiologist available for you." She left the room and returned with two small pills.

"Here's some Demerol," she said, holding me up so I could swallow the pills. "This should help."

It did not help one bit. My contractions got stronger and the pain intensified, spreading from my hips to my back. I was nearly screaming in pain. I'll never forget that they offered me Demerol instead of a real epidural for pain relief. I've always assumed it was because I was on welfare and perhaps my health insurance didn't include having an anesthesiologist administer an epidural. But I know one thing—that Demerol didn't do a damn thing for the pain. I remember feeling like it was more pain than I'd ever experienced in my life. I just wanted that baby out of me.

I was happy to see my family when they arrived—my cousin T-T was there, and Candy, Mae, Bob, Gaye, and my mom. But all I could really think about was how bad I wanted to push the baby out and have the pain go away. When I was dilated ten centimeters and it was time to start pushing, it was just the doctor, two nurses, and my mom standing at the business end.

"Bear down!" I heard someone yelling. "And push!"

I sat up like I was doing crunches and pushed down as hard as I could until they told me to stop. Then I took a deep breath and did it over and over again.

When I finally pushed the baby out, I remember hearing my mom say, "It's a boy!" But that was just wishful thinking. Because the nine-pound child that the nurse put in my arms was a little girl with slanted eyes that made her look like a little Buddha. Everyone had told me that I was having a boy because of the way I carried. So I had lots of boy name ideas. But deep down, I wanted a girl.

I didn't have many girl names chosen, so I had to think. The group Wilson Phillips had been big the summer before, and one of the members was named Chyna. I thought it was a cool name and since she looked Asian to me, I named my daughter Chyna Tahjere Griffin.

The day I gave birth to Chyna, April 1, 1993, Kiy and his crew were shooting a video for their song "Love Me Right." From what I heard, he was living it up in Los Angeles. By the time I had Chyna, he'd bought a Jeep Cherokee and had left the Oakwood and was living in a three-bedroom house with a pool in the San Fernando Valley.

I also heard that he was beginning to act way too big for his britches. But he was allowed to get away with that. I saw folks treating him like his shit didn't stink, and he began to act that way. I'd never dealt with him like that and didn't plan to.

I wasn't in touch with Kiy during those early days of Chyna's life. I took the baby to Kiy's mother's house, but he and I weren't in much contact. I did want Chyna to know her father, though. I'd grown up not knowing anything about who my father was. I didn't want Chyna to deal with that.

So in the summer of 1993, when Chyna was about two months old, I decided to take her to Los Angeles so that her father could see her. I took my best friend Roz and my friend Tara for moral support in case he was still acting weird.

When we arrived at his house, one of the guys let us in and then told me that Kiy was at the studio.

We sat in the living room and waited. Chyna was a chunky little baby, with Kiy's round brown face and slanted eyes. She was just starting to smile at me, and she was always really mellow and laid-back.

A few hours after I arrived, I heard a key in the door. Kiy came into the living room.

"Hey," I said, standing up and walking toward Chyna.

"Hey, Faith," he said, with an awkward smile. He put his keys down on the kitchen table and made a beeline to where Chyna was sitting in her seat. She was wide awake and looking at her father with interest.

"Can I take her out of this seat?" he asked me.

"Of course," I said. "She's your daughter."

He bent down and unbuckled Chyna's straps. He picked her up and held her close to his face.

"You are so beautiful," he said to Chyna. "You are just the prettiest little thing."

He held Chyna close and kissed her chubby cheeks. Then he turned to face me.

"You gonna stay out here for a minute?" he asked.

"I'll be here for a few days and see what happens," I told him. "I just want you to get the opportunity to see Chyna and spend some time with her."

"Thanks. I appreciate that."

Kiy seemed like he was happy to see Chyna, but he was still all over the place. He was in and out of the house entertaining women and all kinds of guests. I couldn't say anything. It wasn't my house. But it still wasn't the best situation. After a few weeks, I was through. And when he pulled another disappearing act to Arizona, I knew it was time for me to go.

I went back to my grandparents' house with Chyna and just hung out for the rest of the summer, getting used to motherhood and trying to figure out what my next step would be. Since Kiy and Christopher

Williams and the rest of the guys were in LA, I wasn't in the studio. I wasn't doing much writing or performing. I hung out a lot with my friend E-Jay, who had a record store in Newark.

I was a single mother who had dropped out of college. People who knew me from around the way probably looked at me and just shook their heads. I was supposed to make it out of the hood. I wasn't supposed to be in this situation. But even then, I knew that my future would have to be different than it seemed. I wasn't doing anything to change it. I wasn't taking any classes or trying to get back in school. I wasn't even looking for a job. I was just living. But I knew that it wasn't the end of my story.

Within a year of my return to Newark, Kiy and his crew were back in Newark, too. I never got a definitive answer about what happened. But the house in the valley and the Cherokee and the videos and the albums—all of that was over.

My situation wasn't much better. I had no plan and no focus. I was completely in limbo. My next step was whatever was right in front of me.

By the end of 1993, Kiy and the crew began going to Unique Studios, in Times Square. They were working on music with an R&B singer named Al B. Sure.

In the late 1980s, when I was just starting high school, Al B. Sure had put out his first album, *In Effect Mode.* His first single, "Nite and Day," had done really well. He was a pretty boy: light skin, "good" hair, and a unibrow. And the girls loved him. Coming from the church, I wasn't used to his breathy and light falsetto. But I was learning that secular music was a lot more varied than gospel music. Al had style, he was a heartthrob, and his music had a good sound. His sophomore album had come out a year or so before he started working with Kiy and it hadn't done so well. But he was still a pretty big star at the time.

In addition to performing and recording, Al also wrote and produced for other artists. He was even trying to get his own label deal off the ground. So he was enlisting other producers to work on songs and help him get them placed with different artists.

Kiy was spending a lot of time up at the studio with the rest of the guys and Al B. Sure. Every once in a while, I would bring Chyna to the studio to see her dad. I wasn't really paying attention to what they were working on. I was simply there with my daughter, visiting my baby daddy. I spent most of my time in the studio lounge, watching television.

A few weeks after they started working together, Kiy played a song for Al that he'd been working on. It had some of my vocals on it, and Al B. Sure asked who the female vocalist on the song was. Kiy told him it was me. I was in the studio lounge at the time. He called out for me to come to the booth. For a minute, Al B. Sure just stared at me.

"This is *you* singing?" he asked.

I just nodded.

"Why didn't you say anything!" he said. He looked like he was actually angry. "I can't believe you can sing like this and never said anything!"

"I wasn't here to sing," I explained to Al.

"But you have a gorgeous voice," he said. "You're hanging out in the lounge every day with a voice like that? What's wrong with you?"

I know some people would have been walking through the halls singing at the top of their lungs any chance that they could. But that wasn't my way. I wasn't the type to advertise my talents. No one had ever asked me to sing. So I didn't. I still knew what I was capable of. But I was always very conscious of not overstepping my bounds and looking too eager for something. If it was meant for me to be involved in something, I believed it would happen naturally and that I wouldn't have to push it.

Al immediately started having me lay down vocals for different songs he was writing. There was still nothing formal about it. If I was around and he needed a female voice, I would sing it.

And then Kiy disappeared again. I could tell that Al B. Sure was frustrated. He was trying to get a production deal, trying to sell the songs he was writing, and Kiy, who was supposed to be helping him, had his own agenda.

I don't know what Kiy was dealing with then. It's obvious looking back that he must have had some serious things going on in his life. Maybe he had some opportunities in different places or maybe he just had issues he needed to deal with and didn't know how to explain it to anyone.

Even though Chyna's father was MIA, Al and I had our bond at this point so I was still in the studio helping out in any way that I could.

"I need more help in the studio," he said to me one day.

"What do you need?"

"I'm writing songs and I need someone to demo them. Are you interested?"

"Of course," I said.

"I need you here every day," he said.

I thought about my Bronco and how it was falling apart. I wasn't even sure if it would make it through the Holland Tunnel every day.

I didn't want to have to keep calling my grandfather if it stalled, although I knew he would come. But I couldn't let the car stop me. I had to make it work.

"Don't worry about it," I said. "Let's make it happen."

After my first week working with Al, I got an envelope with a check for two thousand dollars. I was still on welfare at this point. And this dude was paying me two grand a week! I felt like I had won the lottery. Except it was better. Because I was doing it my way, using my talent and living my dream.

Just as I had always prayed for, I was going to be able to make my living with my voice and my musical ability. I was thrilled and excited. And with that kind of money, I'd be able to move out and take care of my daughter. I really felt like I had made it.

I was twenty years old, a new mom with an interesting new job that would pay me more than I could ever have dreamed. In the back of my mind, I thought I might even be lucky enough to do more background vocals. For me, the true joy was in being able to sing professionally, even if I wasn't the main attraction.

Freeze-frame on me for just one second. I'm standing in a recording studio with Al B. Sure, my first paycheck in my hand, and a big smile on my face. Chyna is only six months old, and I haven't lost any of the baby weight. I'm in a skirt outfit, made out of a knit fabric, laid-back and unassuming. Not really a super-fly, look-at-me type of girl. I'm happy as hell about my new job. And I am clueless to all the changes that are about to happen to me.

Fast-forward this frame one year and my life would be so different that some of my closest friends wouldn't be able to recognize me.

CHAPTER SIX

The First Lady

*E*very day, I would pack up Chyna for the drive over to Manhattan in my beat-up Ford Bronco. Most days, I had to whisper a silent prayer as I strapped my baby into her car seat.

Please, God, let this car get through the Holland Tunnel today.

I wanted to be really professional, and I wanted Al to know he could count on me. But that car was on its last legs. There were many days I'd have to coax it into Manhattan after it stalled a few times and then call Al to let him know I was on my way.

One morning, I'd been up late with Chyna, who wasn't feeling well. I had a hard time getting up and it was just one of those days. I could have easily called the studio and told Al I wasn't going to make it. But I wasn't about to do that. I had a job that I knew some people would kill for. I'd have to summon up some strength to get through the day.

I took a shower, got dressed, and then got Chyna dressed. My Bronco was parked on the street right in the front of the house, and I opened the back door to buckle Chyna into the car seat. She looked up at me and laughed.

"Hey, baby girl!" I said to her. "You ready to make some music?"

I got into the driver's seat, said my usual prayer, and pulled off down Grumman Street toward Route 78. The ride was bumpy, as usual. The truck needed shocks really bad and there were a few other things that needed to be done when I got some money together.

But for now, it was getting me back and forth into Manhattan—barely. And I was hoping I could soon get a new car instead of investing money in a hunk of metal. It was a blustery winter's morning. There were snow flurries blowing around but not quite sticking to the ground. It was just enough for me to go slow on the roads. And it was cold enough that I worried if the car would make it.

As soon as I pulled through the tollbooth of the Holland Tunnel, I felt the car start to buck and sputter.

Oh God no, I whispered. *Please not here.*

I pushed on the gas, my hands gripping the steering wheel. I thought if I just focused really hard, I could somehow *will* the car to move. But it died, ten feet into the Holland Tunnel. Other cars trying to get through began to honk as I sat there helplessly. The snow started to come down harder, and there was a heavy wind blowing the flakes into the tunnel. Traffic began backing up for miles outside the tunnel, all because of that damn Bronco. I started to cry.

Some guy came up to me and tapped on my window.

"I think I might be able to push you through," he said.

"God, I hope so." I told him.

The guy brought his truck up to my back bumper. I put the car in neutral and steered as he drove his truck, nudging my car slowly through the tunnel. I made it to the other side and thanked the guy over and over. With the car on the side of the road, I still needed to get the car towed away somewhere and get to the studio on time. I took Chyna out of her car seat and threw her up on my hip. I checked to make sure she was bundled up properly and then I pulled my own coat tight around me to shield me from the bitter cold. With Chyna holding on tight to my neck, I walked down Hudson Street to find a pay phone. I called my grandfather and begged him to come and help me.

As usual, he told me he'd be right there and I waited as patiently as I could, watching the clock the whole time.

My grandfather drove out from Newark and did something to the car so that I could drive it just long enough to get it to an auto body shop near the studio. Then I grabbed Chyna again, dipped into a nearby deli to pick up a sandwich, and hauled ass into that studio and up to the third floor where Al was waiting for me.

"Hey, Faith. How are you this morning?"

My ears were freezing because I hadn't been wearing a hat. But the rest of my body was hot because of all the walking I'd done. I was sweaty, out of breath, and hungry. Chyna was cranky and I didn't know how we were getting home that night. But Al didn't need to know any of that.

"I'm doing great this morning," I said with a bright smile. "How are you?"

I loved my new gig with Al B. Sure. I knew he had been a popular singer but I didn't know he was a good songwriter, and I began to respect him as a musician. He taught me quite a bit about production and studio work. I didn't know he'd written and produced stuff for Tevin Campbell. And most importantly, I noticed right away that although he didn't really play instruments, Al B. Sure knew exactly what he wanted in terms of sound. No matter what producer or musician he worked with, his music still had the same readily identifiable sound. From watching him work, I learned that producers didn't always have to be able to play music. They just needed to know what they wanted to hear, then give this information to the right people and make it happen.

I worked on a number of different songs, recording demo versions and arranging the vocals if necessary. It wasn't much different from the tinkering I had done with recording in Tyrone's home studio. I had an ear for how to make songs sound more melodic and the best way to enrich the voices on the track. Al B. Sure began calling me "the Doctor" because of my ability to take a track and doctor it up into something special.

It was a calm, relaxing work environment. His wife, Jackie, was nice, too. I can remember complimenting her on a beautiful pair of boots she was wearing and the next day she bought me the exact same pair, which I thought was really sweet.

For six months, I worked with Al as a session singer. And I knew that he was also trying to sign me as an artist to the new label he was hoping to get off the ground. I was hopeful. But after seeing what Kiy and the guys had gone through, I knew that the record business was extremely unpredictable. So although I knew he was trying to make something happen, I wasn't holding my breath.

In the meantime, I was doing okay for myself. I had a car. I was making two thousand dollars a week and still using the last of my food stamps. My child was taken care of and I even had a little change to go to Mannie's jewelry store in the diamond district, where JT used to take me, and buy my own little gold rings and earrings. I set up my own bank account and at the age of twenty, I was finally starting to feel like an adult.

I was occasionally still hanging out with Kiy and his crew, mostly so that he could spend some time with Chyna. Once in a while they would need a ride to a studio session, and I would take them. They were no longer working with Al B. Sure. But they still had other connections in the industry.

Once, they had time booked at a studio called the Hit Factory. It was early 1994. I had just gotten my own apartment in East Orange, New Jersey, and I was one of the few people whom Kiy and Ike and

Floyd could depend on to get a ride somewhere. I drove them to their session and planned to wait so that I could drive them all back to Newark. Kiy's crew had been hired by Puffy to work on a track for a new singer, a fifteen-year-old named Usher Raymond.

A lot had happened to Puffy since I'd come down to the studio in LA when I was pregnant with Chyna to sing on a track they were working on. Andre Harell had fired Puffy from his job at Uptown. And now Andre Harrell was having a string of successes while people were wondering what the next move for Puff would be. He was still producing many artists and LA Reid, the head of LaFace Records, had hired him to executive-produce Usher's debut album.

And now Puff had invited Kiy and his CK Blunt Productions to see if they could contribute something to Usher's album.

Even though I was working with Al B. Sure, I still didn't go to the studio with the guys in any capacity besides just hanging out. I brought Chyna and planned to just wait in the studio lounge for them to be done and go back home.

I sat on a couch in the studio lounge, watching television with Chyna in my lap. The lounge was small and sparse. There were two tattered leather sofas, an ancient television bolted into the wall, and a few end tables with a telephone on one and stacks of take-out menus and magazines on the other.

I turned to put my legs up on the sofa and situated Chyna beside me so that she could take a nap. I was flipping through a magazine when Ike Lee came into the lounge.

"Mama. We need you. Come on."

"Need me for what?"

"We need a woman's voice on one of these tracks. Come *on*."

"Okay, okay," I said, shifting Chyna, who was sleeping, away from my body and positioning her on the sofa.

I followed Ike out of the lounge and down the corridor in the direction of the studio. My mouth had gone dry and my hands were cold and clammy. I'd sung for Puff back in LA, but he'd become much more accomplished since then. Everyone knew who Puff Daddy was, and now I was about to come face-to-face with him.

I took a glance at myself in one of the framed photos that lined the hallway as I walked behind Ike. I had on a pair of wide-legged palazzo pants that I'd worn a lot when I was pregnant with Chyna. And I had on a brown-and-beige knit sweater and brown slouchy suede ankle boots. I looked okay. But I was still self-conscious. I looked like I was going to run errands—not sing for a popular music producer.

I walked into the studio behind Ike with my head down. The room was loud; people were laughing, talking, and joking with each other while a track played on the speakers that were embedded into the walls around the room. The only people I recognized were Kiy, Ike, and Floyd, who were all sitting on folding chairs to my left. They looked nervous as they talked about which songs they were going to play for Puff.

To my right, there were three men sitting at the mixing boards, pushing buttons and twiddling knobs to adjust the way the music sounded pulsating through the speakers. One guy was standing up, leaning over the men at the mixing board. His back was to me and even though I couldn't see his face, I knew it was Puff from the sound of his voice.

"That shit ain't hot," he barked at one of the guys. "I need to hear some strings on that shit. Don't none a y'all niggas know how to play some guitar? Make that shit sound full. I want it to be on some old operatic shit!"

The guy swallowed and then wiped his face with his hand. "I was gonna try that but I need to get out of here—"

"Did you just say you needed to get out of here?"

Puffy spun around to face the rest of the room.

"This nigga just told me he needs to leave. Do y'all believe this shit?"

I didn't even really remember what he looked like from before.

So it was like seeing him for the first time. He was only a few inches taller than me, but the intensity of his attitude made him seem like he was over six feet tall. His words rushed together very quickly, and his normal speaking voice came out like a yell.

"This *is* your home, nigga!" he said to the producer. The guy jumped slightly and then tried to smile.

A young guy, about sixteen or seventeen years old, opened up the studio door and poked his head in. Puffy waved him in. The kid gave him bottled water and a sandwich and then disappeared.

"My time is too fucking valuable for y'all to be bullshitting." He took a swig of his water, swished it around his mouth, and then swallowed.

"Now I need to hear this Usher song with some female vocals on it."

Ike stood up from the far side of the room where he'd been sitting with Kiy and Floyd. "We got somebody right here." Ike came up to me, put his hand on my shoulder, and walked me over to Puff.

"Mama can sing," Floyd said.

Now, I have to make this clear: I was *not* there to sing that day. It was nothing but the work of God that brought me into the studio with Puff.

The engineer started the song, and Puff reached for a piece of paper on the console that had the song's lyrics on it.

When the beat started, Puff started nodding with his eyes closed. Then he looked at me and started waving his arms like a conductor and singing.

His voice was comically bad. He was hitting the right notes — sort of. But there was no tonality or vibrato. Still, I understood what he wanted. He sang it a few more times and I just stood there listening and nodding.

"You hear that?" he said. "You hear how those harmonies fall into place? I want some rich harmonies right there."

I nodded again.

Puffy handed me the paper with the lyrics on it. "Here," he said. "Go over this and I'll be back to hear it." He turned to walk out of the studio.

"I'm ready now," I said.

Puff turned around and looked at me. "You ready? You ain't even listen to it."

I could barely speak. This was all a shock. You have to remember—I was *not* there to sing. I was there to wait for the guys and drive them back home. So to suddenly be thrust into this situation was really crazy.

I just started making my way to the booth. I got halfway there and realized that the room was too bright. I couldn't take everyone just staring at me. I felt so self-conscious with my Anita Baker layered haircut and my going-out-to-dinner outfit. I was so not fly like Puff and his people. The guys were all wearing the latest Karl Kani denim outfits and Timberland construction boots. I knew I looked out of place.

"Can someone turn the lights down a little?" I asked. The room went dim, and I continued walking toward the booth.

Inside, I began laying down the vocals for the chorus. But it didn't feel right.

"Excuse me?" I asked Puff.

Puff turned around and looked at me.

"Um. I was just wondering...Would you mind if I changed up this line a little bit."

"Do whatever you need to do," he said, pointing to the engineer to start the track over.

I was so nervous, I could hear my heart beating in my chest. Even though this wasn't the superstar Puffy that he would later become, he had a presence that meant business.

Still, I had a feeling that he didn't know how I was about to straight kill those two little lines he wanted me to sing. I stood up straight and calm, just like I did when I sang "Let the Sun Shine In" at Emanuel Baptist. I took a deep breath and belted out my lines.

I just closed my eyes tight, clenched my fists, and brought my arms up near my face. I leaned into that microphone and poured out those notes like I'd never done before.

When I finished my lines, I came out of the booth, relieved that it was over, and started walking toward the door. I noticed right away that Puffy was looking directly at me. It almost felt like his eyes were boring into my face. I looked away. I wasn't sure if he liked what I'd done or not. I just wanted to get back to the lounge and check on Chyna.

He gestured to where he was sitting, on a piano bench pulled up to the mixing boards. I glanced over to my left where Kiy, Ike, and Floyd were sitting. They were watching me intently as I walked back over to Puff and sat down next to him.

Puff leaned in and said something to me but I couldn't hear a thing because the music was so loud. The track I'd just sung to was still looped up and the engineer was working on it, so the whole room was deafening.

"Did you say something?" I yelled.

Puff leaned closer until his mouth was right near my ear. "I said I love your voice!"

I smiled and looked down at my lap. My stomach was starting to bubble up, and I felt tingles on my neck. I knew I had a good voice. I'd always known I had a gift from God. But hearing this from some-one like Puff—who seemed to be so discriminating—was exciting.

"Thank you," I told him, and then stood up to leave.

He pulled on my arm and gestured for me to sit back down. He turned to face the mixing board. I turned around, too. Now our backs were to the guys.

"I'm starting my own label," he yelled. "It's called Bad Boy Records."

I knew he wouldn't be able to hear me if I said anything over the noise. So I just smiled and nodded.

"I want to sign you."

I froze in place and my eyes grew wide. I slowly turned my head to the left to look at Puff.

"What did you say?"

"I said I want to sign you to my label!"

It was surreal. And also, it felt kind of awkward. Kiy and Ike and Floyd, who were there to play some tracks for Puffy, were sitting right across from us. It was so loud that they probably couldn't hear what he was saying. But they must have known something was up.

"Are you interested?" Puffy asked me with a smile. "You wanna be signed to Bad Boy Records?"

"Yeah," I yelled over the music. "Hell yeah I'm interested."

Before I could say another word, he whipped out a piece of paper and a pen, propped it on the mixing board, and started writing.

"How does this sound?" he asked, pointing to a complicated set of numbers he'd scribbled down. My head was swimming. He wanted to negotiate a deal right there in the studio just two minutes after he heard me sing for the first time? I didn't understand any of the pay structures he was talking about.

"I think I should talk to my lawyer first," I blurted out.

"You got a lawyer?" he asked.

"Absolutely. His name is Stuart Levy. You should send everything to him."

I sounded way more confident than I felt. I didn't know what was happening. But I remembered some of the conversations I'd had with Stuart Levy when I was still in high school and I knew I shouldn't be talking numbers with Puffy.

That was Puffy's way, even in the very beginning. He was all business. Through the years, people have talked about how Puffy will take advantage of his artists financially. They expect him to be a certain way because he's young. But from the very first day I met him, he was about his business first. I should have taken his example. Instead, I would end up learning the hard way that it was up to me to stay on top of my business interests. Because Puffy would always stay on top of his.

After the session was over, we all piled into my Bronco to head back to Newark. I'd come in the role of a chauffeur. And I was leaving as a potential artist on a new label headed by one of the hottest producers in the industry.

Kiy sat in the front seat; Floyd and Chyna were in the back. Floyd moved up to get closer to me.

"What did Puff say to you?" he asked.

"You're never gonna believe it," I told him.

"Tell me!"

"He said he wants to sign me to his new label!"

Floyd let out a loud whoop and then clapped me on the back. "Get the fuck outta here! Are you serious!"

I stopped at a traffic light right outside the Holland Tunnel and turned around to face Floyd. "I couldn't believe it, either!"

I looked in the rearview mirror at Chyna sleeping in her car seat. I didn't know what this would really mean, or if anything would actually come out of this new development in my life. But I was damn sure happy that a path seemed to be laying itself down before me. All I needed to do was watch closely and follow it carefully.

I knew one thing already: The phase of my life with Kiyamma was over. I have to say that he was a blessing in disguise, even with all the drama. Without him, I would not have had Chyna. And I might not have ended up singing for Puffy on that fateful day. God works in mysterious ways.

My lawyer, Stuart Levy, got in touch with me as soon as he received the contract from Puffy. It was a standard arrangement for the time. I was going to receive a seventy-five-thousand-dollar advance. That kind of money was new to me, and I thought it was fair. However, Puffy was requiring that 50 percent of anything I earned for publishing went to him. Stuart Levy told me that this was a standard thing for a new artist. I wasn't really bothered by signing over half of my publishing rights. What bargaining chip did I have? I had just moved out of my grandparents' house. I was about to get seventy-five grand. That would be enough to set myself up for real.

The next time I went to the studio with Al B. Sure, I told him about the deal Puff was offering. Al had told me months before that he was trying to secure his own label deal and would sign me whenever it came through. But it didn't look like that was going to happen. I was so grateful to him for giving me a start in the business but I had to move on. I was thankful for Al believing in me and my skills and I told him so.

"Faith, you know you gotta do what you gotta do," he told me.

"Thanks, Al. You have been so good to me!"

"And I ain't trying to hold you back. You better sign that deal and take over the world!"

I hugged Al and promised him I would do my best.

While the contract was being negotiated, Puff's girlfriend, Misa Hylton, gave birth to their son Justin. I actually knew Misa already. Her cousins were good friends with some of my people from Newark and occasionally attended my church.

I took a ride up to Scarsdale with my friend Dave and took a present for Justin. Puff was still living with his mother. All the producers and songwriters and executives who would form the backbone of Bad Boy Records were in and out of the house, helping to get things ready before he moved into his new office space.

Things were coming together well for Puff. He soon moved the operations for the label from his mother's house to a Manhattan office that was full of young folks bustling and making things happen.

There was Harve Pierre, who worked on getting Bad Boy songs on the radio. He would go on to produce several hit records; he still works with Puff today. There was Derek "D-Dot" Angelettie, who worked on the street team and also began to produce. Hilary Weston, who worked in marketing, ended up managing Lil' Kim and still does today. And there were people like Jay Black, a rough dude from Westchester who was always getting into something but also made sure everyone always had a good laugh. I liked that Puff seemed to really try to help his people get jobs. There was an intern named Tinker who was like family. And Groovy Lew, a stylist for the label, was also from Puffy's neighborhood. That's just the way it was. Everyone was extremely close — even when they were beefing with each other. We all managed to work hard together and party hard together.

It was a very special, familial atmosphere. And many people who went on to successful careers in the entertainment industry got their starts with Puff.

After the contract was signed, I met with Puffy at the brand-new offices for Bad Boy at 8–10 West 19th Street.

I wanted Puff to know that I was taking all of this very seriously. Although I didn't think I really looked like a recording artist at the time.

"Now, I just had a baby a year ago," I told Puff. "This is not how I usually look."

"Don't worry about that," Puff said. "We gon' take care all that."

Puffy cocked his head to one side and looked at me thoughtfully. "We gotta do something about your hair, too."

I put my hand up to my hair. It was dyed blond at the time and was a bit damaged from all the processing I'd done to it.

"I know," I said. "I'm sure we can come up with something hot."

"You gon' be my mature balladeer. For the grown and sexy folks," Puff said. "So everything you rock gotta be classy."

I just nodded.

"And you way too pale!" he said.

I laughed. "Well, what am I supposed to do about that?" I asked.

"You going to a tanning salon," he said. "There's one right near the office."

Now, I knew nothing about stylists and fashion—or tanning. So I had to just put all my trust into his vision. The thing is, I didn't know much about what was hot, as far as the industry was concerned. I just knew what I liked. Puff knew what was hot but he was under so much pressure because I was *his* artist on *his* brand-new label. There was a lot on the line, and he wanted everything to be perfect.

I will always have love for Puff for seeing something in me before I had any kind of a look. I was dope with just what God gave me. But the way things happened with Puff was truly divine order.

Before I even signed my contract, Puff had me in the studio observing and contributing to music from the other artists he was working on at the time, including Usher and Mary, who was putting together her second album.

My early days as a Bad Boy artist were varied. One day, I might come to the studio and he would take me to the house of Eddie F, one of the producers, to work on a song. Some days, he would walk with me down to the tanning salon in the Village for my mandatory tanning sessions.

Every day was a new adventure and I loved it. A few weeks after I signed all the paperwork, Puff told me to go to a hotel in Midtown Manhattan and pick up Usher Raymond, the singer whose album he was producing.

Usher was Puff's top priority at the time. LA Reid had entrusted him to produce his first album, and there was a lot of buzz surrounding him. Puff knew I'd done some writing with Al B. Sure, so he asked me to try some things out with Usher during a few of his sessions. We'd started meeting nearly every day at the studio; I'd help him arrange the vocals on whatever songs he was working on or write a bridge or a chorus for a song.

I'd finally replaced that Bronco with a Toyota 4Runner that I bought for cash from a repossession yard in Brooklyn. So one afternoon, I drove to Usher's hotel, found a parking spot, and went inside. I told the receptionist who I was there to see, and she directed me up to his room.

A stern-looking woman looked me up and down as soon as I walked into the room. "Can you wait out here please," she said, pointing to a sofa in the living area. "Usher's not quite done with his schoolwork yet."

"Sure. No problem."

Usher's tutor went back into his room, and I could hear them discussing one of the battles of World War I. After a few minutes, I heard his tutor giving him a homework assignment and telling him he was done for the day. He bounded out into the living area, clapped his hands, and stretched.

"Hey, Faith! Let's get outta here!"

Usher was only fifteen. He was very slim with the same round head and heart-shaped nose he still has today. His hair was close-cropped and in waves, and he was always running his hand over his head out of habit. He had a big smile and he used it often. He was bright-eyed and eager and in awe of being in the music business.

"Let's go!" I said.

We headed out into a sunny spring afternoon and climbed into my truck. I eased the car into the thick midday New York traffic while Usher rolled down his window and took in all the sights.

"Faith, I am *starving*," he said. "Can we order some food before we get started?"

"Absolutely. Can't sing on an empty stomach."

Usher sat back in his seat and exhaled. "I got something I've been working on that I want to try out in the studio," he said.

"Good. I've been telling you that you need to write."

He kept looking out his window. "Yeah, I know. But sometimes when I get in the studio, I feel like no one thinks I can really write a hit record. Even if it sounds really good, they just dismiss it 'cause I'm young or whatever."

"Usher. It don't matter how old you are. A good song is a good song. You just gotta get Puff's attention and make him really listen."

Usher turned away from the window and looked at me. "Get his attention? How am I supposed to do *that*?"

We both laughed as I pulled into the parking lot next to the studio. I ordered him a lunch of peppered steak and potatoes from our favorite diner, a place called Lucky Strike. After we ate, we went into the studio and had the engineer cue up the latest track we'd been working on, a song called "Think of You."

Usher had a smooth voice. And for a teenager, he had good control of it. "Think of You" had a strong, bass-heavy beat and heavily stacked harmonies in the chorus. I was trying out a few lyrics with the music as Usher observed. Although he was very young, he was very motivated.

"You have to be very aggressive if you want to write," I told him. "Be prepared when any of the producers come around and speak *up*. If you want to be taken seriously as a writer, you have to act like one."

We continued ad-libbing some lyrics until Puff breezed into the room with a few assistants. Whenever he came in, it was like he brought a tornado of energy with him. He would be carrying on two or three conversations at the same time, looking over paperwork in his hands, and listening to the song, too.

"Aiight, Usher," he said. "What's going on in here? Y'all working or what?"

Puff pointed to our empty take-out containers. "Look like y'all doing more eating than working…"

I gestured to the engineer to start playing the backing track to "Think of You," and Usher's voice came through the speakers, clear and vibrant. Puff's face was completely blank, just like when I sang for him in the studio. And I couldn't tell if he liked our lyrics or not. Usher and I both looked at him, searching for some kind of encouraging sign on his face.

"I like it," he said, finally. I saw Usher exhale silently and sit back a little in his chair.

"Me *and* Usher wrote that line," I said to Puff. I winked at Usher, who smiled at me.

Puff turned to look at Usher. "Oh word. You writing now, too."

Usher cleared his throat. "Yeah, I was telling you that's what I want to start doing..."

"Well then do it," Puffy said. "Just make it hot. If it ain't hot, don't bother."

When Puff left, Usher was exuberant. "You think he really liked it?" he asked me.

I went over to my food and took a final bite. "If Puff don't like something, believe me, you'll know it."

A few weeks later, Puff took me and one of his producers, Chucky Thompson, to work with an R&B singer named Pebbles who lived in Atlanta. Pebbles was LA Reid's ex-wife, and because of that connection Puff was enlisted to work on her next project: her first solo record on her own label, Savvy Records. Pebbles had several hit records under her belt, including "Mercedes Boy," from her first album released in 1987, as well as a duet with Babyface called "Love Makes Things Happen" that had come out three years before. But she was best known at this point as the woman who discovered pop trio TLC and had them signed to her label. Their album *Oooooooohhh... On the TLC Tip* had been a runaway success two years before, and they were bona fide stars.

I was honored that Puff had enough confidence in me to send me to work with someone who'd had a good bit of success in the music industry.

Puff put us up in the Hotel Nikko in the trendy, upscale Buckhead neighborhood. There were koi ponds and Japanese gardens, and I settled into a super-large room that I had all to myself.

Candy, Pebbles's assistant, gave me a ride to Pebbles's house, where she had a home studio. I couldn't believe how extravagant the property was as the vehicle brought me closer and closer to the front entrance. There were acres of well-manicured lawn, and several groundskeepers were tending to planted shrubs and flowers. The house was set back far from the road, with no other homes in sight. Pebbles, with her waist-length hair and flawless skin, was standing right out front, signing for a package, when I pulled up.

"Faith, it's nice to meet you!" she said before ushering me inside.

I tried hard to keep my cool. But I had never been in a house like this. Each room was professionally decorated, and the architecture was intricate and detailed. There were high ceilings and windows with elaborate coverings. The guest house out back was bigger than most of the houses on Grumman Street back home.

After a brief tour, Pebbles took me into her home studio. She had it set up just like a professional studio. There were benches tucked under the console of the mixing board, a small vocal booth with microphones set up, and speakers all around the small room. I thought about how two years before, I'd sit in my bedroom and make songs with one pathetic device—my answering machine. And now I had a whole room of equipment at my disposal.

"I've heard some of the things you've been working on," Pebbles said. "And I like it. I want my music to have a soulful sound."

Pebbles also had an all-male group in town working with her on some songs. She introduced me to the four guys, and we began to listen to the tracks she had cued up and the verses she'd started to come up with. We spent the afternoon writing and laying down tracks. It was exciting to help an established singer come up with new ideas. I wasn't sure if any of the tracks we worked on would actually appear on her album; I was just happy to be there.

When it was time for me to go, I took a cab to a studio in downtown Atlanta. Puff wanted me and Chucky to check out a group he was thinking about signing to Bad Boy. He wanted our opinions on whether or not they were any good. And once again, I felt very special. I was a part of Puff's inner circle, and I was flattered that he valued my opinion on something as important as signing a new group to the label.

We went into a live recording room at the studio. These are really large rooms used for recording an orchestra or any sizable group of musicians. So there was space for at least a dozen people to sit. A piano and several chairs were set up in front of a few microphones.

"I'd like to introduce to you the members of 112," said the group's manager as the guys came into the room and took their places at the microphone. "This is Q." A tall, thin young man smiled and waved at us. "And over here we have Daron," the manager continued. "And on the end, Michael and Marvin."

Chucky and I smiled at the guys and waited for them to begin singing. They were really clean-cut. I could tell they were bred in the church. They just had that look. And when they opened up their mouths to sing, there was no *doubt* that they grew up in church. They sang a ballad they'd written themselves, and it was beautiful. The four-part harmonies were on point. When they got to a powerful crescendo in the song, my mouth dropped. I leaned over to Chucky and whispered in his ear, "Now these mu'fuckas can *sing.*"

"I know that's right!" Chucky said.

They sang a few more songs while Puffy stood in the back of the room with the manager. I turned around to sneak a peek at him. As usual, his face was blank and his arms were folded tight across his chest. He didn't move one muscle in his face or even blink. I looked back at the guys; they stood there clearing their throats and looking around at each other nervously.

"Well damn!" I finally said. "Y'all niggas gon' make me catch the Holy Ghost up in here!"

The guys in the group laughed, and a little bit of the tension evaporated.

"Chucky, Faith, can I talk to y'all for a minute," Puff said.

I gave the guys a thumbs-up sign and then followed Chucky and Puff into the studio hallway.

"What did you think?" Puff asked us.

"Sign them *now*," I said. "Are you kidding me? Them niggas can blow!"

"Yeah. They got a nice sound, right?" Puffy said.

We all talked briefly, and then Chucky and I went back into the studio while Puff talked to the manager.

Chucky and I joined the guys around the piano and began harmonizing on different gospel tracks. Every song I named from groups like Commissioned, the Winans, and the Clark Sisters—they knew them all. We spent the next hour singing, harmonizing, and making jokes. By the time I left the studio to return to my room at the Hotel Nikko, I had a feeling that the members of 112 were going to be my label mates—and also very good friends.

I was beginning to enjoy being in the music industry. Although I wasn't yet working on my own material, Puff made me feel like I wasn't just an artist. I was helping him fulfill the vision for Bad Boy. He trusted my opinion, and I was honored. And he was more like a friend than a label head or a boss.

In fact, soon after I was signed his grandmother passed away, and he asked me to sing "His Eye Is on the Sparrow" at the funeral.

It was a song he often asked me to sing if we were around executives from Arista or BMG, the parent companies for Bad Boy.

I think part of the reason me and Puff became so cool was because I was cool with his girlfriend Misa. Puff was surprised to see that Misa and I knew each other. I think it made him even more comfortable around me.

I liked Misa. She was spirited and full of energy. She's the kind of girl you want to hang out with on a Friday night. And once I was officially on the label, we became cool enough that we started running the streets together. Misa was helping Puff with styling the acts on the label. So we were all working hard. But we would play hard, too.

My relationship with Misa would also bring me into the cipher of Mary J. Blige. At the time that I was newly signed to the label, Misa hung out a lot with Mary. Mary was in the studio with Puff working on her sophomore album, the follow-up to *What's the 411.*

Puffy asked me to work on "Don't Go," a song that would appear on Mary's new album. Of course I agreed. But I was really nervous about working with her. I'd heard that Mary was difficult.

When her name came up, sometimes people would raise their eyebrows or just shake their heads. There was some talk going around that she'd gotten into it with a journalist during an interview. I knew she had a feisty personality and I wasn't quite sure what to expect. Also, I wasn't sure if she would treat me differently because of my friendship with Misa. She and Misa were very good friends at the time. And Misa and Puffy were always on and then off and then on again. So all of these intermingled personal relationships could have made things go any kind of way.

Puff wanted me to sing some backgrounds and write a vamp melody for "Don't Go." When I went in to add my backing vocals, Mary wasn't in the studio yet. I added my vocals and then went back to the lounge. I saw her when she came in and went directly into the booth. I waited for some kind of reaction to come out of the room they were working in. I didn't hear a word. A few hours later, she was gone. I wasn't sure if she liked what I'd done or not. I listened to the finished version with her vocals added and it sounded great. But I still wasn't sure if she liked my contribution.

Soon after that session, Mary appeared on a BET music video program. The host, Sherry Carter, asked her who she liked in the music industry at the time.

"There's a new artist named Faith Evans that Puffy is working on," Mary said. "And I think she's dope. Everybody needs to look out for her."

I was watching the show at home in New Jersey and I felt a warm rush of pride when I heard her say my name. I had always had confidence in myself, but hearing it from Mary was an even bigger boost. The biggest R&B singer on the scene had told the world that I was someone to watch for! I was inspired and honored.

One day I went to the studio to work on a song and on my way out, I saw Misa and Mary talking together in the lounge. I knew Misa and Mary were friends, and while I knew Misa pretty well, I hadn't really been formally introduced to Mary, so I didn't want to just walk up and start talking to them.

"Hey, Misa," I said.

"Faith, where you going?" Misa asked me.

"Probably home. Why?"

"Why don't you come out with us?"

I shrugged. "Okay," I said. "Where we going?"

"The only place to go on a Sunday night," Mary said. "The Tunnel!"

We all left the studio together and took a taxi to Mary J. Blige's apartment on Park Avenue and 66th Street. It was just turning to dusk when we got out of the cab, and the whole city had a warm glow. I looked up at Mary's building in total awe. She was really living it up. From the street level, I could barely see the very top of her high-rise. And up and down the streets were prim and proper ladies with steel-gray hair walking little dogs and doormen congregating on corners having conversations. Her neighborhood was like another world for me. I was staying in a one-bedroom apartment in East Orange, New Jersey, and was happy to have that. Living in an opulent building with a doorman was more extravagant than I could imagine.

When we got to the heavy glass door, a uniformed doorman opened the door. "Good evening, Ms. Blige," he said, bowing slightly.

"Thank you so much," Mary said.

I walked into Mary's apartment and fell in love with it instantly. It was huge. Her living room was mammoth, with floor-to-ceiling windows showing off an awesome view of Manhattan. Mary's entire apartment was tastefully decorated. Nothing over the top. It was simple but very elegant and modern. I followed her and Misa into Mary's bedroom, where she threw open her closet and started looking for something to wear.

There were dozens of shoes and boxes of brand-new clothes all over her room that had been gifts from stylists and clothing designers.

"What about this?" she asked, holding up a black spandex one-piece catsuit.

"You can rock that," Misa said, "with those black boots right there."

Mary stood in front of the mirror above her dresser and adjusted her hair. It was a platinum-blond shoulder-length weave; she had a thick black headband covering her bangs.

Misa was going through a box of clothes sent by a stylist, holding up different outfits to see if Mary liked them. There was another box near the armchair where I was sitting, and Mary told me to open that one and see what was inside.

There were lots of sweaters from a clothing line called Coogi that was very popular at the time. They were known for brightly colored knits in different zigzag patterns.

"Damn, this shit is hot!" I said, holding up a knee-length Coogi knit dress.

"Keep it," Mary said. "I'm not gonna wear it."

"Seriously?" I asked.

"For real, girl! Rock that shit!" she said.

I was too happy. I had a little money in my pocket, but I wasn't really paid like Mary. And although I was officially on Bad Boy Records, I was still an unknown.

After we were all dressed and ready to go, we had a few glasses of champagne and then went outside, where Mary's doorman hailed a taxi and held the door for us as we climbed into the backseat.

"Where to?" our driver asked.

"Eleventh Avenue between Twenty-seventh and Twenty-eighth," Misa said.

The driver shook his head as he pulled off. "Nothing but trouble at the Tunnel," he said.

The Tunnel nightclub has been closed for years now. But in 1994, it was ground zero for the hip-hop community. DJ Funkmaster Flex, one of the most popular radio DJs in New York, commanded the turntables all night. And everybody who was anybody waited in lines that stretched down three city blocks to get in.

One thing I liked about Mary—she knew how to have a good time even though she was a huge celebrity. She didn't go straight up to the VIP section and just drink and watch the crowd. When me and Misa and Mary hit the clubs, we went directly to the dance floor and partied like the regular folks.

I started hanging out with Mary and Misa on the weekends. We always had a good time going to different parties and clubs, drinking, dancing, and flirting with guys. We would usually start our night out at Mary's place, trying on clothes, fixing our hair, and having a glass or three of wine.

When I came over, Mary usually had some company in her living room. Usually, it was her boyfriend, K-Ci, and his brother JoJo. They were in the group Jodeci, and I knew their history as members of a traveling gospel quartet. So it was surreal to see these famous folks lying on Mary's sofa, drinking beer and watching television. After a while, though, I got used to it, and I would kick it with them briefly before I went into Mary's room.

"What up, Faith," K-Ci said to me one Friday night when I came over.

"I'm chilling. How you doing?"

"I'm waiting to hear some music from you," he said. "I keep hearing you the shit!"

I smiled. "You'll hear something soon, I promise. Is Mary back there?"

"Yeah. She in there…," he said.

I went into Mary's room and saw her sitting at her vanity, applying her makeup and fixing her hair. She looked like she was pissed off about something.

"What up, girl," I said, sitting down in an armchair behind her. "You ready?"

Mary took in a really deep breath, closed her eyes for a second, and then exhaled slowly. I didn't have to ask any questions. I'd heard that she and K-Ci had a very volatile relationship, though I'd never seen anything happen. But it was obvious by the look on her face that she was going through it. I could relate to that.

"Let's go," she said, standing up and stretching her arms out. "I'm getting out of here and I'm having a good time tonight."

We always had fun. But looking back, I think she was going through a lot at the time, even though she had so much going on for herself.

Of course today, Mary is very vocal about the troubles she was going through at the time. But I didn't know anything about the drug abuse back then. And I knew only a bit about her relationship with K-Ci.

I spent a few months working on Mary's album. I ended up co-writing and singing backing vocals on several songs, including "Don't Go," "I Never Want to Live Without You," and "You Gotta Believe." I also worked on a song that wasn't on her album, "Everyday It Rains," which appeared on the soundtrack for *The Show*.

At the time, I knew very little about how the industry worked. So even when I was co-writing and doing vocals and vocal arrangements for certain tracks, I wasn't always being properly compensated for it.

If you aren't really focused on the business of music, you will be taken advantage of. It sucks. But it's life. I was always adamant about making sure I was credited properly on an album. Probably because I'd always obsessively studied album credits myself. But I wasn't as knowledgeable about making sure the money was right.

And of course, I didn't have a manager, who would have been in charge of making sure I was credited and paid properly. Like so many newcomers to the music industry, I was completely on my own, learning as I went along.

When I'd first met with my attorney, Stuart Levy, a few years before, he'd explained the basics of publishing and writer's royalties to me. He even drew me a few pie charts to help me understand how things were divided.

Soon after I signed to Bad Boy, I met Kamala Gordon, who worked in publishing at BMI, the company responsible for making sure writers are compensated properly when their music is played. She explained to me that anytime a song was written, someone—sometimes the producer or the artist's manager—fills out paperwork outlining the "splits" for a particular song, meaning how credit for the song would be split. If a sample is used in a song, the original composer asks for a certain percentage of the publishing. It can be as little as 10 percent. And if necessary, it can be 100 percent.

If 50 percent of the publishing goes to the composer or producer of the original song, the remaining 50 percent is split between the new producer or composer and the songwriters. Here's where it gets tricky: You have to agree with the other songwriters on how much of the percentage you should be credited for.

When I worked on Usher's first single, "Think of You," and about seven other songs on his album, I sang background vocals and helped to write a few bridges and hooks. I'd made sure to send in all my paperwork so I could be credited and paid properly.

Today, when I look at my statement from BMI, I see that I am credited for 11.5 percent of Usher's first single. Which is fair for what I contributed. That means if BMI collects $100.00 from radio for playing Usher's first single, I'll get a check for $11.50.

But with the things I worked on for Mary, it was a different story. I can't blame anyone but myself for not staying on top of my business. With her album, everything was all over the place. You can't submit paperwork for splits until the song is complete. But after I'd finish my part of a song, Puff would be in and out of the studio for weeks, tweaking things, adding and perhaps removing different elements of the song. Sometimes, I couldn't keep up with listening to the final version of a song to note how much of what I'd contributed ended up there.

For example, for the song "Everyday It Rains," I am credited for something like 0.00001 percent. That is completely inaccurate. I wrote the bridge and sang on the bridge, which I felt should be considered at least 10 percent of the song.

"I did more than it says on these papers for some of these songs," I complained to Kamala Gordon from BMI. "I didn't even send in my paperwork. Who sent this information in?"

She just looked at me and shook her head. "Faith, you can't just go in the studio and start working without negotiating these things. The first one to submit the information basically wins."

"So that's it?" I asked. "I can't tell someone that there's been a mistake?"

"At this point you can appeal," said Kamala. "That means a letter will be sent to everyone listed as a composer or writer on the song. But that will take months, and you won't get any money while you're waiting."

With the way things were, I was getting between eleven hundred and fifteen hundred dollars every two or three months for the things I was credited for. I didn't want to appeal. I just wanted to keep getting my money and make sure my paperwork was straight in the future.

And I knew I had to talk to Puff about giving me a writer's fee. I was thrilled to be signed to the label, and I was learning about recording and preparing for my own album. But I also knew I needed to be paid for coming into the studio and writing for these artists. Record labels have a budget that includes paying songwriters just for coming into the studio. And here I was, coming into the studio every day, contributing lyrics and vocals to these albums, and not getting paid anything. I was working with songwriters like Big Bub who was working on Mary's album. I'm sure he was getting a songwriter's fee, and I thought I should be, too.

I actually didn't want to say anything at first—I had my own apartment in East Orange. I had finally gotten rid of that broke-down Ford Bronco and bought a '91 4Runner. I had what I needed. But something kept gnawing at me. I thought of my grandmother, underestimating her worth and not getting payment from the people who left their children with her. I knew I had to approach Puffy.

I waited until the next time I saw him in the studio and we were talking about one of the tracks I was working on for Mary.

"Puff, I think I need to set up a fee for my writing sessions," I said.

He looked at me with a blank expression on his face. He suddenly morphed from friend to all business.

"What are you talking about?" he barked. He had this rapid-fire way of speaking where everything came out in one jumbled phrase. I wanted to just say never mind. But I knew I couldn't.

"Look," I said. "If you want me to go to someone's session, I think it's fair to work out something."

"How much do you think you worth?" He asked.

"I want fifteen hundred per session," I said, holding my breath and not making eye contact.

Puff didn't say yes or no. He just mumbled something and walked away. But I did start receiving payment for my studio work with artists. And of course looking back, I should have been paid more than I was for those sessions. I was slowly starting to see how Puff could be ruthless when it came to money and business. But that was a very small taste of what was to come.

I was getting the hang of the songwriting and musician side of the business, but when it came to being an artist, I was nervous. I was grateful for the opportunity and I knew how fickle the music industry could be. I was only going to have one shot to make it happen.

I was aware that physical appearance was going to make a big difference. In gospel music, it doesn't matter if you are plump. As a matter of fact, in some cases the bigger the better. Gospel greats like Mahalia Jackson never had to worry about being thin. But pop music is a completely different story.

Even before I signed to the label, back when I was still doing session work for Al B. Sure, his assistant had gotten me a gym membership and I'd started working out regularly. The weight was coming off—very slowly. But my stomach was still not looking right at all.

I called my girl Toni, the young lady from Compton I'd met

when I stayed with Kiy at the Oakwood. She was working in an office building out in LA. On a different floor in the same building was a well-known plastic surgeon.

Toni did some research for me and then I called to make an appointment for a tummy tuck. It was very expensive—nearly ten grand. I had just received the seventy-five-thousand-dollar advance from signing to the label. And I figured it would be a good investment in my career.

This was long before plastic surgery was something everyone did. I didn't know anyone who'd had a tummy tuck back then. I'm kind of surprised when I think about it now. I was only twenty years old, traveling to LA, alone, to get major surgery.

I left Chyna with my grandparents and flew out to the West Coast for the operation in the early days of summer. I didn't tell Puff or anybody from the label what I was going to do. I didn't even tell my grandparents or any of my family. As usual, for the big important stuff, I wanted to do it on my own and in private. I didn't want anyone to try to talk me out of it or make me have any doubts.

My friend Curtis Baldwin and his girlfriend, Carolyn, who used to live with Kiy at the Oakwood, took me to the hospital and picked me up. The pain after the surgery was unreal. It was almost worse than what I'd experienced having Chyna the year before. They cut you from hip to hip and bring your stomach muscles together. It's really brutal and quite a shock to your system. And then I had this serious scar and all these stitches around my belly.

I was not a pretty sight when that surgery was over. I stayed in an aftercare facility for ten days. For a few days after that, I stayed with Hailey, a friend who lived near the hospital. He was so gracious. But he had lots of pets and liked to cook. I couldn't move off his sofa, and the waves of nausea from his menagerie and his cooking were killing me. So I called my girl Toni and told her to get me out of there.

For the rest of my recuperation, I stayed with Toni and Brian or

Curtis and Carolyn. I could barely walk and I was grateful that they all took such good care of me, helping me change my bandages and cooking for me.

Every day when Toni came home from work, she'd helped me up to look in the full-length mirror.

"How do I look?" I'd ask her.

"Girl, when you get these bandages off you are going to be *fierce*."

"It better be worth all this pain."

Toni led me back to her sofa and helped me to lie down. "It will be! All the stars do this. It's all about the image."

I rubbed my sides, which were still sore and achy. "I chopped off my hair, I went to a tanning salon, and now I've had fat sucked out of my belly. What's next?"

After a few weeks, I definitely saw the results of the surgery and I liked it—a lot. The only thing I didn't like was my tummy-tuck scar. Not only was it huge and very noticeable, but it was crooked! I figured I could get it fixed one day. For the moment, though, I was just going to have to deal with it.

A few weeks later, Puff gave me the name of a doctor who prescribed me some weird diet pills that made me jittery and anxious. But they worked, and I shed a few more pounds. But I was still nervous about looking my best when it was time for me to start performing. I could see that being in the music industry was going to be a lot more than just standing in front of a microphone and singing a song.

In June 1994, I turned twenty-one years old. In just three years, I'd crammed in a lifetime of living. I'd tried going the straight-and-narrow route, finishing high school and going to a highly regarded university. Then I was pregnant and shacking up with my pseudo-boyfriend in Los Angeles. Before I could even blink, I was back at home, a single mother with no plan. Then fate guided me to Al B.

Sure, and I was a working musician. Another fateful meeting and I'm singing for Puffy and then signed to his label.

But as far as I was concerned, it would remain to be seen how Puff's new label would perform. The artists he had signed were pretty varied. There was me: I was supposed to be the classy, mature balladeer. There was a girl group I'd seen around the offices named Total. They were a sexy pop trio from New Jersey. There was Craig Mack, a rapper with a distinct raspy voice and a playful style.

And there was another rapper I'd heard a little about here and there but had never met. I would learn later that the guy everyone called Biggie or just Big had seen me coming in and out of the Hit Factory while I was working with Usher. He thought I was a background singer and had asked a few people about me. I remember hearing that a rapper on Bad Boy would be in a session on some of the days I was there working with Mary or Usher. And I'd heard the remix to Mary J. Blige's "Real Love," which featured a brief rap from a rapper going by the name Biggie Smalls. But I knew absolutely nothing about Christopher George Letore Wallace, aka the Notorious B.I.G., until I met him shortly after my twenty-first birthday.

CHAPTER SEVEN

Brooklyn's Finest

*E*verything was coming together for Puffy's new label. He set up a promotional photo shoot for advertisements that would appear throughout New York City, announcing his new stable of artists. I didn't know anything about what to expect at a photo shoot. Puff just told me to come to an address in SoHo near Houston and Broadway. I left my apartment in East Orange and first drove to Newark to see my girl Roz. At Roz's house, my friend Gloria was visiting. Gloria, also known as rapper Hurricane G, was down with Redman and the whole Hit Squad, and we'd been cool for years. I ended up bringing her with me so that I wouldn't be completely alone.

We walked into a cavernous room on the top floor of an office building. In the center of the room, a tall, thin white guy was setting up a tripod and camera while barking orders at two assistants. He took some Polaroids of the assistants and then they huddled around and waited for them to develop. In one corner was a long table set up with benches tucked underneath. Two girls I didn't recognize sat there, laughing and talking. On the other side of the room, a well-known makeup artist named Nzingha was unpacking makeup brushes and other tools from a large canvas bag and spreading them out on a black mat. Everyone seemed to know exactly why they were there and what they needed to do. Except me. Nzingha happened to have a curling iron with her, and she offered to help me do something to my hair.

"Don't worry about a thing. You look cute," she said.

She took a step back and looked at me. "You've got a great pair of legs," she said. "That little skirt is doing it."

I ran my hands down my skirt. "You think so?"

"Absolutely."

Afterward, I went to the bathroom to make sure I looked okay. I was wearing this denim mini skirt and a matching vest I'd bought from a shop in downtown Elizabeth. I didn't see a stylist with racks of clothes so I assumed that I'd be wearing what I'd arrived in.

I sat at the long table with Gloria and waited for someone to tell me to do something. From where I sat, I could see everyone coming into the large room. As soon as I sat down, I saw a tall brown-skinned guy with a very distinctive voice. I recognized him as Craig Mack, who was signed to the label and had a hit song out that summer called "Flava in Your Ear." He came in laughing out loud with one of his friends, and they headed straight over to the two girls sitting at the far end of our table.

And then Puff came in, a whirlwind of noise and energy as usual. He had an assistant struggling to keep up with him as he walked quickly into the room.

"What up people!" he yelled out. "Let's make it happen!"

The photographer and his two assistants made a beeline toward Puff and showed him the Polaroids. Puff nodded and gave suggestions. Then Craig Mack came over to him; they exchanged greetings and an elaborate handshake before talking about a remix to "Flava in Your Ear" that he was about to record.

"We getting LL on that joint," Puff said to Craig Mack. "Big and Busta, too. It's gonna be ridiculous!"

The photographer told us he'd be ready to begin in five minutes. I wasn't even sure at that point who was actually in the photo shoot. I went back to the table with Gloria and cased the room again.

I saw Puffy barking orders at an assistant. I knew he'd be in the photo. I saw Craig standing by the open window, yelling down to the street level. I knew he was on the label, too. I knew the group Total was signed to the label, but they weren't at the shoot. I knew Mary wouldn't be there because although Puff worked with her quite a bit, she was signed to MCA and he hadn't been able to bring her from Uptown to Bad Boy after Andre fired him.

There was only one other person there who could possibly be there for the shoot. And he was standing five feet away from me, leaning up against the wall of the studio and listening to two young guys standing in front of him argue back and forth.

The guy was tall, well over six feet, dark-skinned and huge, close to three hundred pounds. I put it together very quickly and realized this was the Notorious B.I.G., also known as Biggie Smalls or just plain Big, which is how I'd heard people refer to him around the studio and in the offices at Bad Boy.

I knew there was a rapper named Big signed to Bad Boy. But somehow, we'd never crossed paths. I gave him a quick once-over. He was wearing a patterned flannel shirt and oversize Karl Kani jeans that were so big, they made a puddle of fabric around his Timberland construction boots.

"Let's go," the photographer said. "Puffy, I want you right... here. Faith, come over and stand this way. Put your arm up on his shoulder. Craig? Where are you? Stand on the other side of Puff. Perfect. Now, Big. You stand behind all of them. Good. Puffy, throw your hands up."

The photographer bent down to look into the camera and kept barking out orders to us.

"Faith, bring your chin up, sweetie. A little more. Hold your head up. Goood. Now turn a bit toward Puff. Perfect."

We posed for the cameras but we weren't really smiling. It was more like mean-mugging, like we just knew it was all about us.

We took a few breaks throughout the shoot and I stayed to myself, talking to Gloria occasionally. I was just there doing my job, and I didn't make much conversation. I was also quiet because I felt kind of awkward. All of this was so new to me. I wasn't sure if I was dressed right, if my hair was right. I didn't know if I was posing the right way—or if there was a right way. I just wanted to do what I was told and get it all over with. At the same time, I was enjoying stealing glances around the room and absorbing the scene.

I was used to having attention on me. I'd performed lots of times by now. But this was a lot different from the gospel realm I was familiar with, and it was a bit overwhelming.

During the lunch break, I was showing Gloria the pictures I'd recently had developed from my twenty-first-birthday celebration. From out of the corner of my eye, I saw that Big was walking over in my direction. He sat down right next to me—a little too close. I just looked up at him and waited for him to speak.

"Can I see your pictures?" he asked.

I picked up the envelope and passed it to him. Big sat back and leaned against the table, stretching out his legs in front of him. He was pretty bold, plopping down right next to me and flipping through my pictures like he'd known me for years when I'd never seen him before.

"Who is this?" he asked, pointing to one of my pictures.

"My cousin."

"What about him?"

"That's my uncle."

Big just nodded. He wasn't facing me. But every once in a while he would look over at me, and I noticed that he had a lazy eye. He'd look at me but only the left eye would focus; the other one was still. And he definitely wasn't a pretty boy. But there was still something about him that was magnetic. I just couldn't put my finger on it. Part of it was definitely his self-confidence.

As he glanced through my pictures, he kept up a steady stream of questions in a voice that was low and deep.

"Where you from?" he asked, keeping his eyes on the photos.

"Jersey," I said.

"Where in Jersey?"

"Newark."

"How old are you?"

I gave him a look. "I'm old enough."

"You driving?"

"Yeah, I'm driving."

"You got kids?"

"A daughter."

"Word? Me, too."

The photographer was ready for us to continue the shoot, and Big gave me back my envelope of pictures. We followed the directions and posed for another hour before the shoot was over. No one made any moves to leave right away. We just all went back to standing near whomever we'd come with and continued talking while the photographer packed up his equipment.

I was standing near the window with Gloria, talking about getting something to eat before I took her back to Brooklyn and then returned to Jersey.

"Let's go," I said to Gloria. "I don't want to get stuck in traffic."

"I'm right behind you," she said.

I went over to Puff and said good-bye and then headed for the exit. As soon as I got to the doorway, I heard someone calling my name. I turned back and saw Big walking toward me, slowly. He had a lopsided gate. Between his size and the way he wore his jeans three sizes too big, he had a slouchy, pigeon-toed way of walking and took forever to get to where I was standing. At one point, he had to stop, hike up his pants so they wouldn't fall to his ankles, and then continue walking.

"Where you 'bout to go?" he asked.

"I'm taking my friend home to Brooklyn."

"Word. Can I get a ride to Brooklyn?"

"Yeah, I'll take you," I said. "You ready?"

"Oh, you gotta take my boys home, too."

I followed his line of vision to a group of guys who had been standing in the corner, cracking jokes and being silly during the photo shoot. It was Lil' Cease, age sixteen; Chico, who was twenty-four; and Nino, seventeen.

"Are y'all ready now?" I asked. "'Cause I gotta go."

Big turned around toward his boys, who were play-fighting and slap-boxing each other. "Yo! Come on. We getting a ride back to BK."

We all piled into my '91 silver Toyota 4Runner for the ride. Big sat in the front seat; Gloria, Cease, Nino, and Chico were in the back. Right away, I saw that Big and his boys were jokesters. They teased each other — and anyone nearby — incessantly. It wasn't anything mean. It was just the way they got down. You had to be tough if you were going to be around them and their brand of humor. They were familiar with Gloria because they knew Redman and the other guys in the Hit Squad, so they joked and teased her, too.

I noticed that B.I.G. was stealing looks at me here and there. "This your car?" he asked me.

"Yeah, it's mine."

Big didn't say anything. Just silently nodded like he was making a note of it. I could tell he was impressed. My truck wasn't anything fancy. It wasn't even brand new, and it didn't have fancy accessories like rims on it. But it was mine. I didn't know anything about Big's financial situation, though he obviously didn't have a car — or his own apartment, as I discovered after I dropped off Gloria and then took Big and his boys to 226 St. James Street in Bedstuy, Brooklyn, where Big lived with his mother in a three-bedroom apartment on the third floor of a brownstone.

It was an early evening in June, and there were dozens of kids running up and down the streets, enjoying the first few days of their summer vacation. And the neighborhood was loud. Although the sun was just about to set, there were still Italian ice vendors ringing their bells, little kids screaming over a kickball game being played in the middle of the street, and cars speeding by blaring rap music.

Cease, Chico, and Nino got out of the car, quickly surveyed the block, and then sat on the stoop of the building. Cease pulled some dice out of his pockets and began throwing them against the side of the brownstone. The three of them began to whoop and holler as their game of cee-lo got more intense. Big and I just watched them quietly for a second.

"Ma? How you know your way around Brooklyn?" Big asked.

"Sometimes I go to Hezekiah Walker's church around here," I said.

Big nodded. "You a church girl, huh?"

"That's right. You don't go to church?"

"Nah. If I ever walked into church a brick would fall on my head."

I laughed. "Why would you say that?"

"I done did too much grimy shit."

"Like what?"

Big propped his arm up on the window and cupped his chin in his hand. "Whatever you can think of."

He was quiet for a second and we both watched Cease and Nino arguing over who owed who some money.

"You going back to New Jersey?" he said after a long minute.

"Yeah, I am."

Big opened his car door and lumbered out. He stood up, straightened out his jeans, and then leaned down into the open passenger's-side window before I could pull off. His face was intriguing to me. It was so round and soft. He was a grown man, and people who just glanced at him might think he was aggressive. But I saw the face of a little boy, sweet and gentle.

"I'ma call you," he said.

I had not given him my number and he knew it. "Oh really?" I said.

"Yes, really." And then he walked away.

I rolled my eyes and pulled off. I picked up Chyna from my grandparents' and went home. As soon as I walked into my apartment, the phone rang.

"What up, Faith?"

I recognized Big's voice immediately. I was trying to play it cool but I knew I hadn't given him my number and I didn't know how he got it.

"Hey, what's up?"

"Told you I was gon' call you."

Later on, he told me that my number had been written on the envelope containing my newly developed pictures. So as he had been skimming my pictures during the lunch break, he'd been putting together a plan as well. But at the time, I had no idea.

"You should come to Brooklyn and hang out," he said.

"I should?"

"Yeah, Ma. You'll have fun. I promise."

"How'd you get my number?"

"You gon' come out here and chill?"

I sighed. But I was also grinning from ear to ear. "Aiight. I guess so."

Now, Big was not what you would call eye candy. He was heavyset, and he dressed in all-purpose clothes that weren't flashy or expensive. This guy had a dead eye and seemed to pay no attention to how he was perceived physically. And yet, despite all that, there was something about him that I was drawn to. He was bold and confident. And he had no doubts that I would go out with him.

So I did.

The next day, I drove out to Brooklyn after dropping Chyna off at nursery school. I can't say my first time out with Big was a date. It was more like a crash course in his life. Looking back, I see that he was probably trying to see what kind of girl I was and if I could mix with his way of life.

As soon as I pulled up to the house, I saw Big, Cease, Nino, and Chico all sitting on the front stoop. It was as if they hadn't moved in the twenty-four hours since I'd last seen them there.

"What up, Faith?" Big said.

I leaned up against the railing leading up to the house. "Hey everybody...," I said.

"Yo, where you get that outfit from?" Cease said.

I looked down at what I was wearing. I'd found a seamstress in Jersey who would make outfits for me. So I'd pick out fabrics and she'd make me a matching short set or a two-piece suit. I usually used a knit fabric, and she'd make it with a hood on the sweater. It was a cute little set and, most importantly, it was something I knew no one else would be wearing. I'd wear some knee-high boots and my Finnish raccoon fur coat I'd ordered out of the Spiegel catalog a few years before — straight-up ghetto-fabulous.

"I had it made," I said. "Why?"

Cease had this wicked little smile on his face. "I'm just saying, you look mad...matchy."

Everyone on the stoop started cracking up, including Big. I think I was being tested. To see if I would get offended. They didn't know I could take it and dish it.

"Nigga, I know you not talking," I spat back. "But I see your boots are."

"Oh shiiit!" they all yelled out. "She got you, Cease! She got you!"

"Yo, Ma, you hungry?" Big asked, still laughing.

My mom, Helene, with her sisters, Missy and Hope, and brother Morgan (© Faith Evans)

My mom, my grandma Helen, and Madeline, her Irish sister-in-law— Dade City, Florida, early 1960s (© Faith Evans)

Me at nine months (© Faith Evans)

My mother and me in Florida (© Faith Evans)

Me, age four, at Emanuel Baptist Church children's choir anniversary (© Faith Evans)

My mother and me at a fair in Jersey City (© Faith Evans)

Me and my mom at a fashion show (© Faith Evans)

On my trip to Orlando after winning the Miss Fashion Teen pageant (© Faith Evans)

On my way to Orlando—all smiles (© Faith Evans)

Johnnie May and Bob Kennedy (© Faith Evans)

Me, at age fifteen, chillin' on Grumman Avenue—check out the haircut! (© Faith Evans)

Mae and a few of the kids she raised (© Faith Evans)

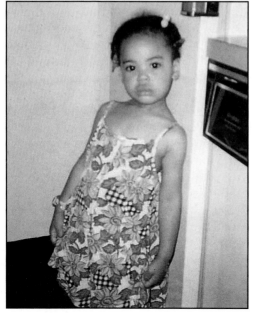

Chyna posing at my apartment in Brooklyn (© Faith Evans)

Me and Mark Pitts at Big's album signing (© Faith Evans)

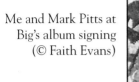

Mark Pitts and Big at our apartment in Brooklyn (© Faith Evans)

Big at an album signing—wearing the shirt I begged him to wear (© Faith Evans)

Walter, me, my friend Stephanie,
and Cheryl on the night I was thrown
through a window in Atlanta
(© Faith Evans)

My friend Curtis Baldwin
at a party given in my honor by
Flavor Unit (© Faith Evans)

Me and Nzingha
getting ready for
a video
(© Faith Evans)

Me at my
"You Used to Love
Me" video shoot
(© Faith Evans)

Me and Big at my "You
Used to Love Me" video
shoot (© Faith Evans)

Me and Big at
Busch Gardens
(© Faith Evans)

"I can eat."

He stood up and looked both ways down the busy Brooklyn street. An older man with no front teeth came riding by on a bicycle, with one flat tire waving at the guys on the stoop. They all laughed and hurled harmless insults at him.

"Come on," he said. "Where we eating?"

Getting teased about my outfit by some little kid was not my idea of a typical first date. But I quickly realized that nothing about Big would be typical. We all piled into my car, and I took them to the corner of Washington and Myrtle to a restaurant called Kum Kao Kitchen. There were at least six cars double-parked out front—a sure sign that the food was good.

"You ain't never had Chinese food this good," I told Big.

Kum Kao's was a grimy spot. I'd started going there with my friend Dave, the guy who drove up to Scarsdale with me to take a gift to Misa when Justin was born. Dave was from Brooklyn; whenever I went with him to Hezekiah Walker's church, we went to Kum Kao afterward.

The front of the restaurant had this deep thick glass protecting it from the drama that could go down in Bedstuy. There was an area where you could eat in the restaurant. But most people got their food to go. The inside was small, about the size of a bodega, and no more than about a dozen people could fit inside at any one time. As you order, you can see the entire kitchen where the cooks are jiggling hot pans with white rice inside and flipping the food around to cover it with sauce.

"What you want?" I asked Big.

He looked up at the menu thoughtfully. "I'ma let you decide since you know the spot."

I ordered my favorites: fried chicken wings and broccoli with brown sauce. We took the food back to the stoop of 226 St. James and spent the rest of the evening eating, smoking weed, and talking shit.

The whole week was more of the same. I was there every day.

And just that quickly, I had become part of the crew. Drinking Hennessy and Coke, smoking weed, and driving Big to different studios to do remixes and freestyles.

My friend Roz, her cousin Markie, and even my daughter, Chyna, became part of the crew. Sometimes, I'd bring them to Brooklyn to hang out and we'd sit out on the stoop, talking and laughing. Chyna has always been a very precocious child. When I met Big, she was less than two years old. But she was already talking up a storm and had so much personality. She would have Big and his friends cracking up with her sassy and fearless attitude.

One time we were sitting on the stoop. There were some girls nearby whom Cease, Nino, and Chico were admiring.

"Yo, Chyna," said Big's friend Damion. "Go tell them girls to come over here."

Chyna walked over to the group of girls. "My uncle Damion said come over so he can holla at you," she said.

The girls erupted into laughter at the sight of this little baby talking like a grown woman.

I was twenty-one. I was signed to Bad Boy, had a little paper in my pocket, and was feeling blessed. I was also feeling impulsive. And hanging out with Big was fun and just a tiny bit rebellious. I was raised in the church. I'd dated JT, a small-time drug dealer, and I'd dated a married man twice my age. But hanging in Brooklyn with Big and his boys was a bit different. There was just a feeling of go-for-broke in the air. We were just living in the moment, doing whatever felt good.

Nothing was scheduled. Every time I came home to Jersey, I wondered if he would want to see me again. I was not gonna sweat him and call him; I'd always wait for him to call me. And sure enough, many mornings, after I returned from taking Chyna to preschool, my phone would ring.

"Yo, Faye, where we eating today," Big would say. And that would become a sort of code phrase that meant he wanted to see me.

I was enjoying spending time with Big. But there was no definitive spark that had me really open—until he kissed me. It may have
been the fourth or fifth consecutive day that I was hanging out with
him and his crew. We were sitting in my car in front of his house,
after another day of Brooklyn-style running around. There weren't
many places we could have privacy since he was *always* surrounded
by his boys. So we spent a lot of time sitting in my car.

On this particular afternoon, I was dropping him off before I
went back to Jersey to pick up Chyna from nursery school. Big
leaned over and, with no warning, he kissed me. He kept his hands
to himself—there was no trying to feel me up. And it was passionate
but in a thoughtful way.

Even though in the streets, he cursed up a storm, drank and
smoked all day, and talked crazy with his boys, in that car he was
warm and sensitive and that kiss sparked something serious inside
of me. I realized that I liked him. A lot. Nothing else happened that
night, which made the kiss even more special.

Two weeks into our courtship and it was as if I had been hanging with Big and his friends all my life. Big and his friends had jokes
for days. Every time I came around, they would start cracking on
my fake designer-made outfits. I took no offense and laughed right
along with them.

Another source of laughter was my beatbox skills. I can actually
do a pretty decent beatbox. My cousin Isaac, my aunt Hope's son,
taught me how to do it years ago, and it was just one of those quirky
things that you would never expect me to be able to do. So we'd be
on the stoop and Big would start rapping in a real slow, old-school
simplistic rhyme style—*Well my name is Big, but you can call me
Biggie...*— and I would chime in with the beatbox and we'd all be
in stitches with laughter.

Eventually, I started hanging out inside Big's house as well as in
the streets of Brooklyn. The three-bedroom apartment he shared

with his mother, Voletta Wallace, was always kept very clean and neat—at least the parts of it she had control of.

At the time that I started coming around, Ms. Wallace's sister was living with them as well as her brother and his family. Like most immigrants, Ms. Wallace made her home available to family members who were trying to make it work here in the States, the way others helped her when she had come here from Jamaica in the early '70s.

I didn't see Ms. Wallace during my first visits. She was usually at work. But I knew she was a teacher and I could tell she wanted to keep a nice home. The apartment was simple but nicely furnished. The foyer led to a dining room with the typical dining room set and matching china cabinet. Next to that was a small sitting area that was connected to her bedroom and separated by sliding doors. All the way at the end of the hall was Big's room.

Big's room was very different from the rest of the house. It was tiny, just big enough to fit a full-size bed. And sometimes it was pretty cluttered. I could tell Ms. Wallace probably didn't go back there too often.

There was nothing going on in that room. Just his bed and an oversized boom box with a cassette player. A window with a fire escape faced the back alley.

That was Big's headquarters, that tiny bedroom. It was where he smoked and drank and listened to music with all his friends. And I was quickly added to the guest list. Ms. Wallace was so aggravated with Big by then: He'd been arrested for selling drugs, had dropped out of school, and was now supposedly a rapper—something she didn't understand at all. She'd kicked him out once before, and he returned. So now they lived together but kept their distance. She was barely tolerating him, and so that back bedroom was where he spent most of his time.

Even though I was now spending a lot of time with Big, I was still out with the rest of the Bad Boy camp as well. Puff and Big didn't hang out back then, so I usually ended up chilling with them separately. For example, during this time, Puff invited me to a dinner at Benihana, in celebration of Misa's birthday. There were a few Bad Boy executives and artists who met up at the restaurant. Of course, Big was invited; I'd even reminded him about it the day of the dinner. But he didn't show up. It wasn't really his type of crowd. He was most comfortable in Brooklyn with his boys, getting into something grimy. It would be a little while before he'd be comfortable going to a place like Benihana with people like Puffy and his boys from Howard University who'd helped him to create Bad Boy. And by then, Big would have changed in a lot of ways.

Within a few short weeks, Big and I were officially a couple. We'd never openly said it. It was just understood. I wasn't dealing with anyone else. And I assumed he wasn't, either. I knew he had a daughter, but I had never heard anything about her mother or what their status was. And a few times, as I made my way up to his apartment, I would see familiar faces, girls who would hang out at the studio, coming down the stairs. But I had lots of guy friends and I assumed that it could be the same for Big. We were together so often that I just assumed that we were exclusive—and he never gave me reason to believe otherwise.

Big was thoughtful, funny, and sweet. And he was smart. Sometimes, out of nowhere, he'd ask me the meaning of a random word like *epiphany* and then he'd ask me to spell a really difficult word.

I would give him a look and he'd say something sarcastic like: *Just because you went to college don't mean you smarter than me.* It was true, his vocabulary was ridiculous, and he was extremely intelligent. I assumed he was asking so that he could put them in his rhymes. But I knew he didn't need to spell a word correctly to use it in a song. I think sometimes he was just testing me. I had to remind him often that I won the second grade spelling bee.

I tried to get Big to come with me to church. But he never would. He always said that karma would punish him if he ever walked through the doors. I knew better, though. Big had been raised in the church and had gone to Catholic school. He wasn't nearly as far from religion as he pretended to be.

One thing we didn't talk about much was the business. We were label mates but it just didn't come up. There has always been a huge misconception about my relationship with Big. He was not a super-star when I met him. He wasn't a star at all. He had been originally signed to Uptown before Puffy got fired. And at that time, Puff was still trying to clear up the paperwork and get Big signed to Bad Boy and Arista, the parent label. I had been directly signed to Bad Boy, and my advance money had already come through. So I was doing better than Big financially at that point. In addition, I had been in the studio, co-writing and arranging and making money from that, too.

I wasn't hanging out with Big for any other reason except that I liked him. I had heard him rap. I'm sure I must have heard his guest verse on the remix to Mary J. Blige's "Real Love," but I didn't make the connection. Actually, at the time that we met, he'd already shot the video for his first single, "Juicy." But I hadn't seen the video and knew nothing about the song.

I went to a few studio sessions with him during those early days of hanging out. He was doing freestyles, guest appearances, and other random tracks. His own album was pretty much finished and I hadn't heard much of it.

One day a few weeks after we started dating, I tagged along with him to D&D Studios where he was working with the legendary DJ Premiere. They were working on a track called "Unbelievable," one of the last songs he was recording for *Ready to Die,* his debut album.

While Big was in the control room with DJ Premiere, I was out front near the pool tables with Monie Love, a British rapper whom I'd become friendly with and remain friends with today.

Many years later, Premiere told a reporter from *XXL* magazine that Big had told him that day he was going to marry me. Which is funny. Because that day, I remember wondering who all the different girls were who were coming in and out of the studio. I was too insecure to just ask Big who these random chicks were. Meanwhile he's in there telling Premiere that I'm his soon-to-be wife.

Although his album was scheduled to be released in a few months, Big was definitely still up-and-coming just like me. I didn't even realize he was on the cusp of superstardom until June 19, 1994.

It was Father's Day, and Puffy threw a huge party at a club near York Avenue in downtown Manhattan. It was going to be my very first industry party. I was signed to one of the hottest new record labels around and I was co-writing songs for Usher and Mary J. Blige but I had never been to an industry party before. I was so green and naive. I didn't listen to a lot of popular music so I didn't know what was really hot.

I bought a new outfit for the occasion: an A-line linen dress with brown buttons. It was fitted at the top and then flared from the waist down to the knee. I wore a pair of cream linen spectator pumps with brown leather accents. The dress showed a touch of cleavage but nothing over the top. I'm sure I looked like a recording executive, not an up-and-coming entertainer.

The nightclub was dark when I walked through the narrow doorway into the large room. The music was so loud that I couldn't hear a word anyone was saying. I headed straight to the bar to have a drink, calm my nerves, and survey the scene from a neutral location.

I saw Puffy leaning in to someone's ear and speaking animatedly. It looked like he was giving some kind of directions. Across the room I could make out Craig Mack and his crew, gesturing for a group of girls to come over to them. And there were fifty or more people on the dance floor, dancing wildly to the remix to Craig Mack's song "Flava in Your Ear."

Groovy Lew, one of the guys who worked in marketing for Bad Boy, came over to the bar and grabbed my hand. "Come on, Faith," he said, pulling me to the dance floor. "We going all-out tonight!"

I danced with Lew and a few other folks from Bad Boy for two hours straight, having the time of my life. And then the music went down a little and Puff appeared on a stage near the front of the club.

"Ladies and gentlemen," Puff said. "I present to you, the notorious one, the nigga that's about to take Bad Boy to the next mutha-fuckin' level. The one. The only... Biggie Smalls!"

The track for his song "Juicy" came on, which uses a sample from the song "Juicy Fruit" by Mtume. It was loud and pulsating, and the crowd on the dance floor rushed to the front of the stage. I looked around confused. I knew Big's album hadn't come out yet. So why was there all this attention on him? People were jockeying for position. I just stood back to see what the hell was going on.

A dull roar came up through the crowd as Big sauntered on to the stage. He walked slow, with his baggy pants dragging just like the day I'd seen him at the photo shoot. He came out there with a drink in one hand and a microphone in the other, grunting a few ad libs.

Uh... Uh...

Just the way he threw out a random sound made everyone in the crowd throw their hands up. The introduction of the song kept playing, and then Big started his verse.

After the first line, I barely heard anything else from him because the crowd took over, yelling out every line and waving their arms in the air.

I felt the same way people like Al B. Sure and Puffy must have felt after hearing me sing in the booth. I had no idea he could move a crowd the way he did. He didn't dance but somehow he had this electric stage presence. I watched, transfixed, as he just swayed his big body from side to side, holding his drink high in the air, throwing his head back, and spitting out his rhymes into the microphone he held close to his mouth.

He was so confident and self-assured. He stood on that stage like he owned it. I couldn't believe that was the same silly jokester I had been running around Brooklyn with for the past two weeks.

Big pointed his microphone toward the crowd. All of the girls in the audience began to sing the chorus.

I didn't know the words to the song that everyone was singing. I realized at that moment that I'd never heard any of Big's songs. I knew he was talented. But this was something else. I actually felt kind of silly because I had no idea how revered he was, even at that time. He had this raw energy on stage; his breath control—essential for a good singer or rapper—was awesome. And he put on a great show.

When it was over, Big saw me standing near the front of the stage. "What you 'bout to do?" he asked.

"I'm about to leave," I said.

"I'm leaving, too," he said.

"Where you going?" I asked.

"I'm going wherever you going," Big said.

There were dozens of people milling around, waiting to congratulate Big on his performance or just give him a pound and a hug. But he had tunnel vision.

"Let's go!" he said, gesturing toward the door.

I grabbed his hand and we began walking out of the club, onto the street and toward my car. For the entire walk, random folks were yelling out to him: "Yo, Big! Where you going?" And the answer Big gave each person was the same. He'd hold my hand up in the air and yell back: "I'm going wherever she's going!"

It's one of my favorite memories: me and Big holding hands, bustling through the club with all eyes on us. Puff had just introduced him to the world; his new single was bubbling on the radio, and the reaction had been awesome. He could have gone anywhere in the world that night. And he could have been with any woman in that club. There were lots of girls there wearing clingy spandex dresses and stilettos. And there I was, in a church-girl outfit and sensible shoes. But he was clinging to *my* hand, letting me know that he didn't want to be anywhere but with me.

"Where we going, Ma?" he asked after he climbed into my truck.

I steered out of the parking lot and toward the Holland Tunnel. "We going to my spot."

"Whatever you say," he said.

I thought about Damion, Cease, L, Nino, and all the rest of his boys who would be waiting on the stoop of his building as we pulled up. I was ready to have some private time with Big, and Brooklyn wasn't going to cut it.

"You are coming to Jersey. It won't kill you."

"I hope it's worth it."

I looked over at Big and saw that he had a tiny smirk on his face. "I'll guess you'll have to wait and see."

I had no doubts in my mind that we were having sex once we got back to my apartment. The sexual tension since our first kiss had been building up for several weeks by this time.

In my apartment in Jersey, I had this really cute canopy bed in my bedroom. But I didn't get the right base for it, so I had fire logs under it to keep it steady. I rarely slept in the bed. And when I brought Big over, I knew I wasn't going to let his oversize frame onto that bed. We would have both ended up on the floor.

Instead, I made sure we were comfortable on my living room sofa. We smoked weed, laughed, and talked about the party and his performance.

With our first kiss a week before, he'd made the first move. But this time, I wanted to be in control. I was a little afraid of him being on top of me and wearing me out. So when I was ready, I attacked him, climbing on top of him and smothering him with kisses.

That night, the spark I felt from the kiss multiplied. It wasn't acrobatic lovemaking. It was just the basics, but I remember feeling very emotional about the whole thing. The fact that he'd left everything to come home with me that night just made the physical interaction more powerful. He made me feel like I was far more than just someone he'd come home with. It felt like he wanted to be with me on a much deeper level. I knew it was too soon for either of us to feel that way. But I also knew it was going to be way more than just a one-night stand.

The next morning, I hooked him up with steak and eggs, just so he knew I was talented in the kitchen as well as in the bedroom. Then I drove him back home to Brooklyn and came right back to Jersey.

I made a point to give him some space. I didn't want to crowd him. If he wanted to see me again, he knew where I was. I was barely back home before my phone rang.

"Yo, where you at?" he said.

"I'm *home*," I said. "I just got back."

"Where we eatin' today?"

I laughed and told him I would come back later that day.

CHAPTER EIGHT

I Do . . .

ig and I became truly inseparable after that night. I was in Brooklyn just about every day—although it was hard to get him to come back to Jersey to my place. That man loved Brooklyn like it was his wife, and it was like pulling teeth to get him to leave, even for one damn night. So I was joined at the hip not only with Big but with Chico, Nino, and Cease, too. If we went to the movies, they were sitting behind us. If we went to Kum Kao, they were waiting in the car. If we were having sex in that back bedroom, they were out on the stoop.

About two weeks after the Father's Day party, we went to a movie and somehow ended up alone for once. We came back to St. James and hung out in the car for a while.

"You know I'ma marry you...," he said. Just like that.

"Yeah, whatever," I said.

Big turned to face me. "I'm serious. You have to be my wife."

I wanted to say, *Do you even know what a wife is?* It was strange to hear Big talking about grown stuff like marriage. He still lived with his mother. And he was a baby in many ways. When he went on promotional trips for Bad Boy, he didn't even pack his own bag. And like many New Yorkers, Big didn't drive — no license and no car. His life was about getting a new pair of Timberland boots, freestyling on mixed tapes, playing cee-lo, and smoking weed. And he wanted a wife?

But after a brief discussion on the subject, I realized he was serious. And I wasn't quite sure what to think. I've been known for not necessarily thinking things through. Just like when Kiy invited me out to LA. Now here I was twenty-one years old, a single mother just starting to live out my dream.

These were heady, intoxicating times, and meeting Big and falling in love with him so quickly just felt right. I hadn't yet met his mother. I'd had only minor interaction with his daughter. He hadn't met my family at all. Did I mention he was still living with his mother? And yet, I had met the sweetest, most romantic guy and he wanted to marry me. Why the hell not?

I'd met and hung out with all the people who were important to Big, except two of the most important — his mother and the mother of his child. I had been parked on the corner of Fulton Street one afternoon with Big in the passenger's seat as usual when I saw a woman in my rearview mirror walking toward my truck. I was bracing myself for something. I'd had my share of dealing with women over dudes so I was ready for anything.

I'm not sure why but I assumed that it was Jan Jackson, the mother of Big's daughter. I had been wondering why they broke up but could never get the full story out of Big. I don't know if she wanted to step to me or not. But Big got out of the car and talked to her for a few minutes. And then she continued on her way and he got back in the car.

"Was that your baby mama?" I asked him.

"Yeah," he said. "That was her."

And there was no more discussion about her. I had questions but I didn't want to seem like I was intruding into his life. If he wanted to share stuff with me, I would listen. But I didn't want to pry. I have to admit, Jan and Big seemed like a good match. She seemed very low-key, just like Big. And she was an around-the-way girl, very comfortable in her Brooklyn hood, just like Big. I already knew how much he loved their daughter T'yanna.

And I just trusted that he was handling his relationship with Jan and his daughter in the right way.

Although I had seen Jan around and she may have known who I was, Big kept stalling on introducing me to his mother.

"You don't understand," he would say. "My moms is off the hook."

"So what are you gonna do?" I'd say. "Marry me and never introduce me?"

"I will, I will. Just give me some time."

I hadn't pressed the issue when it came to meeting Jan, but I thought meeting his mother was important. Still he kept putting it off and telling me it would happen at some point.

In the meantime, I took him to meet my grandparents and other family members at a cookout we had for the Fourth of July. My whole family was there. And I told my grandmother that I was going to marry Big. I could tell she was worried that we were moving too fast. But of course, true to her nature, she didn't say a word about it. She just welcomed Big with open arms and made him a plate of food.

My mom was a different story. As soon as she heard that we were planning to get married, she made her feelings very clear.

"Married? Please. Ain't nobody ask me about getting married," she said.

I was concerned about my mom being perceived as abrasive because of the way she always just spoke her mind. It was never her way to hold back. I just sucked my teeth and ignored her. I guess she wasn't quite sure how to react. But I didn't think it was appropriate. I felt like I was grown. And that she should be able to accept it.

Of course, now I completely see where she was coming from. And she had every right to feel that way. But I was in my own world then.

Everyone was pretty cordial and accepting, and we had a great time. But it just made it more glaringly obvious that I hadn't met Big's mother, and I stayed on him about it. He kept promising me it would happen when the time was right.

In the meantime, I started planning our quickie wedding. My friend Donovan, my partner from Newark, had recently gotten married in upstate New York. He told me about the quick process and how you didn't have to wait for a marriage license.

I called Big to tell him about it.

"It's up in Rockland County," I said. "But you know, we don't have to do this…"

"Let's do it," he said.

"We need a witness…," I said.

"I'll call Cease," he said.

"Big, it has to be someone of legal age."

"Oh," he said.

"And they have to have valid ID."

"I'll find somebody," he said. "When we going?"

Big and I both had a few studio sessions throughout the week.

"We can go on Thursday," I told him.

"Aiight," Big said.

He got in touch with Man, the older brother of Nino, one of the guys in Junior M.A.F.I.A. I knew I wouldn't have time to get a ring for the ceremony, but I did want to have something nice at some point. So I headed down to Mannie's, my favorite jewelry store.

It was the same place I'd often visited with JT years ago. Back when I used to go there with him, I noticed that Mannie always had signed pictures of his celebrity clientele on the wall. When I got my record deal, I came to Mannie's on my own to get a few things. But when I went to pick out a wedding ring, I ended up looking in the window of a place across the street from Mannie's.

It was called Diamond Quasar. The jewelry on display was much more expensive than Mannie's stuff. But there was a gold ring with diamonds studded around it that caught my eye. I looked inside and saw a man with thick, dark wavy hair behind the counter. He looked up and saw me standing there and smiled and beckoned me inside. The store was small and identical in design and layout to all of the other stores in the diamond district—very utilitarian, nothing fancy. The small shop had glass enclosures on either side with jewels laid out on velvet cases.

He straightened his tie and walked over to me. "Hello, miss," he said. "What would you like to see?"

I pointed to the diamond band in the window. "How much is that ring right there?"

The jeweler came from behind the counter, opened up the glass enclosure, and took out the ring.

"This is eighteen-karat gold. Two full carats of diamonds around the band. Good quality. Here, try it on."

He slipped it onto my finger and I stuck my hand out to get a good look. It was beautiful.

"You like, right?"

"I love it."

"It's five thousand dollars. Good price."

I raised my eyebrows. "Wow. Well, I'm getting married," I said. "That's why I'm looking at these rings."

"Congratulations!"

"I want my husband to come pick this up. Can I just give you something to hold it until he can pick it up?"

"Sure," he said, packing the ring and putting it behind the counter.

He took out a pad to take down my information. And I gave him five dollars—all the money I had on me at the time—for him to hold on to it.

"He's a big, dark-skinned guy," I told the jeweler. "He'll be here next week."

The jeweler offered me his hand. I shook it. "My name is Jacob," he said. "Pleasure to meet you."

Big did end up buying that ring for me. And then he purchased some things for himself while he was there. Then he told Puffy about the spot. And word began to spread. Eventually everyone in the music industry would get their jewels from "Jacob the Jeweler," all because I'd looked in the window and seen something I liked the day before Big and I got married.

On the morning of August 4, 1994, Big and I drove up to Rockland County with his friend Man in the backseat. We talked and smoked weed for the entire hour-long ride.

"You scared?" I asked Big.

"Nah...," he said.

I wore my white sleeveless linen dress, the same one I'd worn to Puff's Father's Day party when Big had spent the night at my place for the first time. And Big was wearing his usual uniform: jeans and Timberlands.

I knew what we were doing was serious. But it was also a fun adventure. We got to the office and there was the county clerk and his secretary. We went into the clerk's office, and he came out from behind his desk and stood in front of it. Big and I stood facing him. The clerk instructed us to repeat after him.

"I, Christopher George Letore Wallace, take you, Faith Renée Evans, to be my wife..."

I wasn't as nervous as I thought I would be. In fact, it felt like the most natural thing in the whole world as I repeated my lines to Big. "To have and to hold, from this day forward, for better or for worse..."

We each went back and forth, pledging to be there for each other in sickness and in health, for richer and for poorer, to love and to cherish...

The county clerk looked at me to repeat the last line.

"Till death do us part," I said.

"By the power vested in me by the state of New York, I now pronounce you husband and wife," said the county clerk.

Big and I stood there and waited for the part where we were supposed to kiss each other.

"Now, since this is a civil ceremony and not a religious ceremony, there is no need to kiss the bride to make this official," the clerk said.

Big kissed me anyway.

I slipped a cheap, two-hundred-dollar ring I'd bought for Big on his finger. And it was over. I was Mrs. Christopher Wallace.

Big and I had known each other for barely two months. And we were now married. I don't know where the legend of us getting married after nine days comes from. Granted, two months isn't a long time, either. But unlike what's been printed so many times, we didn't get married nine days after we met. I don't know if getting married two months after meeting is any better. But still. I need to clear that up.

That afternoon Man, Big, and I stopped at a diner on our way back into the city. And then I drove them both back to Brooklyn. I was back in Jersey in time to pick up Chyna from preschool.

It wasn't the most traditional way to start a life together: smoking weed on the way to our wedding and stopping for greasy french fries on the way home. And we didn't even have plans for a household set up.

They say love is blind. And I was so in love with Big that I couldn't see a thing.

CHAPTER NINE

F.E.W.

The next day, we went up to the Bad Boy offices to tell the staff about our little secret. The night before, I'd called my friends Donovan and Roz, my grandparents, and my mom and told them what we'd done. No one was particularly jumping for joy. But they didn't say anything negative, either. The first people we saw were Mark Pitts and Wayne Barrow, Big's managers, who would later end up managing me as well.

Mark was one of the people that had gone to Howard University with Puff. Along with Derek "D-Dot" Angelettie and Harve Pierre, these guys helped Puff start Bad Boy up from the ground. They'd practically lived with him at his mother's house in Scarsdale while they plotted out the future of the label.

But it also meant that they were learning as they went along. And that the main goal was to keep Puff happy. Which is why it looked like the blood drained out of Mark's face when I told him the news.

Mark and I had gotten along well, and we had a friendly relationship. He called me Sugarfoot, and I called him Mudfoot. I have no idea where those nicknames came from. But they stuck.

"Hey, Mudfoot," I said. "Gotta tell ya something. Me and Big got married yesterday."

Mark sputtered and his eyes opened wide. "You did *what*."

I smiled. "We got married!"

Mark looked faint. He cleared his throat and ran a hand across his forehead. "I didn't even know y'all were dating!"

I told Mark it was really true and that I was happy. He wasn't upset. Just shocked.

"Are you sure you wanna do this?" he asked me.

"It's already done!" I said.

And then he said something I would hear over and over again from everyone else in the office that day: *Did you tell Puff?*

I had never even given any thought to what Puff would say. I had completely separated myself from Faith Evans, Bad Boy recording artist. I'd always planned to have a life of my own, and I knew my life would include marriage and babies. (To this day, I've always tried to be sure I make room for life outside of the music industry. I've had to turn down a lot of interesting projects because of it. But in the end, I'm glad I can come home to a normal family life no matter what is going on in the record business.)

Of course, Big and I hadn't known each other very long. I knew we were being daring and impulsive. But what I did on my downtime had nothing to do with Puff. I wasn't running anything by him or looking for his approval. So I didn't understand why everyone was so concerned with what Puff was going to say.

Big and I went into Puff's office together that afternoon. Big had told him we were coming by and needed to talk to him. The door was open when we got there and Puff was sitting at his desk, wearing a basketball jersey that spelled out the words BAD BOY in fancy script across the front.

Puff's office had just been completely tricked out in wood with chrome detailing, and he was really looking the part of an executive. He was on the phone when we walked in. Me and Big sat in two chairs facing his desk.

I didn't understand what the big deal was or why we even had to tell him anything. I was only signed to his record label. That was my job. I didn't think it had anything to do with my personal life. But Big seemed to think we needed to tell him in person, so I was there.

Puff got off the phone and clapped his hand together. "Aiight," he said, "what's going on?"

Big looked over at me and then looked at Puff. "Me and Faye got married yesterday," he said.

Puffy didn't say a word. His mouth just dropped. For a long minute, it was quiet.

I looked over at Big. He just shrugged, and we both waited for Puff to either close his mouth or actually say something.

Puff's eyebrows were arched really high and there was some kind of small noise coming out of his mouth. It sounded like he was gasping for air.

"You're married? When did y'all start *dating*," he finally said.

Me and Big both laughed. "Yeah, it was kind of a spur-of-the-moment thing," Big said.

Puff looked over at me, and I just smiled. "Are y'all serious?" Puff said.

"Hell yeah, I'm serious," Big said. "This my wife. Straight up."

Puff's head was still. But his eyes kept shifting from me to Big and then back to me again. I could see he wasn't happy about this new turn of events. But it seemed like he was holding himself back from being visibly upset.

"Ain't that some shit," he said, with a nervous laugh. "Y'all married. Wow."

Big stood up and motioned for me to get up as well, which I did. "Aiight, I just wanted you to hear it from me, you know what I'm saying?"

"No doubt," Puff said. They shook hands, and we left Puff standing there at his desk scratching his head and mumbling something under his breath. He was completely perplexed.

Looking back, Puff's anxiety was understandable. Big was his marquee artist. And in addition to that, Big was the only one on the label or employed by the label who didn't seem even the slightest bit intimidated by Puff. It made me even more enamored of Big. I felt protected by him because he didn't seem to be tripping off anyone in the music industry. Not even Puff. Later, I would see that most of the rules Puff had in place for Bad Boy employees and artists didn't apply to Big. Like smoking weed in the office and in the studio. Puffy strictly forbade it. Except for Big. (And in time I would take that to mean . . . and Big's wife, too.)

We were only in Puff's office for about fifteen minutes that day. We left while his head was still swimming. In a few days, he was shipping Big's first single "Juicy" to radio. A lot was riding on the success of the song. And now, he was going to have to figure out how to handle his marquee artist being married to another artist on his label.

I had my own issues. We were now married, after a whirlwind courtship, and I *still* had not met Ms. Wallace. And now I was a Wallace, too. It was not a good situation. Two days after we were married, Big told his mother. And she didn't believe him. Then a family friend heard Big on the radio telling the host that he'd recently gotten married. The family friend told Ms. Wallace, and she asked him if it was really true. He told her it was, and she hit the roof.

Ms. Wallace was very upset, and rightfully so. Her twenty-two-year-old son had gotten married and didn't even tell her. Worse yet, she had never met me!

A few days later, I came to the apartment, and Big silently placed a letter on my lap. I could tell from the look on his face that it wasn't good. It was a long, handwritten letter from his mother. She told him how disappointed she was in him that he would do something as important as get married without telling her. She said she would never forgive him. And she said she would never let T'yanna forget what a terrible thing he'd done to Jan. My heart sunk farther and farther into my stomach with every line I read. Especially since I knew she was 100 percent right in the way she felt.

"I told you I should have met her," I yelled at Big.

"I know, I know," he said.

"I have to talk to her." I said. "And I don't want to hear anything from you."

I waited at the apartment until Ms. Wallace came home. Usually I was gone by then or stayed in the back room. But this time, I took a deep breath, walked out of Big's bedroom, and saw her standing in the front hall.

"Ms. Wallace?" I started. I showed her the letter I was holding.

She looked me up and down and waited for me to speak.

"I'm Faith. Christopher's wife."

Not really the way you should be introduced to your mother-in-law. But I had to start somewhere. I was so nervous. I didn't know if she was going to curse me out or ignore me. Big had made it seem like she would bite my head off if we ever crossed paths.

"Ms. Wallace," I continued. "I really need to talk to you. Chris showed me this letter and I know you're upset."

Ms. Wallace just looked at me like she was waiting for me to say something substantial.

"Chris asked me to marry him. And I know it seemed to happen really fast and I know what you probably think of me. But it's not that way. I was raised in the church and still make sure I'm there every Sunday. And I know Chris has a daughter and I respect that because I have a daughter, too. You can ask Puff and Mark and all those guys about me and they'll tell you that I'm a good person. I'm just hoping we can figure out a way for you to get to know me."

"I'm glad you talked to me, Faith," Ms. Wallace finally said, in her Jamaican accent. "But why didn't you come to me sooner?"

"Big didn't want me to meet you," I said. "I'm not sure why."

At this point, Big appeared in the hallway with a sheepish, guilty look on his face.

"I should strangle you," she said to him. "Why would you keep this girl from me?"

I was immediately comforted by his mother's demeanor. She wasn't mean at all. She was no-nonsense and serious. But she was also warm and motherly. She could have continued to be mad about the whole situation. It's a credit to her that she let it go and pretty much accepted me as her daughter-in-law immediately.

Big and I had crossed several hurdles within a week or two of being married. But we hadn't managed to set up house together. I still had my apartment in Jersey. Yet I spent more time in that tiny, cluttered back bedroom with Big. It was like pulling teeth to get him to come to Jersey. Now that we were married, though, it was annoying being up in that back bedroom with all his boys all the time. I didn't mind hanging out; I just thought we needed our own space.

I certainly couldn't live with him at St. James Place. But Big was not trying to leave Brooklyn.

After we'd been married for a few weeks, I'd had enough of spending the night there. I hated commuting back and forth from Jersey, and I told Big we needed to move in together.

"Ma, I ain't moving out to Jersey," Big would say, shaking his head. "It's too far."

"Too far? Big, it's not even an hour away."

"Nah, I gotta be around my niggas."

"Well, look. We're gonna have to find a place in Brooklyn, then. I'm not gonna keep spending the night over here."

"Okay, find a place around here," Big said. "But not too far."

I rolled my eyes. "Of course not. Not too far from your beloved Brooklyn."

While I tried to find a suitable place to live, I was in and out of the Bad Boy offices practically every day. I was just beginning to start working on my album and I was still finishing up things on both Usher's album and Mary J. Blige's album, so there was always some business that needed to be handled. And in these pre-cell-phone days, I often needed to dip into the office and use the phones to handle personal business as well.

One morning, I came into the offices and headed straight to the promo room, where they kept all the posters and new music. That was usually where I went to use the phone. I was trying to find out when I could pick up my first new car, a Toyota Land Cruiser.

When I was done taking care of business, I saw Misa sitting in an office across the hall. I went over to say hello and noticed she was talking to another young woman, a new Bad Boy employee named Cheryl Flowers. Cheryl was six feet tall, slim and brown-skinned, with a small gap between her two front teeth. She had a really friendly demeanor: Anytime someone walked by her office and said hello, she'd call them "honey" or "sweetheart."

Cheryl was going to manage the various producers who worked for Bad Boy, including Chucky Thompson, Nashiem Myrick, and a duo known as Tone and Poke. I was impressed to see this young woman working as an executive for the company. She didn't even know that I was signed to the label. She thought I was just hanging out. I didn't look like a star. My hair was dyed blond but cut into a short natural hairstyle. And I didn't dress the part of a recording artist—yet. I was still mostly a new wife and mother who worked in the studio and was trying to get my home life together as well.

Ms. Wallace put me in touch with a Realtor who sent me to look at a few places in Brooklyn for rent. I fell in love with one place, a beautiful duplex in Park Slope. I took Big around to look at it.

"Hell no," he said as soon as we pulled up.

"You didn't even look at it yet!" I said.

"Does it have an elevator?"

"No, it doesn't. It's only three floors."

"Then I don't have to look at it. They want four thousand a month *and* I gotta walk up three flights of steps? Hell no."

I went back to the drawing board. There didn't seem to be an apartment in Brooklyn that was good enough. It was either too expensive or too far out. I was getting frustrated when one of Ms. Wallace's good friends told me about an apartment for rent in Fort Greene, on the corner of Myrtle and Carlton, right near the Fort Greene projects. It was two decent-size bedrooms and two bathrooms with large windows facing Carlton Avenue. It was larger than anything else we'd seen and it was on the ground floor. The rent was about fifteen hundred a month, which was a good amount of money back then. But it was something we could afford. It was behind a grocery store, which scared me a bit because I didn't want to deal with mice.

But I was still ready to set up house. So Big and I made plans to move in. We needed a couple thousand dollars to move in and buy furniture. I had some of it. And Big told me to get whatever else I needed from Lance "Un" Rivera.

Lance Rivera was one of Big's friends from Brooklyn. I didn't know too much about him. But I remember he had a really nice apartment over on Washington Street. Un lived close to Ms. Wallace. When I was over there, sometimes we'd go by and my daughter Chyna would play with his young son.

After Big signed with Bad Boy as an artist, he and Un decided to start a label. They secured a label deal with Atlantic Records, and the first group they signed was Junior M.A.F.I.A.

I went to Un and got thirty grand. I think this money was part of the advance they got from the new Undeas record label. With that money, I put down the security deposit and paid a few months' rent on the apartment. And then I went out to a Seaman's furniture store in Queens. Mark Pitts's dad was the manager there, and Mark sent me to see him. I bought the typical furniture setup: a teal-green leather living room set, one of those tall lamps with four or five bulbs that sprouted out, and a large glass coffee table that was constantly slipping off the base.

I also bought some stuff for Chyna's bedroom. She wouldn't end up sleeping there much, though. Soon after we moved in, we realized there was an ant infestation in that room, in the carpet. She was barely two years old and petrified of bugs so we usually slept in the living room on a pullout bed.

Big's single "Juicy" had dropped by this time, and he was starting to become more and more known. Sometimes I'd take a nap in the living room, and Chyna would wander over to the big glass window. People walking down Carlton who knew we lived there would yell up to Chyna. "Where Big at? Is he in there right now?"

Once we set up house, we fell into our own routine. My daughter was splitting her time between my grandparents' place in Newark and our apartment in Brooklyn. I was happy to see that Chyna bonded with her stepfather immediately and they got along really well.

They were both very silly and could amuse each other for hours with the most ridiculous made-up games. Big would do something like put Chyna inside a cardboard box and pretend like he wasn't going to let her out.

"Nope, you ain't never getting out," he'd say as Chyna banged on the box.

"Heellllp meee!" Chyna would say, half laughing and half screaming.

And of course, Chyna would get scared for real and start crying. Then Big would let her out. And she'd start laughing.

"Do it again!" she'd yell.

"Nah, you gon' start crying."

"Put me back in that box right now!" she'd yell.

He'd put her back in and rock the box all around the room. She'd start crying for real. Then he'd take her out; she'd start laughing and insist on doing it all over again.

I would just watch and roll my eyes at the both of them.

When Chyna was back in Jersey, I tagged along with Big occasionally to some of Junior M.A.F.I.A.'s recording sessions. I was also spending more and more time at the Hit Factory writing and recording tracks for my own album.

By September, Big's debut album, *Ready to Die,* was about to be released. There was a lot of anticipation for the record. Most of the songs had popped up on a few mix tapes that were being sold on the streets. DJ Enuff, a popular DJ on New York's Hot 97, got hold of the entire album and played it on repeat, which led to a huge buzz. Funkmaster Flex, whom Big name-checked on the song "Juicy," played several of his tracks during his nightly shift and every night that he played in the Tunnel nightclub, where he was a resident DJ. Craig Mack's album was being released around the same time, and a "B.I.G. Mack" campaign was being used to promote it.

I remember I drove down to a Burger King restaurant in downtown Manhattan with Misa to watch as Big and Craig Mack did a photo shoot for promo posters. They had these custom-made boxes made to look like the Styrofoam holders that fast-food burgers were sold in. Stamped on the top were the words B.I.G. MACK. Inside were samplers of Big's and Craig Mack's albums.

Even though he was getting recognized more and more and his album was being critically acclaimed, I'm not sure how much money Big really had back then. I bought him a lot of clothes—Coogi sweaters, Timberland boots, whatever he needed.

Soon after his album dropped, Big had an autograph session scheduled at a record store in the West Village, and I was trying to convince him to change up from the flannel shirts he wore all the time out of habit. I went to a big-and-tall shop and got him a silk short-sleeved shirt.

"Will you wear it?" I asked, holding it up.

Big just shrugged, looking at the shirt kind of warily. Clothes were for function as far as he was concerned. He wasn't really trying to be fly—not yet anyway. But when I went to the record signing, sure enough, Big was wearing the shirt I bought him. And it looked good on him, too.

I sat nearby as he autographed CDs and posters inside the store. At one point, he took a napkin and scribbled an autograph for me. It said: *To FEW, the love of my life. Love, Big.* That was Big's nickname for me. (It was an acronym: My initials were now *F.E.W.*) I took the napkin and someone snapped a picture of me holding it across my chest as he stood next to me with an arm thrown across my shoulders.

As soon as Big's album dropped, it seems like our lives started moving on fast-forward. *The Source* published a story on Big, as did the *LA Times* and a few other notable media outlets. And we started getting a lot more attention when we went out. There's a picture of me and Big at the Shark Bar that was published in one of the urban magazines, either *Vibe* or *The Source*. And Big is sitting there with this mean look on his face, holding up a chrome .22. The funny thing is, it was *my* gun. Not Big's.

Even before I got a deal, I'd somehow gotten into the habit of keeping an unloaded gun in my purse. I don't know what I was thinking. But I believe, in a subconscious way, I didn't want people to underestimate me just because I came from the church. I wasn't going around pulling guns on people or even showing them that I had it. It was just something for my peace of mind, as I started moving in circles that felt unfamiliar. I didn't want anyone to think I was some punk, a little church girl who couldn't handle her business if necessary.

But after I got with Big, carrying a gun took on a whole new meaning and feeling. It represented something totally different. In hip-hop, there's nothing sexier than a woman who will hold you down by any means necessary. There have been countless songs written by rappers talking about how their women will bust guns for them. I wasn't *really* that chick. But having a gun in my bag gave me a ride-or-die demeanor that I know Big liked.

Big and I never went on an official honeymoon. But those first few weeks of our marriage were as carefree and fun as a Caribbean vacation. We were in our own world.

Even though I was all up under Big, I still had to focus on my own music as well. So by the fall of 1994, it was time for me to start working on my own album. The work I'd done on both Usher's album and Mary's album was complete; Big's and Craig Mack's albums were in stores. I was next out of the gate for Bad Boy Records.

The very first song I recorded for my album was a jazzy, bluesy number called "Give It to Me." I had a studio session at the Hit Factory, and Big came to visit while I was working on the song.

When you are in the early days of a really intense relationship, nothing matters except that person. And physically, Big and I could not get enough of each other. We were in the lounge listening to the playback of the song and ended up kissing.

"I gotta go in the booth and lay down these vocals...," I said.

"Nah, you don't have to go right now."

We locked the door to the lounge and had a great time. We giggled every time the engineer or someone from Bad Boy would try to open the door and wonder why they couldn't get in. The lyrics to my new song perfectly matched what was happening in that lounge.

For the next song I recorded, Cheryl Flowers, the producer manager who worked for Bad Boy, came by to check on Chucky Thompson, one of the Bad Boy producers.

"I could listen to you sing all day," she told me. "Your voice is beautiful!"

"Thank you so much!"

"No, I'm serious," she said. "You and Chucky are doing big things together."

"I know we're trying to," I said.

Cheryl flashed me a smile—showing off that tiny gap between her teeth and her wide and expressive eyes. "Would you mind if I came by tomorrow to hear you sing again? When I get off work at that crazy place, I want to just chill. And I love your voice. It's just what I need after a day at Bad Boy."

"Of course," I told her. "Come by anytime."

I loved coming by the studio and seeing Cheryl's tall frame curled up on a sofa in the lounge, waiting to hear me record. Cheryl ended up becoming one of my very good friends, and she got added to the crazy mix that was me and Big's life. She quickly bonded with my daughter Chyna, too, and would keep an eye on her in the studio. Cheryl was someone I could rely on to look out for me and one of the few people I would be able to trust when things really got crazy. And I could always count on her for a fun night, especially when we were with Big.

I remember one time, early on in our new friendship, Big, Cheryl, and I went to this weed spot in Brooklyn. We had plans for the usual: get some weed, go back to our apartment in Brooklyn, and smoke, eat, and just chill. It was early winter and a cold evening so I had on a full-length fur coat. We drove to Big's favorite weed spot, a fake bodega in Bedstuy that had practically no inventory.

"Faye, run up in there right quick," Big said.

"Nah, Big," I said. "You go. This your spot."

"I'm tired. Just run up in there real quick."

"Fine," I said. "Give me the money."

I took the money, got out of the car, and went into the store. As soon as I got inside, the police were swarming the place.

"Everybody down on the floor!" I heard a bunch of cops screaming.

And there I was, facedown on the damn floor with my brand new full-length fur coat on. All because Big's lazy ass didn't want to get out of the car.

The cops started arresting people right and left. I was petrified. I was a recording artist on a major label! This could not be happening to me. But it was. An officer came up to me and told me to get up. They were just about to arrest me.

"Officer, I was only here to pay my rent!" I cried out.

He looked at me closely, searching my eyes.

"I don't know what's going on here," I said. "But my landlord told me to come here to pay my rent and that's it..." I gave him the most pitiful wide-eyed look I could manage.

"Okay, miss, you can go," he said, leading me out of the store.

I got back into the car, still shaking uncontrollably, and told Big and Cheryl what happened. They thought it was hilarious. But it wasn't funny yet to me.

"Yo, Ma," Big said. "Where's the money?"

I had to think for a minute. Everything had happened so fast. I checked the pockets of my fur coat and it wasn't there. And then it came back to me.

"I threw it away," I said.

"You did *what*," Big and Cheryl said.

"I got nervous! I thought if they saw the money they might know why I was there so I threw the money away!"'

Big and Cheryl and I laughed about that night for a long time. It's a great example of the silly yet happy times we all shared together.

Because Cheryl worked at Bad Boy, she had to deal with me and Big when things weren't going well, either. She wasn't just a friend, she was a co-worker. So when Big and I began to argue about various things, she had to be right up in the mix of that as well.

In October 1994, just two months after we got married, we had a huge blowup. Big was about to go on a promotional tour throughout Europe. And we'd hardly spent any time together before he left. He'd been hanging in the studio, in the streets, and God only knows where else. I was pissed off that he hadn't spent any time at home and now he was leaving for Europe, where he would be for weeks.

He had a big duffel bag full of stuff. I got so mad at him, I took his bag and dumped everything in it out the window of our bedroom, which was right over the street gutters. Needless to say, Big was not thrilled. We screamed on each other up until he was about to head for the airport. I stormed out of the apartment before he left.

When I came back, I began cleaning up the apartment. When I made my way to the bedroom, I was in for the shock of my life. I looked into my closet and saw that my clothes had been shredded! Cut to pieces! Dresses, suits, jeans, leather outfits—just hanging in shreds. I started crying. And then I called Cheryl, who was at the airport waiting for Big to arrive because she had to go to Europe with them on the tour.

"What is wrong, Faye!" Cheryl kept asking as I tried to compose myself.

"My—my—my—ahhh...my *clothes*!" I screamed. "That nigga cut up my damn clothes!"

"Who, Big? Why would he do that?"

"I can't stand him. He get on my fucking nerves! Cheryl, he cut up my favorite linen dress!"

I could hear Cheryl take in a sharp breath.

"No, girl. No he did not cut up that dress," she said.

"Yes he did! And all my jeans, too!"

"Wait. Faye. What about the Coogi dress? The one Mary gave you!"

I went to the closet and searched frantically for the Coogi dress Mary J. Blige had given me a few months before. I thought that dress was so cute; I was waiting for the right event to wear it.

I saw it in the back of my closet and breathed a sigh of relief. It looked fine. I took it out and then I noticed. It was shredded, too.

"Cheryl!" I cried. "He cut this one up, too!"

Big had arrived at the airport while I was talking to Cheryl and I could hear Big and the rest of them telling each other the story and laughing.

"Big, why would you do something like that?" I could hear her asking.

"Ask her why she threw my shit out of the window!" he yelled to Cheryl.

Big was lucky he was going out of the country. 'Cause I needed all that time to recover from him cutting up my clothes. I was so hurt. Now when I think about it, I can't help but laugh. But at the time, all I could do was sit in that apartment alone looking at my shredded clothes and just cry.

Big's trip to Europe kicked off a new phase in our relationship. Suddenly we weren't just running around Brooklyn with Cease, Chico, and Nino anymore. He was flying to different cities for shows and I was spending more and more time in the studio working on my album.

We were still together, but it was tough to maintain a relationship when he was gone so much. Yet I did have my own career to focus on. Even though my album was still in the very early stages, I was beginning to see the fruits of my labor in other ways.

Two months after Big dropped his album, Mary J. Blige released *My Life,* the album I'd worked on. The critics gave it very favorable reviews. It was another feather in Puff's cap, and I was pleased that I was able to be a part of it. When the songs I worked on came on the radio, it was a thrill to hear my voice in the background. And seeing my name listed on the song credits had me overjoyed. I couldn't believe it was really happening. I was a songwriter! Just like I'd pored over George Benson's and Rick James's albums, looking at the names of the musicians and songwriters, someone was now scanning Mary's album and seeing *my* name listed as one of the people who'd helped bring it together.

But before I could really revel in the way things were unfolding, the drama that would follow me for the next three years began with a very disturbing phone call from Big. It was November 30, 1994. I was at our apartment in Brooklyn. Big was at the Quad Recording Studios where he was working with Junior M.A.F.I.A., and he sounded a little worried.

"I'm not coming home until late," he said.

"Why? What's wrong?"

"My boy 'Pac just got shot," he said. "I'm going up to Bellevue to check him out," he said.

Although I'd never met Tupac Shakur, I knew that he and Big were cool. Big had always spoken highly of him, and I knew that although they didn't see each other very often, there was a mutual love and respect. The year 1994 had been a rough one for Tupac. Just a few weeks after Big's first album dropped, Tupac had released his album *Thug Life Volume I.* But he was becoming more notorious for his personal legal issues than his music. The year before, he'd been arrested for shooting two off-duty police officers. The charges were later dropped—but just two months later, he was arrested for sexually abusing a woman and beating up a former employee.

I know that much has been said about Tupac feeling like Big and Puff were involved in that attack. I can only go by what I knew of Big and 'Pac's relationship at that time. Big always spoke very highly of 'Pac, and I never got the sense that anything was amiss. They weren't close friends, necessarily. But I know he respected Tupac as an artist, and he was obviously cool enough with him that he called to tell me he was going to the hospital to see him as soon as he found out what happened.

Cease had been standing out on the balcony smoking a blunt when 'Pac got to the studio. They spoke and then 'Pac entered the studio and was ambushed by some guys waiting in the lobby. But 'Pac wasn't going to the studio to see Cease and Big. So it was always assumed that the people he was going to see must have set him up. Either way, the idea that Big had something to do with it was just unrealistic.

I wasn't at Quad. And Big and I were both running around a lot at this time. So I can't speak definitively on anything. But I can say that I truly believe that Big had *nothing* to do with the attack on 'Pac that night.

Tupac getting shot at Quad would be the beginning of a lot of misinformation and miscommunication between Tupac and Big. I don't know if anything could have been done differently that night. I think Tupac was already living in a fantasy world where his enemies were part of large conspiracies to hurt him. But if someone could have convinced Tupac that night that Big had nothing to do with him getting shot, so many things may have ended up differently.

At the time, I didn't give that stuff much thought. I only knew Tupac from his music and his movies. I had never met him and only knew what the average rap music fan knew about him.

I was cool with anyone Big was cool with. But eventually, his alliances and friendships would become fractured and confusing, leading me to make some poor decisions with serious consequences.

The day after the shooting, Tupac was famously wheeled into court on a stretcher to hear the verdict in his sexual assault case. He was found guilty and sentenced to two years in jail. Serving time in prison so soon after the shooting would turn out to be a really bad chain of events.

He went to jail soon after the attack. And he would have some time to stew over whom he thought shot him. And there would be no time for things to be explained and cleared up.

The moment 'Pac was found guilty, a stopwatch began, counting the moments until my life and his would intersect. So much was about to happen that would bring us into the same place at the same time. Unfortunately, I wouldn't see any of the warning signs until it was too late.

Chapter Ten

Changing Faces

While Big was crisscrossing the country, I was still hanging out with Mary and Misa occasionally, going to clubs. Being married to Big probably cemented my place in the crew since he was becoming more and more popular. Mary even came by our place in Brooklyn a few times to hang out. I didn't have a song out yet so I wasn't particularly well known; I could still walk through the hood without being recognized.

So I had Mary in the hood, going to Kum Kao and walking to the bodega with me to get myself a blunt. I got the feeling that she liked hanging out with regular folks. I guess it was like being back in Yonkers, where she was from. I think she liked doing 'round-the-way stuff with us.

When Big performed at Howard University's Homecoming Weekend concert, Misa and I drove down together. Before I went, I bought a few Coogi sweaters for Big and a pair of Timberland boots. I remember the concert was held in a huge venue, something like a converted post office. The show was packed and it was live. We stayed overnight and had a great time.

And I'd driven up to Westchester a time or two, where Misa had an apartment for her and Justin. We were cool mainly because of the irony that we knew each other before I got into the industry. I enjoyed her company as well. But Puff wasn't exactly thrilled about it.

I remember once, Puff stopped me as I was leaving the Hit Factory after a recording session. He knew I was on my way to hang out with Mary.

"Where y'all going?" he asked.

"We just hanging out," I replied.

"Well listen," he said, holding up a finger. "Don't get caught up in this industry shit. That's not what you here for."

I didn't feel like I needed a warning from him, but I filed it away in my mental Rolodex anyway.

At the end of 1994, Big was scheduled to shoot the video for his next single, "Big Poppa." They were shooting it at Nell's, a famous nightclub in downtown Manhattan. For the occasion, I bought a new outfit: a black suede wrap dress and some black boots with white stitching. My hair was dyed platinum blond and curled into ringlets. I had never been on the set of a video and was excited to see how it worked. I knew I wouldn't be *in* the video. But I also knew that since my husband was the artist, I could go and hang out.

As soon as I got there, Puffy walked up to me. His face was all twisted and it was obvious that he was pissed off about something.

"You need to mind your business," he said.

I was stunned. I had no idea what he was talking about. I started racking my brain, trying to think of what he could be talking about. I started to speak but he cut me off.

"I'm just telling you," he said.

My only other connection to Puff was Misa. So I had to assume that for some reason, he was referring to her. But I had no idea what I had done wrong.

I didn't know it then, but Puff and Misa had been having issues. He'd been cheating on her, and she was always suspicious. I'd later find out that at the time, she was trying to figure out what was up with some new chick who seemed to be popping up. I didn't know anything about that stuff yet, though. And if I had, I would not have told Misa anyway. It wasn't my business and it wasn't my place.

To this day, I still don't know why Puff thought I was putting words in her ears. I just know that when he screamed on me at that shoot, I wanted to cry. I was embarrassed and I felt bad. And I knew that he knew better — that wasn't my style at all to get caught up in that kind of he-said/she-said mess.

Maybe he thought since he was doing his thing on the side that I would say something to her. I was hurt because I would never take the initiative to insert myself in anyone's relationship like that. Of course, he hadn't known me for very long at this point. But I was a genuine person, and I thought he knew that.

Hype Williams was the director of the video. It was essentially one big party scene with lots of cameos from artists and other entertainers who were hot at the time, like Mary and Busta Rhymes.

I saw Misa and Mary sitting around a banquette and sat down next to them. I was so naive that I thought it was just like any other night when we all went out and sat around at a nightclub. But this was much different. They had a purpose for being there, and I was just tagging along.

The music started playing and Misa, Mary, and I began swaying back and forth and clinking champagne glasses as Hype filmed us. When he took a break after a few takes, Puff immediately pulled me to the side.

"You can't be in this video," he said.

"Why? 'Cause Big's my husband?"

"You're a new artist, Faith. We're gonna introduce you in a totally different way," he said.

I understand now why he wouldn't want me—a new artist on his label—to be an extra in Big's video. The way a brand-new artist is introduced is very important. You can't go back on your first impression. But at the time, I thought Puff was just tripping because Big and I were married. Misa was in the video, cuddled up with Puff in several scenes. So why couldn't I be?

Hype did some editing and cropped me out. If you look closely, you can see a full head of platinum-blond curls in one scene with Mary and Misa. That's me. And the back of my head is all you can see.

Looking back, I totally get why Puff wanted to keep my identity under wraps. Later on, when Big released "One More Chance," the cassette single included an advertisement for my album. There was a very close-up picture of my face that still didn't make it very clear what I looked like. It just had the date of my album's release printed underneath my name. Puff was trying to keep the mystique going. But at the time of the video shoot, I didn't quite understand all that.

There was another young lady on the set that day who seemed to be near Big during a lot of scenes. And during downtime I noticed she hung out with Nino and Cease and all the guys from Junior M.A.F.I.A. During one of the breaks, she stood next to Big, and an on-set photographer snapped a few photos of them posing. All I remember thinking about her was that she was very tiny. And she seemed really comfortable with Big and the rest of the guys, considering I'd never seen her before.

I asked Chico who she was and he told me it was Kimberly Jones, also known as Lil' Kim. Although I hadn't known Big that long at that point, it was still strange that I had never seen Kim before that day. I definitely had heard her name. I knew she was the girl in Big's crew. But I never saw her at Ms. Wallace's house, and I spent quite a bit of time there in the beginning of our courtship. I may have seen her from afar with a group of girls. And I knew she was often at

Cease's house. She was cool with his sister. But she didn't come up in conversation, and we had never crossed paths.

I've been asked many times what my first impression was of Lil' Kim. And honestly, I didn't have one. She was a young woman in a group signed to my husband's record label. Even as I watched her that day on the video set, dancing around, laughing, and joking, I had no inkling that she was anything more than an up-and-coming rapper. I had no reason to suspect that she had any other link to my husband whatsoever. Considering how things would play out, it seems hard to believe that I didn't know better.

The next day, Misa and I drove up to Westchester for one last scene they needed to shoot. It was a scene I knew I wasn't trying to be in. Puffy was to sit in a Jacuzzi with a bottle of champagne in one hand, surrounded by a bevy of beauties.

"I know one thing," Misa said loudly. "There won't be *no* hot tub scene if I'm not in it!"

Like me, Misa had made sure she was on the set of her man's video. In addition to being a stylist for Bad Boy, she was also keeping an eye on Puff.

And indeed, Misa was in the hot tub scene with Puff. Her hair was also dyed platinum blond and arranged in two Princess Leia–style buns. When the video was later released, I'd hear from friends that some people, who knew that a singer with blond hair named Faith was married to Big, assumed that Misa was actually me, because she had blond hair in that video.

Although Big was becoming more and more popular, he didn't let that change my status. I was still his wife and he treated me as such. I cooked for us, kept the house clean (although he spent more time in the studio than at home), and took care of him.

Just about every day, I was in the Hit Factory with Chucky Thompson, writing and arranging tracks. And sometimes, after I was done, I was catching the first flight to whatever city my husband was in.

I would see Puffy backstage at a show, and he would do a double take. "What are you doing out here?"

I would give him a look. "I'm out here to see my husband."

"You should be in the studio working."

I'd give him my latest recording to listen to. And that would be the end of that discussion.

No matter how often I traveled to see Big on the road, I was working hard in the studio. And Puff loved every single song I played for him. So he really couldn't complain.

My visits with Big were simple: We'd smoke weed, order room service, and have sex. That was pretty much it.

I remember going to Chicago to see him. When I got to the room, it was pretty late; Lil' Kim and some of his boys were in the room. We all exchanged greetings, but I made it clear that I was tired and wanted some private time with my husband. They all left. While we were in bed that night, the phone rang. I could tell that he was talking to a woman but I didn't know who. I heard him say something about "chilling with my wife for the night." When he hung up, I asked him who it was. And he said it was Kim. I assumed she was calling about the show the next day or something else business-related. There was no reason for me to think otherwise.

Over the years, Kim has talked about how she and Big were supposedly childhood sweethearts. So much has been said about her relationship with my husband. All these years later, people still don't know what to believe. I do know this. When Big and I were together, she played her position—in the back. *Way* back. When I came out on tour dates to see Big, she either was not around or made herself scarce when I arrived. I knew Big was working on her image and trying to make her marketable.

After my tummy tuck, I was still in the gym working out so that my body would be right when it was time for my album to drop.

"Yo, take Shorty to the gym with you," Big asked me one day.

"Who? Kim?" I asked.

"Yeah. Take her to the gym with you. Show her how to work out."

I agreed and let Kim tag along with me the next time I went to the gym. I just did the basics on how to use a few of the machines in case she went back on her own. Soon after that, Big gave me another assignment.

"Where you be getting your clothes and stuff from?"

"Misa and Mary put me up on Patricia Field," I told Big. "It's in SoHo."

"Take Kim with you the next time you go shopping," he said. "She need some help getting her style right."

I did what he asked me to, taking her with me, even giving her a dress of my own. It was a champagne-colored satin mini dress I'd had made for me that didn't fit properly. I gave it to Kim, and she wore it to a few of her first performances.

I wasn't a fitness guru. And I wasn't a stylist, either. I think Big just wanted me to introduce Kim to the things I'd been learning since getting into the industry. I was no expert by any means. But Big had seen me exploring certain things, like eating healthy and working out and trying to get my gear right. So I guess he just wanted me to try to help Kim since she was a brand-new artist. And because she was the only female in a rap crew of grimy boys, I'm sure Big wanted to make sure she'd get the right attention.

Most of what I knew about Kim, I picked up from hearing the other guys in Junior M.A.F.I.A. talking about her. They always had something slick to say.

I didn't know the deal with her. But from seeing how the guys dealt with her, I got the impression that she was in a vulnerable situation.

Big didn't seem to treat her with the utmost respect, either. I remember one afternoon she came by the house and Big wasn't there. He called and before I could start talking, she made a face and gestured for me to not tell him that she was there. He ended up finding out anyway.

"Why you got that chick up in the house?" Big asked.

"Why not?"

"Nah," he said. "I don't want Shorty in my house *ever*."

Even before we moved to Brooklyn, I noticed that Big was kind of rough and abrasive toward Kim. I once heard him screaming on her at his mother's house although I had no idea why.

"You think you special?" he screamed. "I'll go get Inga right now." While Kim cried, Big kept yelling at her. "We don't need you for this group. Inga would be happy to be down." (The "Inga" he was referring to was a sixteen-year-old rapper named Foxy Brown who would go on to be Kim's nemesis.)

"You ain't special," he said. "I will replace your ass with the quickness. Don't forget that shit!"

I think seeing the way they talked to her and about her made me dismiss her. I usually have Spider-Man senses when it comes to other women. But with Kim, there was nothing.

I remember going to a hotel room in Manhattan where Big was staying. And when I got there, Kim was on her way out. She ended up hanging around for a bit longer and getting a ride back to Brooklyn with me.

"I know you're Big's wife," she said, as I drove us over the Brooklyn Bridge. "We're more like brother and sister."

I just nodded. My Lil' Kim bullshit detector was still set to OFF.

CHAPTER ELEVEN

Disappearing Acts

*I*t's easy to understand why I couldn't see that Kim wasn't being honest with me. There were too many other signs that Big was beginning to stray. I was suspicious of so many other women that I had no time to give a second thought to what Kim and Big's relationship might be.

The first time I caught him cheating happened before the end of 1994. He went out to Chicago for a show, and when he returned he was acting weird. He kept checking his pager and then trying to be discreet when returning calls. He'd make a call and then go out of his way to keep his side of the conversation brief and vague.

I am a super-sleuth when it comes to sniffing out infidelity. So the next time he got a page and then went to the phone, I made sure I was close by when he was done. He left soon after, and I picked up the receiver and hit REDIAL. It was some chick in Chicago.

"Who the fuck is this?" I asked.

She told me her name and that she had met Big at a show.

"So why are you calling him now?"

"'Cause now I'm pregnant," she said.

I confronted Big as soon as he came home. "Who the fuck is this bitch talking about she's pregnant?"

Big sucked his teeth. "Ain't nobody pregnant by me!"

I told him about the phone call, and he just walked away from me. "Who is this girl?" I asked.

"Just some chick I met after the show."

"Well, did you have sex with her?"

"Yeah, Faye. I did."

I was stunned. He just admitted without any hesitation that he'd cheated on me. And he looked me right in the eye when he said it, too. This was my first introduction to how Big could be brutally, painfully honest. He could look me right in my eye and tell me had sex with some other woman. And he wouldn't even blink. It was almost like he was daring me to do something or say something about it. Which just drove me crazy.

"So how do you know she's not pregnant by you?" I asked.

"'Cause I know," he said. "That bitch is straight lying."

"You can't go out of town without fucking somebody else?" I said. "I'm not gonna be able to trust you when you have to go away!"

Big just rolled his eyes like he didn't even want to deal with it. He went to the telephone and dialed a number. I didn't realize he'd called the girl in Chicago until I heard him cursing her out.

"...And bitch, you know you ain't pregnant with my baby so you better stop saying that shit, too."

He slammed down the receiver. And I never heard anything else about that chick. I don't know if she really was pregnant. All I know is I never heard her name or anything else about her again.

I was hurt that so early on into our marriage Big would go away on tour and cheat on me. That was not cool.

Of course, I don't know what exactly I expected. We rushed into our relationship and rushed into our marriage. We were way too young. And he was on the verge of stardom. It was irrational for me to think that we would be a typical American family. But I truly loved Big, and knowing that he wasn't faithful hurt even though I knew he didn't take those other women seriously. I was mostly concerned that the woman in Chicago was more than just a fling, and Big assured me that she wasn't.

He was in and out of town, still doing dates on the "B.I.G. Mack" tour, and I was holding down things at home. But after the incident with the first chick, things just kept getting progressively worse.

I flew out to Daytona to see him, and before I could even get settled in the room, I saw a notepad with a girl's name and phone number on it. The name looked familiar. I think I'd seen it somewhere before. And it wasn't Big's first time in the area, so I put two and two together right away. Big was in the bed sleeping, and I called the number immediately.

"Who is this?" I asked. "And why is your phone number in Big's room?"

"Um, this is Maria."

"Hi there, *Maria*. I think the three of us need to have a little chat."

"Look. I'm not trying to cause any trouble," the girl said.

"Too late," I told her. "Where you staying at?"

Turns out the girl was staying in our hotel, just a few floors down.

"You need to come up to our room," I told her. "Big needs to talk to you."

While I waited for the girl to show up, I slipped into bed with Big and woke him up.

"Your little friend Maria is on her way over here," I said.

Big didn't miss a beat. "Oh, word? Cool."

Maria knocked on the door. I got up and opened it, then got back in bed with Big.

Maria came into the room and just looked at the two of us.

"My husband has something he wants to tell you," I said.

Big sat up a little bit. "Yo, shorty. This right here is my wife. So you need to know I ain't fucking with you like that."

I gave Maria a smile. "Now get out," I said. "And close the door behind you."

Of course, Big probably had sex with that girl as soon as I got on a plane back to New York. But back then, I just wanted these women to know who I was, and I wanted Big to acknowledge me. And he always did. He never hesitated to tell any woman he crossed paths with that I was his wife and no one—except his daughter and his mother—came before me.

Me and Big always made up pretty quickly. In Daytona, I forgave him for the little Maria incident and ended up talking him into going on a two-hour ride from Daytona to Tampa so we could go to Busch Gardens. We went the next day—with Cease and Nino and Chico tagging along, of course.

I remember that being one of the truly fun and carefree days with Big. It was a gorgeous sunny day, and we were running around the amusement park like little kids. I got on a few roller coasters and begged Big to get on one with me.

"Come on," I pleaded. "You will love it. I promise."

"Faye, you crazy," he said. "I ain't getting on that shit. My big ass gon' end up flying out into the parking lot somewhere."

"I'll be right next to you," I said. "I won't let nothing happen to you."

"You ain't gonna be able to do nothing to help me," he said with a laugh.

"Forget it," Chico said. "You ain't getting Big on no rides."

"I bet you I will," I said.

I worked on Big for the rest of the afternoon. Telling him how fun it would be, daring him to do it, teasing him for being afraid, and just being a pain in the ass about it. Finally, at the end of the day, he agreed.

"I can't believe I'm 'bout to do this shit," he said.

I grabbed his hand and took him to the line. Chico and the rest of the guys couldn't believe it. They started teasing him about how he'd let me talk him into something he said he'd never do.

When we got all buckled into our seats, I looked over at Big. "You ready?"

"Few," he said, calling me by my nickname. "I am *not* ready."

"Too late now!" I screamed as the ride started. We flew up and down across the tracks, upside down and backward, until we were both sick. We screamed and laughed, exhilarated and scared at the same time.

That roller-coaster ride would become symbolic of our relationship—many ups and downs, some within minutes of each other. We moved forward very quickly and then backward just as fast. But through all of it, we were right next to each other, holding our hands, closing our eyes, and enjoying the ride.

A few days after we got back home from Tampa, I noticed a strange number in Big's pager. It had a 215 area code, and I knew he'd recently done a show in Philadelphia and was scheduled to return there soon for another show.

I listened to the message. It was from a girl named Tiffany who sounded as if she worked for a record label. She was asking Big a bunch of questions about when he was going to be arriving for a concert. As always, I made a mental note: There was some chick named Tiffany in Philly who sounded suspicious. And when Big went to Philly for the next show, I planned to be right up in the audience to see if I could find any signs of another woman.

I did attend the show in Philly. I ended up driving down there with my friend Doobie. Doobie was actually a friend of Big's. But he'd become my friend, too, and we hung out in Brooklyn a lot with his friend, a guy we called Creamy.

In Philly, I didn't see any signs of another woman. But by then, Big had already started getting carried away with the infidelity. I had way more things to deal with than suspecting an anonymous chick in Philadelphia. There was all sorts of drama going on right at home.

Big and I had developed a dangerous pattern. He'd cheat on me. I'd find out. Then I'd curse him out and stop speaking to him. And then we'd get back together and start all over again.

A prime example occurred when Big went on a tour date in Virginia with Junior M.A.F.I.A. He usually checked in with me after they landed and gave me the number to his hotel room in case I needed to be in touch. But this time, when Big got to Virginia, he called me up acting strange.

"Yo, Ma," he sad. "L is going to be using my room so I won't be in here."

I was immediately suspicious. Big was the artist; the other guys packed his bags and served as roadies and hype men. Why the hell would he give up his room to L?

I told him I would talk to him later and got off the phone.

I walked around our apartment, getting more and more pissed off with each minute. Did he think I was stupid? He would never give up his room. He was obviously trying to get away with something. And I knew it had something to do with a woman. I fed Chyna, got her ready for bed, and then called Big's hotel room. The line was busy. I continued calling on and off for hours, and the line was always busy. I went from annoyed to furious.

Finally, I decided to act. I couldn't let Big think I was going to just take this kind of behavior. I knew I couldn't stop him from cheating on the road. But I damn sure wasn't going to let him think he could tell me some bullshit lie to keep me from finding out.

I called Continental and made a reservation for a ticket to Norfolk. The next flight out was leaving at 6 AM. I called Cheryl, my new friend who worked at Bad Boy, and told her to come over and watch Chyna.

But before I could leave for Virginia, I had to go to the studio. I had time booked to work on a new song with Chucky. So even though I was anxious and upset, I had to hold it together for a few hours in order to do my job.

The beat was ready when I arrived. I really liked the idea that producer Chucky Thompson was going for. But it was going to be a challenge for me to write something to such a slow and simmering beat and make it work for my voice. There wasn't a lot of music — just a haunting and spare track that was bass-heavy.

For a long time, I just sat in the studio, thinking about what Big was doing in Virginia and wondering how I was going to write a song to a track that felt like it had no music for me to sing to. I was a bit intimidated in the studio that night. I'd already written several songs that Puff and the rest of the folks at Bad Boys really liked. And I'd worked quickly, too. But this track wasn't as easy.

I was about to give up and call Chucky and ask him to come to the studio and play something to help me. Instead, though, I just starting humming to myself, and something began to take form.

The words moved up and down the scale, as if they were riding the waves of the track. It became a very jazzy, bluesy song that seemed a bit improvisational. The sound was similar to Anita Baker and some of the scats and riffs she would do with her voice.

Once I got over that initial hump, everything came together quickly. Within five hours, I'd completed the song I titled "No Other Love."

And it really captured how I felt about Big.

Even though I had just booked a ticket to surprise Big and see if he was up to no good, I was in love — deeply. And of course, being in love can make you do some very foolish things.

As soon as the song was done, I went home to get my stuff and make sure Cheryl was straight with Chyna. Then I took a cab to the airport and hopped on my hour-long flight to Norfolk. When I landed, I caught a cab to the hotel they were staying in. I was like a ninja when I got up in that hotel lobby. I didn't want anyone to see me and warn Big that I was there. I saw Hawk, Big's road manager, standing at the front desk, paying Big's hotel bill. I snuck behind him and then dashed onto the elevator.

I got to Big's door and knocked. There was no response. I knocked a few more times and then I finally heard Big's voice.

"Who is it?" he said.

I had to think fast. If I said my name, he wouldn't open the door if there was someone else inside.

"Housekeeping," I said, adding a random foreign accent to my voice.

The door opened up, and there was a woman standing there. She was brown-skinned, slim, and had short curly hair. I remember she was wearing a plaid skirt; it looked kind of like a school uniform. I pushed her back into the room, jumped on top of her, and started beating her ass.

"This your little friend?" I screamed at Big. "You think you slick?"

Big was sitting on the bed, just watching with his eyes wide, as I pushed and smacked the girl, who was screaming and trying to duck for cover.

"Yo, Ma, you need to chill!" Big said. "I didn't even fuck her!"

I mashed the girl in the face and then kicked her.

"Yeah well, you should have," I said.

I walked out of the room and back to the lobby, took a cab to the airport, and grabbed the next flight back to New York.

I didn't know it then, but Big was right behind me on the next flight out. And when he landed, he was on a mission to find me and patch things up. We had a two-door Lexus coupe that we were renting at the time while my car was in the shop. As soon as I landed, I jumped in the car and headed to Kum Kao to get something to eat. I saw Doobie and Creamy standing in front of the restaurant.

"Yo, Big looking for you," Doobie said. "He just rolled through here talking about any y'all seen my wife?"

"Whatever...I ain't even thinking about him right now."

I continued on my way, picking up my dry cleaning, going to the beauty supply store to get some stuff to do my hair, running to the post office to mail out some bills. Every time I stepped out of the car, someone would yell out to me: "Yo, Faye! Big just pulled off. Wanted to know if anybody seen his wife..."

I was determined to avoid him as long as I could. But by that evening when I pulled up to our place, I saw him standing in front of the building, talking to a few of his friends. I tried to walk past him and go straight into the building.

"Ma. Come *on*, Ma. I been looking for you all day!"

"I don't have shit to say to you, Big. Just leave me alone."

"You really flew out there just to see what the fuck I was doing?"

"How you gon' tell me L is using your room? What kind of weak-ass lie is that?"

There was a small smile playing on Big's mouth, and his eyes were twinkling with mischief. That was something about that man that could just make me melt.

"You still mad at me?"

I didn't say anything. I just leaned against the door to our building and looked at him.

"Come inside," he said. "I'ma make it up to you."

I followed him inside and even though I wanted to be mad at him for at *least* another hour, I gave up and let him make it up to me instead.

Flying to Virginia to catch Big in a lie was so immature. But that was my idea—back then—of being a ride-or-die chick. My love affair with Big had started off with lots of drama and heat. And honestly, I don't think either of us would have wanted it any other way. I know Big probably got a kick out of seeing how I would go off when I thought another woman was on the scene. But it wouldn't take long for the whole scene to wear me down.

Big started spending more and more time at Unique Studios with Junior M.A.F.I.A. as they finished up their album. If he wasn't out of town for a show, he was in the studio with Junior M.A.F.I.A. Sometimes he would stay at the studio really late, and I'd get a call just as I was getting into bed.

"I'm staying in Manhattan," Big would say.

"Where?"

"I got a room at a hotel. I'm coming home tomorrow."

"You can't just take a car home and go back in the morning?" I'd ask.

"Come on, Few," he'd say. "We got a lot of work to do. By the time I come all the way to Brooklyn it'll be time to come back here anyway."

"Fine," I'd say. "I'll just sleep alone. Again."

I did the best I could to set up a household for us. And he wanted to spend the night in a hotel just a few miles away? And this was the same man who made me leave my spot in Jersey because he just *had* to be in Brooklyn!

Eventually, the hotel stuff started getting out of hand. One night Big was out of town for a show, and I ran into Chico in Brooklyn. Chico usually traveled with Big, so it was unusual for him to be around.

"Why didn't you go with Big?" I asked.

"I did," Chico said.

"So why are you *here* in Brooklyn?"

"Because we came *back*, Faye."

"Wait. Big is back, too?"

Chico started to look uncomfortable. Like he knew he may have gotten Big in trouble.

"Yeah," he said slowly. "Big is back..."

"Well, where is he?"

"He didn't come back to Brooklyn yet," he explained. "We had a session in Manhattan as soon as we landed, and he went straight to the studio."

"When did y'all get back?"

"Like, day before yesterday..."

Big had been in town for two days and hadn't bothered to come home? Or even let me know he was in town? I understood that his schedule was hectic but I felt like he was being disrespectful—and sneaky. And I didn't like it at all.

It seemed like the more Big began to experience fame, the weaker our relationship became. The love was still there for sure. But we were so young and Big was starting to see the world for the first time. He was finally ready to let go of being in Brooklyn every waking moment. As he ventured out of his favorite borough, though, he was venturing away from me as well.

One afternoon, I was in the front seat of Big's Toyota Land Cruiser with his friend Damion. I opened up the glove compartment looking for a tissue and there was a Polaroid picture of a tall, thin, light-skinned girl. There was a phone number scribbled at the bottom.

I felt my blood start to boil. I was like the Incredible Hulk. I could be sweet, unassuming, and naive sometimes. But then Big would do something stupid, like leaving a picture of his latest concubine where I could find it. It was almost like he *wanted* to get caught. I put the picture back and waited to see if it would disappear. It didn't. And when I saw that it was still there a few days later, I sprang into action.

Someone who worked at Bad Boy was able to trace the number for me. It was a girl I'll call Anita who lived in the Parkchester, a sprawling apartment community in the South Bronx. I decided to pay Anita a little visit and show her what happens when you mess with my husband.

I got her exact address and I told Cheryl, my new running partner, and my friend Chris to come with me. But first, I had to go to Harlem to the Abyssinian church for Puffy's son's christening ceremony.

So here we are, up in the church, on a beautiful occasion. Justin, Puff's son, is about eight or nine months old. He's being christened, and Misa and Puff and all of their family members are there. And because this is the very early days at Bad Boy, many of the employees are here as well. It's a very serious and special occasion—and all I'm thinking about is how I can't wait to get out of there and find this Anita chick.

As soon as the ceremony was over, we said our good-byes and jumped in a cab to take a quick trip uptown to the Bronx. We told the cabdriver to wait outside Anita's building. I wasn't expecting what I needed to do to take very long.

When me and Cheryl and Chris got to her building, we rang the buzzer a few times. Finally, a young woman's voice called out. "Who is it?"

We all looked at each other. What the hell were we going to say to get up there: *This is Big's wife and two of her friends and we're here to beat your ass*?

"Who is it?' the girl asked again.

"It's Chris," said my friend Chris. Since Big's real name is Chris, maybe Anita thought it was him. Either way, she buzzed us in.

We went up the elevator. When it opened onto her floor, we saw her open the door to her apartment and look out into the hallway.

"There go that bitch right there," I said.

Cheryl held the elevator door open so we could have a quick

escape. Me and Chris jumped on the girl, pushed her into the apartment, and gave her a brief but thorough beat-down.

Me and Chris dashed back into the hallway and onto the elevator. The three of us ran out of the lobby and toward the waiting taxicab. As we ran, Anita was hanging out of the window to her apartment.

"They just attacked me!" she was screaming. "Somebody call the police! There they are right there!"

While Anita yelled and pointed in our direction, we ran and jumped in the cab and headed back to Manhattan, laughing all the way.

A few years ago, I met a stylist on a video shoot. We started talking and it turned out that he used to date Anita in high school. He stayed in touch with her over the years, and she later told him about when we came up there. He knew the whole story about me and my crew beating her up. He told me that the young lady lived with her father and younger brother and he couldn't believe I'd been bold enough to go into her home and attack her. It was a horrible thing to do. It was Big I should have been fighting. But that was how I dealt with my frustration. I cursed him out, too, of course. But I thought maybe kicking some ass would get the word out that chicks better think twice before messing with my husband.

I would eventually learn that beating the chick's ass doesn't work. There will always be someone to take her place. If your man is going to cheat on you, it's up to him to put a stop to it.

I thought about William and how I'd messed around with a man who had a wife. I thought about how devastated his wife must have been when she found out about me. I'd known it would come back to me. That's just the way karma works. I didn't give that woman or her marriage a second thought when I was sleeping with her husband. So now here I was, dealing with so many women who felt like I did back then. They didn't owe me a damn thing. It was Big who was supposed to be faithful. I had a few options. I could keep running around the country, beating up every girl he messed around with. I could dip out on my own and adopt the two-can-play-that-game stance, or I could just let Big do his thing and focus on an exit strategy.

In time, I'd end up doing all three.

CHAPTER TWELVE

You Used to Love Me

The infidelity issue was really depressing. And like most people who are heartbroken, I threw myself into my work. But every single fight and argument I had with Big and every single make-up lovemaking session seeped into my songwriting for my debut album. Sneaking into the studio to make love became a song called "Give It to Me." Reflecting on what he meant to me became "No Other Love."

Cheryl and I drove down to Washington, DC, to work on a song with Chucky Thompson, who lived in the area. And Big and I were going through it over some chick at the time. I can remember me and Big arguing back and forth over the phone all the way down to DC. Although I was there to work, I was completely stressed.

"I'm getting real tired of feeling like I can't trust you," I said to Big.

I could hear him sighing heavily through the phone. "Faye, you be making shit way harder than it need to be —"

"You fucking anything that moves and *I'm* making shit hard?"

Big sucked his teeth. "Why you even gotta go there?"

"You just don't understand how I feel, Big." I started to cry.

"Yo, Faye," Big said. "Come on, Ma. Don't cry…"

"You don't even care. You just playing all kinds of games."

I could hear some commotion on the other end of the phone and someone was calling Big. "I gotta go to sound check," he said. "I'll holla at you in a minute."

Cheryl, who had been sitting next to me in the car, rubbed my shoulder. "Come on, girl," she said. "We got get into the studio and get this song done. Puff gon' have a fit if we come back home without a song."

When I went into the studio with Chucky and heard the track, the lyrics practically wrote themselves. Especially considering I was still in tears. I wrote that song, "You Don't Understand," in less than two hours, using my frustration with Big to motivate and inspire me.

Now, even though Big and I had our differences, I wasn't thinking about leaving him. As a matter of fact, it was during this time that I went to the Ink Spot in Jersey, my favorite tattoo parlor. I had already had Chyna's name on my left upper arm and my own name with a musical staff near it.

I decided to get the letters B.I.G. tattooed right above my right breast. I didn't tell Big ahead of time what I was going to do. But the next time I saw him, after a show he did in New York, I made sure to wear a revealing shirt that showed off my new artwork.

"I like that right there," he said, a smile on his face.

"Oh really," I said. "And why is that?"

"'Cause now niggas know. You better mark that territory."

We laughed together. But Big knew that his territory didn't need to be marked. If anyone needed a permanent sign to keep people away, it was him, not me.

In addition to our arguments, there were other stresses bubbling up for Big that I didn't know much about. Around the same time that I got my tattoo, *Vibe* magazine published an article about Tupac written by Kevin Powell. 'Pac was in jail at the time, and in the interview he blamed Big and Puff for the shooting at Quad Studios four months before.

Now, I didn't read the article when it came out. Back then, I didn't really keep up with who was saying what in magazines. But I remember hearing Big talk about it.

"Shit is crazy," he said. "He *know* I ain't have nothing to do with that shit."

There were murmurs of agreement from Cease and Chico and Nino. It was obvious that they were all perplexed as to why Tupac was going so hard trying to blame them. And they may have been just the slightest bit worried about how it was all going to play itself out.

I didn't pay much attention to what was being said in the press—or Big's reaction to it—because the early summer of 1995 was a whirlwind of studio sessions for me. I was working on a daily basis to complete my album. Every so often, Puff would come by to hear what I was working on.

I continued to draw on my real-life experiences, mostly with Big, as my songwriting inspiration. Basically, if you listen to my first album, you are listening to the soundtrack of my life with Big during that time.

It began with an interlude, with my famously super-stacked harmonies of my own voice. On the short introduction, I sang about how far I'd come in life. And then the album opened with "No Other Love," the bluesy, jazzy song I recorded just before I snuck up on Big in Virginia.

One afternoon I was in the studio, listening to a track that the Trackmasters produced. Mary J. Blige and her sister LaTonya came by my session to say hello.

"I like this track," LaTonya said. "This is hot."

We all nodded to the beat, humming and trying to come up with lyrics that would work.

LaTonya started singing a random line over and over and I picked up where she left off.

"That's hot," Mary said, urging me to continue.

All I had to do is think about my on-again-off-again love affair to find the words I needed to help the song come together. As with most of my songs, I was done quickly, in less than a full day at the studio. I would record and then wait to hear back from Puff on how he felt about the song. I trusted his opinion: If he said something was hot, I had no doubts that it was.

A perfect example was the song that would become my first single. Chucky put together a track that I loved immediately. As soon as the hook came to me, I got chills.

I laid down the hook and listened to it over and over. I called Puff before I even finished writing.

"Come to the studio," I said. "I want you to hear something."

"I'm on my way," Puff said.

For the song, I used a very gentle and soft approach. The beat was heavy and hard-core, and I didn't want to overpower the song. So although I could have belted the notes out hard, I snuck up on the beat instead. I was learning how toning down my voice could be even more powerful than screaming out the notes.

Puff came into the studio, heard me laying down the track, and went crazy.

"That's that shit!" he screamed out. "That's that shit right there!"

For the entire afternoon that I recorded that song, different music industry folks came through the studio. I remember seeing Heavy D bobbing his head. I distinctly remember seeing Michael Bivins from New Edition. He came in with a friend whom I thought was really cute—I remember noticing that the guy had very distinctive facial hair and a huge Adam's apple. Q-Tip from A Tribe Called Quest was there. Even Andre Harrell, Puff's former boss at Uptown, came through.

Something electric was happening. Every single person who heard the song just fell in love with it, from the producer to the engineer to all of the seasoned music industry executives who were there.

Before my session was even over, I actually felt like I had a potential hit record on my hands.

It was the kind of love song that I knew any woman could relate to. But it was also a song that men would bump in their cars because the beat was crazy and my voice was more smoky than saccharine-sweet. I also knew that it perfectly fit what Puff was going for in terms of being sexy and mature. It was the kind of song I knew that people my mom's age would like just as much as young people.

We decided instantly that "You Used to Love Me" would be the first single. I continued to finish up songs for the rest of the album.

While most of the songs I wrote were written to describe my feelings for Big, I wrote one song with lines that I wished Big would sing to *me*. That song, "Soon as I Get Home," sounds like something I've written to a person I want to spend more time with.

But really, I was writing what I wanted to hear from Big. As he traveled for work, spending time with me became less and less of a priority; I just wanted to hear him say that as soon as he got home, he'd make it up to me. I talked to Big about it all the time. And while I didn't always get the response I wanted from him, I was able to vent in the studio and feel somewhat better.

The songwriting and recording process was coming very easily to me—until Puff brought me a song he wanted me to remake.

"I'm telling you, Faith," he said one day. "This is gonna be hot."

He played me a song called "Love Don't Live Here Anymore" by a group called Rose Royce. I wasn't feeling the song at all. I knew it was considered an old-school classic but I just didn't like it.

"I don't know, Puff," I said. "It don't really do nothing for me."

"Listen, it's gonna be a duet," he explained. "You and Mary!"

I nodded. I loved the idea of working with Mary J. Blige, especially on my very first album. But it didn't convince me that the song was right for me.

I just trusted Puff's vision and learned the song. Mary and I met up at the studio, figured out who was going to sing which verse, and began laying down the track. When Puff came in to hear how things were going, he wasn't impressed.

"What the fuck are y'all doing in here?" he asked, turning up his nose. "I don't feel the pain in this song."

Mary and I just looked at each other.

"You supposed to be like…" Puffy twisted up his lips like he was in pain and sang a line off key.

I tried not to laugh. But it always cracked me up when Puff tried to tell his artists how he wanted them to sound. Even though he couldn't actually hit the notes, I would know exactly what he was trying to get out of me.

"Puff, I just can't get this song," I told him.

"That's 'cause y'all need to get drunk," Puff said.

Me and Mary looked at him like he was crazy.

"You heard me. Get out. Go down the street to that bar on the corner and get drunk. You better be fucked up in the next two hours. Then get back here and knock this shit out. Go. *Now*."

Puff ushered me and Mary out of the studio. We just shrugged and laughed, leaving the studio and walking to the nearest bar. We sat down and ordered a round of tequila shots and Heinekens to chase them down.

"You like the song?" I asked Mary as we downed our drinks.

Mary signaled to the bartender to bring another round. "Rose Royce is the shit!"

"It seems so old-school," I said.

Mary held up her shot glass. I clinked mine against hers and then drained my drink.

"It *is* old-school, baby," said Mary. "That's what makes it hot. I love all the old stuff. Rose Royce, the Isley Brothers, Marvin Gaye and Tammi Terrell? That's all the hot shit."

Mary started telling me about all the music she loved. I was in awe of her knowledge of old and obscure soul records. It seemed like she knew every R&B song ever recorded since the Motown era. I was really impressed.

As soon as we got a nice buzz going, we left the bar and stumbled back to the studio to try out the song again.

I still thought the song was better suited to Mary's voice: earthy and raspy. But I did my best. Puff was satisfied, but I wasn't crazy about it.

"You'll see," Puff said, after the song was completed. "That's just what this album needed. The Queen of Hip-Hop Soul and the First Lady of Bad Boy, together on one track! Trust me on this one!"

CHAPTER THIRTEEN

The Tipping Point

I was really excited about the way my album was coming together and looking forward to the release, which was scheduled for August 29, 1995. In late spring, I was just finishing up the last few tracks and making plans for shooting a video.

While I finished my album, I also went in the studio for a remix to one of Big's songs. His next single, "One More Chance," was being remixed, using a sample from DeBarge's "A Dream."

The original chorus of the song was like a chant.

Puff wanted the remix to be more melodic and radio-friendly, and I was enlisted to help reformulate the song. After listening to the track several times, I began to come up with a different version of the chorus that was a smoother and softer version of the "one more chance" line from the original and synced up with the new song.

I softened it and came up with similar words with a very different vocal arrangement.

Mary came by the studio after I was done and ended up adding her vocals as well.

I was pleased with the way the song turned out, and when the song began getting airplay it quickly became a hit. Even though people didn't yet know who I was or what I looked like, they definitely knew my voice, because that song was being played everywhere.

There was the start of some confusion, though. Both Mary and I sang backing vocals on the song. And the way our voices blended together, it was hard to tell where her voice ended and mine began. Especially since Mary was an established artist and I was brand new. It would take some time for my sound to be identified.

In the early summer days of 1995, all my hard work began to pay off. One night, I was driving alone in my Land Cruiser back home to Brooklyn after a studio session in Manhattan. It was late; I was dead tired and barely listening to what was on the radio.

And then I heard the familiar sound of bombs dropping. It was a sound effect that DJ Funkmaster Flex used on his radio show on Hot 97. Whenever he played a song that he was absolutely sure was going to be a hit, he would "drop bombs" while the song played.

"This is that new hot joint off Bad Boy Records," he said. "The summer is not ready! This joint is *crazy*!"

And then I heard my voice, gentle and soft.

It was "You Used to Love Me," the song I'd recorded that I just knew was going to be a hit. And Flex was dropping bombs on it!

I started crying so hard that I was nearly blubbering. I looked up toward the sky and whispered as I cried: *Thank you God, thank you God. Thank you so much for this...* I truly felt so blessed. I knew how hard it was for someone to get a song on the air. I went to school and church with hundreds of awesome singers who would never hear themselves on the radio.

It had been five years since I sat in my bedroom at my grandparents' house in Newark, writing a melody for my telephone answering machine and stacking my vocals. And now I was officially a professional singer with a hot song playing on the most listened-to radio station in New York City.

I drove home, singing along to my own song, completely over-whelmed and grateful. And I cried like a baby the whole way.

Right after my single started playing on the radio, we shot the video for Big's "One More Chance" in a brownstone in Spanish Har-lem. Puff just wanted me in one scene. During the video, I was to just sing the chorus straight into the camera. I was pretty sure I could handle that. But then I got to the shoot and saw a lot of other female singers who looked familiar: an R&B duo named Changing Faces, the group Zhané, Total, Da Brat, Aaliyah, Miss Jones, Patra, and of course Mary J. Blige, who was also singing on the chorus. They were all going to lip-sync to our voices in the video.

I had no idea that all of these other women were going to be in the video, and it made me more nervous. Not only was it my voice on the song, but it was my husband they were all supposed to be singing to.

Puff had always said that Big was supposed to be a sexy heart-throb. And this video was supposed to showcase all the women who wanted Big as he rapped about his status as a player.

When Hype Williams, the director, put the camera on me and instructed me to start singing, I did what I was told. But it was hard to look directly into the camera. I had no idea what I was doing. I guess Puff could see that I was scared, because he came over to me to give me a pep talk.

"Where's the swagger, Faye?" he asked. " You can't be looking scared now, girl."

"I know, I know," I said.

Puff was like a corner man in a boxing match. "You see all these chicks up in here? But this yo' nigga. You can't let these chicks be hotter than you on *your* shit."

I got my nerves together. For the next take, I did a little bet-ter, relaxing a bit and just focusing on the smooth groove of the song.

After that portion of the video was done, I thought I'd just be able to hang out and observe. They had a scene set up for Big to sit on the edge of a bed as a model lay in bed next to him. The model was getting dressed in a skimpy outfit and preparing to take her place in bed when Big called Puff and Hype over to him.

"I want Faye in this scene," he told them both.

There was some discussion among the three of them. And the next thing I knew, *I* was in bed next to Big as he rapped the second verse of the song. I was shocked that Big would want me in the video for that scene. I figured he'd want some video chick to be next to him. I knew it was Hollywood and not real life. But Big wanted his real-life woman next to him in that scene. And of course, I loved that he was making it clear who the main woman was in his life as well as in the video. The music played, and Big and I nodded to the beat as he began to rap.

If you see the video now, I look absolutely petrified in that scene. My body is really stiff and my arms are tight at my sides. But it didn't matter. The song blew up and went to number one on the Billboard Top 200 Singles chart. The video went into constant rotation on BET and MTV.

And suddenly, I couldn't just walk out of our apartment in Brooklyn and go to the bodega to get a blunt without being recognized. It was both thrilling — and a little scary.

One afternoon, I was wearing a baseball cap pulled down low as I ran out of the house for something quick.

"Excuse me. Are you Faith?"

I had my hat pulled so far down, I was surprised that the young lady had even seen my face.

"Yeah, it's me. How'd you know?"

"I saw your lips," she said. "And that mole! And I knew it was you."

I had to laugh at that one. My mom's lips and her mole that I inherited are very distinct, so it shouldn't have surprised me that I would always be very recognizable.

By the time the summer of 1995 was in full swing, my single was becoming more and more popular and I started performing it at various small clubs. The label had a list of cities they wanted me to perform in to promote the single.

But I needed help. I couldn't go out on the road by myself. I had Chyna, and Big was on the road for his own music. Mark Pitts, who was Big's manager, was now also my manager. But he was on the road with Big and couldn't take care of me on a day-to-day basis.

Cheryl, who was still managing producers for Bad Boy, had become very knowledgeable about all my needs because we were together all the time as friends. And I asked her to be my road manager. She agreed and left her job at Bad Boy to work with me. Puffy wasn't happy about it. But Mark Pitts supported the decision, and we were on our way.

One of my first performances with Cheryl in position as my road manager was an appearance on a video show at BET. At the time, the BET studios were in Washington, DC, and we drove down together for the show. Before we left, Puff picked out the outfit he wanted me to wear—a red satin pantsuit. And he wanted my hair in a "mature" style. While other artists were rocking long weaves with sideswept bangs, I had to have my hair in a French roll with long bangs in the front. I felt like this made me look older than I was, and I assumed that's what Puff meant by mature balladeer.

When we got to BET, we asked one of the assistants where we could go to have a smoke before the show. (We didn't specify that we meant weed, not cigarettes.) They pointed us to an area in the staff parking lot. We went out there and shared a blunt before it was time to get ready. I was nervous about my first major television appearance, and I figured smoking first would take the edge off just a bit. Besides, I had these European eyedrops that burned like hell but would make your eyes super-white.

When we were done, we gathered up all our things and made our way to the studio. Before we even met the host of the show, we were called into the office of one of the producers of the show.

"This performance is canceled," the man said.

Cheryl and I looked at each other in shock.

"Is there a problem?" Cheryl asked, trying to keep her voice steady.

The producer looked across his desk at us with disgust on his face.

"We have been informed that the two of you were using illegal drugs in our parking lot. This behavior is unacceptable and we're not having you on our network."

My heart sank. How could we have been so stupid? We thought no one noticed. And before we left, Big had told me how cool everyone was at BET when he went. He'd told me that he smoked weed with some of the on-air hosts and had a great time. Maybe because he was a rapper, the rules were different. But Puffy's "mature and sexy" balladeer was about to be kicked off BET before she could sing one note.

Cheryl and I stuttered and stammered, trying to apologize and salvage the show.

"We're calling Jean Riggins," the producer said.

Jean Riggins was the senior VP of black music for Arista at the time. Even though I was a Bad Boy artist, our parent company was Arista, the home of singers like Whitney Houston. I knew we were in trouble then.

Cheryl talked to Jean Riggins, who said she would do her best to smooth things over. When Cheryl hung up, she looked at me with tears in her eyes.

"Girl," she said. "Do you understand that Puffy is going to have a fucking *fit*?"

I nodded. Puff hadn't even wanted her to be my road manager. And now our first time out on the road and we were in major trouble. Somehow, Jean Riggins was able to convince the folks at BET to give us another chance, and they let me perform my single. We never told Puff, but he did find out that we'd almost screwed up big-time.

Big had been hard at work, too. In addition to promoting his own album, he was preparing to release Junior M.A.F.I.A.'s upcoming album, *Conspiracy*. Big was on a number of tracks for the album. That July, while he and I were both on the charts with our own songs, Junior M.A.F.I.A. released "Player's Anthem," which also became very popular at radio. It was as if anything associated with Bad Boy was blowing up. Although Junior M.A.F.I.A. wasn't a Bad Boy act, it was still part of the sound since Big was so heavily involved with the project.

Lil' Kim immediately stood out to me on that record, and I thought she was dope as a rapper. I still didn't have much of an opinion on her personally. But when I heard her flow on "Player's Anthem," I knew she was very talented.

And then Total, the R&B trio also signed to Bad Boy, dropped their first single, "Can't You See," from the soundtrack to the movie *New Jersey Drive*. Big rapped on the intro to the song, and it became another instant classic.

You have to understand: The summer of 1995 belonged to Bad Boy. Everything Puff touched shot to the top of the charts, and every act on his label was enjoying success. It was a very exciting time.

In between performing my single at various outlets and putting the final touches on my album, Mark Pitts told me to prepare to go out to LA to work with the legendary Babyface. He was putting together the soundtrack to *Waiting to Exhale* for Arista Records, and I was chosen to perform "Kissing You" for the album. I learned the song, flew out to LA with Cheryl, and recorded the song with Babyface at his home studio in Los Angeles.

What with recording with legends, appearing on television, hearing myself and my husband on the radio, and seeing the reaction from people I performed for, I felt like my career was a high point. But at home in Brooklyn, things weren't as sweet.

Big and I were like two ships in the night. On the rare occasion that we were both in the apartment, we still had good moments, nights when we ordered from Kum Kao, smoked a blunt or two, and had sex for the rest of the night.

But I still didn't trust him. And he was still spending far too much time in hotels in Manhattan when he should have been at home in Brooklyn.

And even though he was the one cheating, he could still be jealous and possessive of me. Dave, a friend of mine who performed in a gospel choir, lived near me and Big in Brooklyn. Dave was the same friend who had taken a ride with me up to Scarsdale to see Puff and Misa's new baby. Once or twice, I'd pointed out to Big the building he lived in.

One day, I ran into Dave outside the home of the woman who babysat Chyna. He hadn't seen Chyna since she was born. So I got Chyna from the babysitter and brought her back outside. Dave and I stood out there for a few minutes, catching up on old times, while he marveled at how big Chyna had gotten. Just as I'm saying good-bye, here come Big, Damion, and this kid named Buck who was one of Un Rivera's cousins. They came speeding down the street in a little tiny rental car and stopped right in front of us.

Big and I had argued earlier that morning about something, and as usual we weren't speaking to each other. But I still didn't expect him to do what he did. Dave was holding Chyna in his arms and looked at the car full of guys warily.

"Yo, my man," Big said. "Bring Chyna over here."

Dave walked over and handed Chyna to Big. As soon as he did, Damion and Buck got out of the car, jumped Dave, and started punching and kicking him. Dave hit the ground and threw his arms over his head to protect himself. He was screaming "Help me!" as Damion and Buck worked him over. I burst into tears and ran to Big's side of the car.

"Big, are you crazy!" I screamed. "Tell them to stop, please! Dave didn't do anything!"

Big just held Chyna and looked at me with a blank expression on his face. He knew I wasn't messing with that dude. He was acting like I'd left the house after our argument and met up with this guy. But he knew that I had gone to pick up Chyna from the babysitter.

"Big, I just came around here to get Chyna! Tell them to stop!"

Big didn't say a word. D-Roc and Buck continued their attack. After about five minutes, they left Dave with a fat lip and a bruised eye, right on the ground in the middle of Washington Street. I helped him up, apologizing profusely, and took him back to our apartment to clean himself up and then call someone to pick him up. The whole scene was horrible. I was embarrassed and I felt so bad for Dave. This was someone I knew from the church and gospel music community! I never saw my friend Dave again.

I couldn't believe Big would have the nerve to beat up my platonic friends while he was messing with other women damn near in my face. I thought that took a lot of nerve.

But of course, even if we were beefing, when our paths crossed professionally we had to suck it up and just deal with each other, even if we didn't feel like being bothered. In early August 1995, just a few weeks before my album was going to be released, we had to perform together at The Source Awards.

We left together from our house in Brooklyn. Lance "Un" Rivera drove with Big in the front seat and me and Lil' Kim in the back. Lil' Kim was going to be performing the single "Player's Anthem" with the rest of Junior M.A.F.I.A., and I was going to do my single. And of course Big was going to perform "Big Poppa."

During the ride into Manhattan, Big was yelling at Kim about something, but I wasn't clear on what was going on. I just know she was upset about it.

The entire Bad Boy roster was scheduled to perform that night. But it didn't feel like we were really all connected. Me and Big weren't speaking. I did my sound check alone. I didn't rehearse with any of my label mates. I didn't even know who for sure was performing or what songs they were going to do. It was definitely a sign of how things were going to play out. Because although I was on the label, as time went on I would begin to feel more and more isolated.

That night, Puff sat between me and Big during the awards ceremony. Me and Big were barely tolerating each other, and I was just trying to focus on what I needed to do. Before our performances, I went backstage to prepare to present an award.

I stood with Chris Webber and Puffy, who were both presenting with me, and we made small talk while we waited to be introduced and go onstage to present. We couldn't hear what was going on onstage. But at some point we heard a low rumble of *ooooohs*.

"Yo, he tried to play Puffy out!" I heard someone say.

It turned out that Suge Knight had gone on stage and dissed Puffy after presenting an award: "If you don't want the owner of your label on your album or in your video," Suge said to the crowd, "come to Death Row!"

Now, at that point, Puff was really beginning to get a lot of shine from being in videos. He was in all of Big's videos; he was in Total's video and Craig Mack's. That was his thing—he was ushering in a new era of branding himself and not staying in the background the way most producers did. Lots of people grumbled about how Puff wanted to be a star as well as make stars. But he was a hit maker—plain and simple. So you couldn't really argue with his methods.

I didn't know why Suge would dis Puff. But I knew he had a reputation. I'd first heard his name years ago, when I was still hanging with Grandpa—aka Christopher Williams. I'd tagged along with them to Uptown Records and heard folks whispering about how someone had attacked Andre Harrell in order to "convince" him to release Mary J. Blige and Jodeci from their management contracts.

I'd never crossed paths with Suge, and The Source Awards was the first time I really felt the energy he was bringing into the industry. I wasn't the only one. Throughout the awards and after the ceremony, there was a certain amount of tension over Suge's remarks.

I took the stage with Puff immediately after Suge Knight was finished. I stood to his right as he addressed the crowd: "I'm the executive producer that a comment was made about a little bit earlier. But contrary to what other people may feel, I would like to say that I'm very proud of Dr. Dre, Suge Knight, and Death Row for their accomplishments. All this East and West Coast shit? That needs to stop."

I didn't take it very seriously. Because Puff was having a lot of success, I knew it was normal for people to start hating on him. And I also knew that there was some validity to some of the things people didn't like about him. It was life. And it was all a part of being famous. At that moment, it didn't seem like the beginning of a dire situation.

As the awards wrapped up and everyone began to make their way to the various afterparties, I saw Mary J. Blige. Her album that I'd worked on, *My Life,* had been released the year before, and she was still riding the success. At the ceremony, she'd taken home a Source Award for best R&B singer. We'd both become very busy so we didn't hang out as much as we had the previous summer, but we were still friendly.

"Hey, Mary," I said when we crossed paths. It was crowded and I knew we wouldn't really be able to stop to talk for long.

But Mary just looked through me, as if she'd never seen me before in her life. I looked at her for another moment, thinking maybe she didn't hear me. But then she just looked at me and then looked away. Then I waved. Nothing. I knew she had seen me. But for whatever reason, she was not speaking to me.

I wondered what the hell that was about. I didn't have time to really stress it because there was so much going on that night. But I did wonder what kind of beef she could possibly have with me.

The year 1995 turned out to be full of questions. And I learned quickly that I wasn't going to like many of the answers.

CHAPTER FOURTEEN

The Truth Hurts

My first single, "You Used to Love Me," was selling briskly and on the airwaves in constant rotation. And just a few weeks after The Source Awards, my debut album, *Faith*, was released.

Junior M.A.F.I.A. released their debut album, *Conspiracy*, the same day. Big was so influential in the album's success that by the end of the summer of '95, Big and I were hip-hop's royal couple — even though we barely got the opportunity to operate as a traditional couple.

I was trying to take my vows seriously. We never even discussed the possibility of breaking up. Although we spent so much time apart that I sometimes felt like I was single. But I was feeling very lonely. And at a time in my life when things were coming together professionally, I felt alone in my personal life.

In August 1995, we were featured on the cover of *Vibe* magazine together, both of us dipped in matching black outfits and sitting in a top-down convertible looking ghetto-fabulous. It was weird because now Puff was completely used to the idea of us being married. And it was considered cool to have us featured together. But we weren't even together like that. We interacted at the shoot. But we arrived separately and didn't leave together.

While Big went out for tour dates, usually accompanied by Puff and our manager Mark Pitts, I went on my smaller tour dates many times with just Chyna and Cheryl. We got a crash course on how to survive on the road. When I look back on how we managed, I'm shocked we made it out alive.

Cheryl was able to start booking me through promoters to do paid tour dates—as opposed to the free performances I did to promote the record. I could get between five and ten thousand dollars to sing my single and perhaps one other song.

The concert business is full of some shady individuals. If you don't have anyone looking out for you, it can be really tough. One time, Cheryl booked me for a show somewhere in North Carolina. It was a small venue—maybe three hundred people. We brought our own backup singers, whom we'd have to pay out of our earnings.

The fee was going to be around eight thousand dollars. The way it usually works is that you get half the money up front, usually before you even get to the city. And then you make sure to get the second half right before you go onstage. For obvious reasons, you don't perform until you have all your money.

At this place, Cheryl had collected the first half of the money before we got to town. When we arrived at the venue, she went to get the second half as I tried to do something with my hair. I was talking to the backup singers about the upcoming performance when Cheryl came into the dressing room looking pissed off.

"This nigga talking 'bout he don't have the rest of the money."

"What!"

Cheryl sat down next to me and put her hands over her face. "He said he didn't make the money off the door that he thought he would."

"So what does that mean for us?" I asked.

"It means we shit out of luck!" she said.

Now, here we are: me, Cheryl, Chyna, and my girl Tammy from Newark. We're alone in North Carolina. We have no security or muscle to get this money. We have these backup singers who need to get paid. And there is a crowd of people who came to see me perform. I could have just skipped out on the performance. But I was just getting started and I had brand-new fans who'd paid money to see me perform. It was important to honor that. They wouldn't understand that I left because I didn't get paid. They would just be pissed off that this new artist didn't perform.

Cheryl found out that the promoter did have some money—but he was using it to pay the security guards.

"How are you paying them?" Cheryl asked the promoter.

"I gotta pay them!" the promoter said. "If I don't they'll fuck me up."

"You giving me half of whatever you giving them," Cheryl said. "Or *I'm* fucking you up."

Cheryl walked that promoter to every part of the club where he could have possibly made any money. She walked with him to the bar, took a cut of that money. Walked him to the coat check, took some of that money. Went to his back office and got some more money. That girl had a lot of heart—she really threatened that guy and got him to give her part of the profits he got from different sections of the venue. We ended up getting a little more than half of what we were owed. I sang just one song and got the hell out of there.

It wouldn't be the last time Cheryl and I had to fend for ourselves in the wilderness of private tour dates. Cheryl would sometimes be paid five thousand dollars in singles, fives, and twenties that the promoter got from the bar. She'd be in some grimy back room at a club, stuffing all this cash in her pocketbook, and then there we were, flying back home with no help and all this cash. It was crazy. But somehow, we made it through quite a few one-off performances.

Our hard work paid off, too. By August 1995, just two months after "You Used to Love Me" was released, it was certified gold. In sixty days, half a million people went out and bought my song. This is something many artists never accomplish in their entire careers. I had done it with my very first single. I was proud and honored for this to happen to me.

I was so insulated in my world of traveling and trying to make my money, I wasn't really on top of what was going on in the rest of the world. So when I was at home in Brooklyn, I didn't really know what was going on around me.

And then, near the end of the summer, I had a conversation with Doobie and Creamy that changed everything.

Doobie and Creamy would check up on me when Big was out of town. They were longtime Brooklyn residents and had an ear to the street on everything going on. Although I met them through Big, we ended up being cool. I could count on them to help me do little things if Big wasn't around.

One afternoon they came by the apartment to hang out while I was in town briefly between tour dates.

"Faith, you know you gotta be careful around here," Doobie said as we rolled a blunt.

"Why?" I asked. "What's going on?"

Doobie sparked the blunt, inhaled, and then passed it to me.

"I've been hearing shit," he said. "Some young cats from the Fort Greene projects been talking about trying to run up here and get you and Big for some of your shit."

"Are you serious?"

"Yeah man," Creamy said. "People know where y'all live...and cats be seeing you on television and shit. Gotta be careful."

I was petrified. And at that moment, something clicked inside me. I'd already known that my marriage was in serious trouble. And now I was living in an apartment practically by myself? I was not going to sit there and wait for some young punks to try to get up into our apartment. Big was hardly there, and I knew I couldn't stay another day. If he wanted to have an apartment in Brooklyn that he barely lived in, that was fine. But if I was going to be living alone, I'd do it on my own terms.

By the time Doobie and Creamy left, I'd already made up my mind that I was leaving the apartment. I had these two huge bags, the kind hockey players used to hold their hockey sticks and bulky uniforms. I grabbed my hockey bags and stuffed them with all my clothes and shoes and Chyna's stuff. I left all of the furniture, the dishes, Big's clothes, everything. I took nothing but my personal effects. And then I picked up Chyna from the babysitter, drove into Manhattan, and checked into a hotel. I would never go back to the apartment in Brooklyn again.

I had gone from a spacious apartment that I shared with my husband to a tiny, bland hotel room in Midtown Manhattan.

I sat on the hotel bed, cradling Chyna in my lap, and tried to gather my thoughts. Professionally, everything in my life was falling into place. I knew I still loved Big and our relationship was not over. Yet. But I wasn't going to let his drama stop me from doing what I needed to do.

For a few weeks before, I'd noticed a high-rise building being built on the West Side Highway. It was a beautiful building, and in the back of my mind I thought I'd like to live there. Now that I was out of Brooklyn, I decided to try to save enough money to move in when the building opened. I knew the rent would be expensive. But if I continued doing shows and kept my expenses low, I could get together a security deposit and move in.

That night, I slept in the bed with Chyna and dreamed of what the next phase in my life would bring. I knew one thing—I needed a break from Christopher Wallace. I made a vow to stay away from him for as long as I could.

For the next two months, I was on autopilot. And my health suffered. I smoked way too many Black and Mild cigars and these Indian hand-rolled cigarettes called bidis. I would drink an occasional V8 juice in a weak attempt to have something nutritious. I was always nauseated, constantly throwing up and extremely stressed out. I was going in and out of town, doing a live show here and there. Then returning to New York, checking out of my hotel if I didn't have the money to stay any longer, and looking for another room so I could start the process all over again.

Every once in a while, I would go to the apartment that the members of 112 were living in over on Broadway and 54th.

Puff had signed the quartet soon after their audition in Atlanta, and just as I'd predicted, I'd become very cool with all of them. Sometimes, I'd bring groceries to their apartment and make them fried fish or pork chops and macaroni and cheese.

I was just barely keeping it together, what with shows and doing promotions and press for my album. Occasionally, I'd get a message from the hotel lobby that Big had called. I wouldn't call him back. And by the time he knew where I was, it was usually time for me to go on to the next spot anyway. I wasn't avoiding him. But I wasn't looking for him either.

I wasn't ready for things to be over with Big. I just felt like I needed him to see that I wasn't going to sit around and wait for him to come home. I felt like he was disrespecting me by not coming home regularly. It was so important for him to be in Brooklyn that I'd set up a household for us there. I didn't feel like he appreciated that, so I wanted to just be on my own for a minute. I knew it wasn't over for good. But things were going to have to change.

Soon after I moved out, Big left to go on a huge tour. Every act who was big in hip-hop and R&B was scheduled to be on this tour: Naughty by Nature, Jodeci, Mary J. Blige, Da Brat, Junior M.A.F.I.A., Total. The established acts, like Jodeci and Mary, were being paid.

Some of the newer acts, were performing for free as part of promoting their new music.

It's customary for new artists to go out on tour and open up for the headliners as a way of getting exposure. And usually, they are given a small daily stipend for meals. But there is no payment for actually performing.

Mark Pitts called me up soon after the tour began. "Faith, you need to get your bags packed so you can get ready to join the tour."

"Can you find out how much Puff's gonna pay me for each date?" I asked.

Because I had a single that had sold over five hundred thousand units, I felt like I should be paid something for going out on the tour. I was doing small dates across the country and getting up to ten grand for singing two songs. I was not about to give up good money to perform for free.

"But this is a great opportunity for you, Faith," he said.

"Nothing? Well then I'm not going to be able to go."

"I really think you should," Mark said.

There was something in his voice that made me uneasy. "Why? Why do I have to tour and not be paid anything?"

Mark hesitated. "I...I just think it's a good idea. It'll be good exposure for you. You need to perform at larger venues...and, um, Puff really wants you to do it."

I realized that if Puff wanted me to do something, Mark was going to try to make it happen. I wanted a manager whose main goal was getting the best deals for *me*. Mark and I got along great, and I really liked his easygoing and respectful personality. It was a good antidote to Puff's intensity.

But he was not only my husband's manager—which could be seen as a potential conflict—he was Puff's boy. This was going to be a decision I would have to make on my own.

"I'm sorry, Mark," I said. "I'm not touring for free."

Mark sighed heavily into the phone. "Aiight, Faith," he said. "I'll let Puff know you're not interested in touring."

I knew what that meant: I'd be hearing from Puff soon. And I was not looking forward to that.

Puff had a way of getting me to do things I didn't want to do. He could fast-talk me into stuff and afterward I'd think, *Damn, why did I agree to do this?* From my hairstyles and clothes to certain songs he wanted me to record.

Like with the photos for my album cover. On the front cover, there is an up-close portrait of my face, which was cool. But on the back, I was dressed in combat boots and a fedora, holding on to a cane. I remember feeling like it was too similar to Mary's style at the time, but Puff just blew me off. And I didn't have the nerve to insist on a different look.

And then I always wanted to perform with a live band and constantly asked Puff if I could. The answer was always no. Of course it's more expensive to have a live band, but I really thought it would help establish my sound.

When Mark came at me about the tour, I knew I was going to hold firm. I was *not* going out on that tour for free. It didn't help that Big was on this tour and I wanted to avoid him.

I felt trapped. I was now trying to avoid my husband and the president of my record label. I was waking up some mornings, not sure if I was at a hotel in Virginia or back in New York. I was developing some sharp pains in my stomach, the beginning of an ulcer caused by all the turmoil. And it would only get worse.

I was driving to the studio one afternoon and turned to Hot 97 to listen to radio DJ Wendy Williams. Lil' Kim was her guest on the show. She was supposed to be promoting Junior M.A.F.I.A.'s recently released album. But Wendy has always been known for trying to get good juicy gossip from her guests.

She asked Kim something about her relationship with Big. I turned the radio up as loud as it would go.

"Isn't Big married to Faith Evans?" Wendy asked.

Kim laughed. "Please," she said. "They broke up. They not wearing no wedding rings. She moved out. They ain't together no more."

I was stunned. Why the fuck was Kim on the radio telling people about my business with Big? And why did she sound so gleeful that we were having some problems in our marriage?

That night, I ran into Doobie and Creamy. "Yo, y'all heard Kim on the radio today?" I asked.

They both nodded but didn't make direct eye contact with me.

"The way she sounded," I said, "you would think she was fucking Big or something."

Creamy and Doobie didn't say one word. They just looked at me.

And just like that it dawned on me. All this time Big had been fucking Kim. And it took a year for my dumb ass to figure it out. So many things began swirling in my head: the late nights that he was in the studio with Kim and the rest of Junior M.A.F.I.A.; the tour he was on with her at that very moment; the ride back to Brooklyn when she made a point to tell me that Big was like a brother to her. Big telling me to take her to the gym and to go shopping. They both played me out—big-time.

Big had never explicitly said that he wasn't messing with her. I'd never asked. I had no reason to think that. And I was so busy beating up every other chick up and down the eastern seaboard that I missed the one right in my damn face.

And it wasn't just Kim, either. Right before I found out the truth about Big and Kim, Junior M.A.F.I.A. was about to shoot a new video for a song called "Get Money."

In the song, Big is berating a woman who wants him solely for his money. I remember being in the studio when he and Junior M.A.F.I.A.

recorded it. It was a catchy song, and I knew it had potential to be a big hit. But when the song came out, people assumed that Big was dissing me. He had a line describing the girl: *tattoo on titty saying B.I.G.* But that was the only thing I had in common with the fictional character in that song. And Big and I were together and happy when he recorded it. But by the time the single was released, we were beefing and people knew that. So they took everything in the song literally. A few weeks before Kim got on the radio, Lance "Un" Rivera had called asking me to be in the video.

"Are you crazy?" I told him. "People already think he's trying to dis me in the song."

"Exactly," said Un. "But you know better. So you should do it just to fuck with people's heads."

I did give it some thought. If Big had approached me about it personally, I might have. But ultimately, I decided not to. I was still pissed at Big. So he got some girl from Philly to play the woman in the video. I found out that it was the same Tiffany who'd paged him when we returned from Daytona months before.

In the video, this Tiffany chick was wearing a blond wig and a fur coat and Big and everyone in Junior M.A.F.I.A. was dissing her and ended up throwing her out of the house. Some people, including industry folks, assumed that the song was about me. And having this girl in the video wearing a wig in my trademark platinum-blond color just sealed the deal.

So between realizing the truth about Big and Kim *and* having to deal with people thinking this Tiffany chick was supposed to be portraying me in a video, I was *too* through and ready to beat some ass.

As soon as I left Doobie and Creamy, I called Cheryl.

"Get me on Wendy's show," I told her.

"I'ma call right now," Cheryl said.

Looking back, I can't *believe* I voluntarily went on Wendy's show to talk about this new beef with Kim. It's not something I would *ever* do today. Airing out my personal grievances on the radio was not a smart move. But at the time, my good judgment was clouded by anger.

I knew, without a shadow of a doubt, that I was going to get Kimberly Jones's ass. And I felt that she—and the rest of Wendy's listening audience—should know.

I went on Wendy's show the very next afternoon.

"You have something you want to say about Lil' Kim's comments yesterday," Wendy asked.

I pulled up close to the microphone and leaned in. "The only thing I have to say is, Kim—you better watch your back. 'Cause when I see you, it's *on*."

"And what about the rumors that he's messing with some chick from Philly," Wendy asked.

"Yeah, there's some illy from Philly out there," I told Wendy Williams. "But that ain't me in that video. She ain't me and could never be me. She better watch herself, too."

From the radio station, I went to confront Big. He was staying at a hotel in Manhattan as usual.

"What's up with you and Kim?" I asked, trying hard to keep my voice steady.

As usual, Big didn't hesitate. Not even for one second. "Yeah, we get down like that."

"All this time?" I asked. "You've been fucking this girl all this time?"

"Yeah...," he said.

There was nothing left to say. So of course we had sex for the rest of the afternoon. But for me, it wasn't like the emotional and passionate nights we shared over the past year. It felt more like closure. I loved Big and I knew I always would. But that afternoon, as we lay in bed together, I felt like a chapter of my life was closing forever. I was going to live my life. Alone, if necessary. And if Big wanted to fuck the entire world, that was on him.

CHAPTER FIFTEEN

Hustling

iss Evans," said the receptionist at the Millennium Hotel in Times Square. "You have an outstanding balance of seven hundred forty-two dollars. I can't rent you a new room until you pay the balance."

"Okay, I'll be right back," I said, knowing that I wouldn't.

While Big and the rest of Bad Boy were on tour, I continued bouncing from one hotel to the other, dragging Chyna and my two hockey bags filled with all my worldly possessions. I would leave her with my grandparents in Newark to do a show, and then pick her up and find a new hotel to stay in for another week or so. My life was scattered and I had no focus. I was just barely keeping up with the daily grind and had no idea what the future would bring.

I was making money, but I didn't always have cash in hand. So I'd run up a bill at one hotel and then have to check into a different one if I didn't have the money to pay it. I came by the apartment where 112 was staying one evening and cooked dinner for them. I was cleaning up and talking to Q, one of the members of the group I was closest to.

"Q, I might need to chill here for a minute," I said.

"Ma, that's no question," he said. "Do what you gotta do."

Q cleared it with their road manager, Bear, who also lived there. Bear was gracious and told me I was always welcome.

That night, Chyna and I slept on the pullout sofa in their apartment. For once I wasn't lugging my hockey bags, and I was grateful. I asked the guys from 112 if I could leave my stuff there as a temporary home base while I got myself together.

The guys were all cool about it. Now, keep in mind, it was only a two-bedroom apartment—and there were four of them. And the apartment wasn't that big. But they didn't hesitate to let me stay there when I needed to. I will always have love for them for that. I shared a little bit with them about what was going on with Big and with Puff wanting me on that tour. But since we were label mates, I didn't want them to feel like they were in the middle, so I kept a lot of stuff to myself.

Although I didn't spend the night at 112's apartment all the time, I did keep my hockey bags there. And if someone needed to get in touch with me, they could leave messages for me there. When I wasn't out of town doing a show, I was camping out at their place. In return, I cooked for the boys whenever I was in town. They loved my cooking, and I loved not having to find a new hotel room every week. So everyone was happy. The guys had strict instructions from me: *If anyone calls, I'm not here.* I knew Big would eventually be looking for me to talk about reuniting, either for a night or for the long term. He would even ask me about going on this tour for free. So I was completely incognito, dipping out of town to perform and staying low-profile otherwise.

A few times, Big called the apartment for me.

"It's Big," Q would say, covering up the mouthpiece.

"Tell him I'm not here," I'd whisper.

Sometimes, Big would catch me if I answered the phone. "What up, Faye," he'd say.

"Hey. What's up?" I'd keep my voice as level as I could.

"You supposed to be out here on tour," he'd say. "Where you at?"

"Nah, I'm good on that," I'd say.

And then I got a call from Kirk Burrowes, the general manager at Bad Boy, that really took me over the edge and made me feel like I wanted nothing to do with Puff or anyone else on that tour.

"We have a problem with your album," said Kirk.

"What is it?"

"The song you did with Mary? We have to take her vocals off it."

I had been standing in the kitchen at 112's apartment, preparing to make a pan of lasagna. When I heard this, I went into the living room and sat down hard on the couch.

"What do you mean? The album is already out! I've sold half a million copies!"

Kirk sighed heavily into the phone. "When we press up the next batch of records, it has to have a new version of the song on it without Mary's vocals."

I thought about how Mary had ignored me at the Source Awards and wondered if that had something to do with this.

"I don't understand..."

"You need to talk to Mary."

"*I* need to talk to Mary? I don't need to say shit to Mary. I didn't do anything to her!"

"All I know is we have to do this before the next pressing..."

"And no one can tell me *why* I have to re-record this song?"

"I'm not sure what's going on, Faith. I'm just telling you what has to happen."

I'd never even wanted to do the song in the first place! And now I had to re-record it without Mary's vocals before my album could be restocked in stores. I was angry. But I wasn't just angry that Mary wanted her vocals off my album, I was angry that I was not in the loop as to *why* she would feel that way.

I asked around, and no one would give me a straight answer. One person told me that Mary and Puff had a disagreement about money and how much he was getting off her album as a producer, and that she ordered him to take her vocals off my album as a result. Someone else told me that she felt like Puff was trying to mold me in her image. And then people started speculating on why Puff had hired me to work on Mary's album.

I'd gone to a radio station in the Midwest while in town for a few shows, and the DJ asked me if it was true that I had given Mary vocal coaching. I didn't know where that had come from, and I told him it wasn't true. But because I sang backing vocals on much of her second album, that rumor persisted, and I heard that also made her upset. I tried to let it go. I went into the studio and re-recorded the song without Mary's voice. And I didn't like it at all. Even when we did the duet after several rounds of tequila, I'd thought Mary's voice was better suited to the song. And now that it was just me on the song, I liked it even less.

I would end up not earning any royalties on that album for over ten years until the record label was able to recoup all of the costs of re-recording and pressing up new copies of the album and removing and destroying all of the copies with Mary's vocals.

But at the time, I had no time to dwell on the Mary situation. I was becoming more and more in demand as a songwriter. I worked with Heavy D, Monifah, Soul for Real, and other artists. I was charging between five and seven thousand dollars per song as a writer's fee, and I charged more if I was to appear on the song. In an attempt to take control of my career, I started talking to Queen Latifah and her partner Shakim Compere about letting their company, Flavor Unit, manage my career. I'd met Shakim through my attorney, Stuart Levy, who represented him. And although nothing had officially been signed, they were helping me to secure writing gigs and a few shows.

Before long, I had saved enough money to move my hockey bags from the apartment 112 shared into my own place. The high-rise on West End Avenue had finally opened up, and I rented a two-bedroom apartment. It was open and well lit. I loved that it was brand new. And the location was ideal: I was doing so much work in Manhattan, I couldn't live in Jersey or in Brooklyn. The rent was twenty-six hundred a month. I paid a few months' rent in advance, then went to a furniture warehouse in Brooklyn and bought a huge pine bed and began to set up house.

I decided that Chyna would now be living with me full-time. My friend Roz agreed to travel with me to care for Chyna if I needed to go on the road. I appreciated my family keeping her when I was traveling or whenever I needed to get things done. But I was starting a whole new way of life. And I didn't want to leave her with anyone unless I had to. She would no longer split her time. Chyna was going to live with me all the time.

Meanwhile, I heard through the grapevine that Big was planning to move to New Jersey. Before I'd left the apartment in Brooklyn, he'd decided he was ready to look at houses and I'd taken him to look at a few, including the three-bedroom, three-bathroom duplex he eventually purchased in Teaneck.

Once we'd both left the apartment in Brooklyn and set up our own separate households, I was only in touch with Big very sporadically. A few times, when I was staying with 112, he was able to reach me on the phone; I always kept the conversation as brief as I could.

But of course we were still married and had business and personal affairs to take care of. I called him once at the house in Teaneck, and a woman answered the phone.

"Can I speak to Big?" I asked.

"He's not here. Who is this?"

"Tell him to call his wife."

After calling another time and hearing the same voice, I assumed it was the girl Tiffany from Philly. I'd heard she was often at the house. A few months before, I would have been looking to kick her ass. But I had no intentions now of crossing paths with Tiffany. I was done with beating up the women whom Big was messing with. (Except for Lil' Kim; as far as I was concerned, I still had some shit to settle with her.)

I felt a little less stressed after I moved into the apartment on West End Avenue. Chyna and I would go to the studio and come home and be greeted by our doorman, Lucius, an older gentlemen who was always friendly. I finally had my own place that was safe and quiet. And my main goal was to keep the money flowing in.

I did all the promotional tour dates that Bad Boy and Arista set up for me, and I did the paid tour dates that Cheryl was able to secure for me as well. One of the markets that I visited often was New Orleans. I loved that city; it was warm and sultry, and every show I performed there went well, with an enthusiastic crowd that sang along to all my songs.

I was so focused on earning money and avoiding Big that I very quickly found myself in a rut. I was performing, which I loved. And the money was coming in, which was great. But something was missing. And the next time I went to New Orleans, I figured out what it was.

During a performance at a small dinner-theater venue, I saw a tall dark-chocolate man with clear skin and a wide bright smile come in and sit at a table very close to the stage. He looked familiar—I was almost sure that I'd seen him at my shows the last two times I'd been in the area. Now, I don't normally notice if someone in the audience is checking me out. But something about this guy stood out. He was really tall, for one thing. And he usually came alone, while most of my fans would come with a date or in a large group. He was handsome and regal and as I sang, I kept finding myself looking at him and then trying to look away. He definitely had my attention and planned to keep it. Toward the end of the show, I looked in his direction, and he held up his wineglass to me as if he was making a toast. I felt myself turning red from the attention as I said good night to the audience and the show ended.

After the show, I sat backstage relaxing with Cheryl and my three background singers. One of my singers, a guy named Chuck, was a former basketball player.

"Chuck, who was that guy near the front of the stage?" I asked him.

"You mean the one who was staring at you?"

Everyone laughed. I tried to keep a straight face. "I didn't notice all that. Do you know who he is or not?"

Chuck got up and walked over closer to me. "Everybody knows him, Faith!" he said in a loud whisper. "That's Roger Short."

"Why does everyone know him?" I asked.

"Because he's in the NBA. He's from this area. But he plays for a team in the Midwest."

I just nodded and tried to look noncommittal. But I was intrigued. He was handsome, and every time I caught his eye, something stirred in me that I hadn't felt in a very long time.

I was married. But I was also feeling very resentful about Big and his exploits. He was screwing anything that moved—including Lil' Kim, a chick he had me befriend! He was blatant in his deception and infidelity and showed no signs of slowing down. And I was supposed to just take that and remain loyal and faithful? Um, *no.*

The next night, I had my final engagement at the nightclub. And sure enough, as soon as the house lights went down, I saw Roger come in through a side entrance. Someone escorted him to a table right near the stage and brought him a glass of wine. He was wearing a sharp navy-blue suit that fit him so well, it had to be custom-made. He stretched out his legs and crossed them at the ankles and then looked up at me and flashed that dazzling smile again.

The heady mix of performing, a few pre-show glasses of champagne, and the attention I received during the show from Roger made me feel extra-bold. When the show was over and we were backstage, I wrote down the name of my hotel and the room number on a small slip of paper and gave it to Chuck.

"Go," I said. "Give it to him before he leaves."

Chuck's eyes grew wide as he took the paper out of my hand. "Are you serious?"

"*Go.*"

I packed up my things, said good night to everyone, and took a car service back to my hotel in the French Quarter. I took a long bath, thinking about what I was about to do. It was scary even to think that I could break my marriage vows and be with someone else. But I was a human with feelings and needs. And the odds were that, at this very moment, Big was somewhere getting his groove on.

I got out of the bath and put on some loungewear that was comfortable but not over-the-top sexy. I went out into the living room area, poured myself a drink, and turned on the television.

Within an hour, there was a knock on my hotel door. I stopped by the mirror in the hallway before I answered it. I looked relaxed and fresh-scrubbed. I tucked my hair behind my ears, rubbed a little lip gloss on my lips, and took a deep breath.

"Hi, Roger," I said.

"It took you long enough to invite me over," he said with a smile.

He came in and I poured us both a drink. We sat on the sofa and made small talk about where he was from and how long he'd been in the NBA.

"The first time I heard your voice on the radio I knew I had to see you perform," he said.

"Really?"

"Yeah, I've been checking out your live shows for a while."

"And now that you've met me in person...?"

Roger gave me a shy smile.

"I guess I'd like to get to know you better..."

I leaned in close to Roger and kissed him. He smelled really good, and I couldn't resist. I think he was probably shocked at how forward I was. But I knew what I wanted and I wasn't going to waste any time.

Now, I ain't one to get all into the details about what goes down in between my sheets. I'll just say this: Roger and I had a great time that night. It was impulsive, and that just added to the whole experience. He was a careful and attentive lover, and that morning I felt more alive than I had in years. And yes, I did feel guilty. I was married, which meant what I'd done with Roger was a sin. I knew that ultimately, just because Big was doing wrong didn't mean that I had the right to do the same. And yet, that night with Roger felt like it took years off my life. And at the time, I only regretted it for a second.

I came back home to New York and continued setting up my new apartment, booking show dates, and working on my album. I continued to focus only on myself and not worry about whatever Big and the rest of Bad Boy were up to.

Not long after I returned from New Orleans, my good friend Rufus came over to visit me. Rufus and I had met years before, back when I was working with Al B. Sure. He was a singer and songwriter who would often work in the same studio on different projects.

"Now, Faith, you know I don't normally do this. But I met this songwriter who is *dying* to meet you..."

"Really?" I asked. "Who is it?"

"Her name is Missy. We were talking about you, and she went nuts when she found out I knew you. She's been begging me to introduce you guys ever since. Do you mind?"

"Nah, it's cool," I told Rufus. "Bring her by here whenever you want."

A few weeks later, Rufus brought Melissa "Missy" Elliott by my apartment to meet me.

"Yo, your album is *crazy!*" she told me during our first conversation.

"Thank you so much," I told her.

At the time, Missy was trying to make a name for herself in the music industry. In the early 1990s, she'd worked on Jodeci's albums; she was a member of a collective called the Swing Mob that included Ginuwine and Timbaland. She'd also been a member of a short-lived girl group called Sista that never released an album.

Missy always had her hair styled in finger waves, and her wardrobe was mainly nylon tracksuits and matching sneakers. I'll never forget that she always carried a brown paper bag with her instead of a purse. Usually it was filled to the brim with candy. She had a serious candy habit. So she'd go to a convenience store, load up on all kinds of junk, and then carry her money and whatever else with her in her candy bag.

I liked Missy. She was bubbly and energetic and she made me laugh. And she also had a certain amount of hustle that I respected. Just a year before, I'd been much like her — writing music for other people and trying to navigate the music industry. So I liked the idea of being able to give her an encouraging word or two about the business.

A new phase of my life started to take form, and it felt good. Missy started to come over regularly, hanging out with me, Rufus, Cheryl, and Chyna. I was still going out on paid tour dates. And I loved my new apartment.

I did feel very disconnected from my label mates. Now, I was cool with everyone, and when we did see each other it was all love. But I just had a different agenda. Puff was out on tour with the rest of the acts on the label. And I knew he was pissed that I wasn't there. But I was doing what I felt was best for me. And at that point, I was not about to be on a tour with the husband whom I wasn't speaking to *and* two of his girlfriends.

I heard through the grapevine that there was a lot of drama on the tour. K-Ci, who was performing with Jodeci, was supposedly getting into physical altercations with Mary J. Blige. I heard Big and Kim got into some kind of fight on a tour bus. I was just grateful that I wasn't dealing with any of that mess. I was on my own, in charge of my own schedule and my own money and my own plan.

It was the fall of 1995. My entire entry into the recording industry had become so summed up by my relationship with Big, I was ready to do things on my own and make a name for myself.

At the same time that I was making these major changes, Tupac Shakur was making some major changes as well. Suge Knight and his attorney David Kenner bailed Tupac out of prison in October 1995. He left the Clinton Correctional Facility in Dannemora, New York, and got on a private plane to LA. Had I known this — the choices I'd make in the next few weeks would have been radically different.

The alarm clock that started ticking the night he was shot at Quad Studios was getting closer and closer to going off.

CHAPTER SIXTEEN

The Danger Zone

I'd lived in Los Angeles with Kiy and his crew when I was still a teenager. So by the time I started traveling back and forth to California for songwriting sessions and performances, it didn't feel like a foreign land, the way it did for some folks on the East Coast.

And although there were a lot of grumblings about tensions between the West Coast and the East Coast, I didn't think any of that stuff had anything to do with me. I was on Puff's label. But I wasn't interacting with him on a daily basis. I was estranged from Big. Essentially, I was on my own.

It was in Los Angeles that I really discovered how popular I was. I was in LA one weekend to work on music and I decided to go out with my good friend Toni, whom I'd known since the days at the Oakwood. Missy was in town as well, and she came out with us. We went to a nightclub together, and when we pulled up, there was a line down the street.

"We're not getting in there," I told Toni and Missy. "There is no way." As soon as we got out of the car, we heard my song "You Used to Love Me" pulsating from within the club.

"Girl, you crazy!" Toni said. "That's *your* song! We in this motherfucker tonight!"

And sure enough, as soon as we got near the door, they waved us in. We had a great time.

I got lots of love in Los Angeles. Whether it was a packed-to-capacity show at the House of Blues or just a meet-and-greet at a record store or an interview at a radio station, I always felt like the folks of Cali really supported my music and me.

After one party, I went back to my hotel and I was told I had a message. It was from Roger, the NBA player I'd hooked up with in New Orleans. I called him back at the number he left for me.

"How are you?" I asked.

"I'll be better if you come and see me," he said.

"Where are you?"

"I'm staying at the Ritz Carlton. I'm in town for the NBA All-Star Game."

"I don't know, Roger..."

"I'll see you at ten."

I did go to Roger's room that night. And we picked up right where we'd left off in New Orleans. There weren't any fireworks, but I did actually like Roger. He was a Southern boy, so he was sweet and mannered. He made me laugh, and his appreciation of my music made me feel good. But I knew there was no long-term potential there.

Interestingly enough, I remember telling him that I was married but separated. He had to know who my husband was, but any conversations about that were really brief, and he didn't seem to be worried about it. Although he should have been. But I was very careful. Although we didn't see each other much at all, I did end up meeting his mother when I visited his hometown. If that got back to Big, I *knew* there would be problems.

During that same trip to LA, I met a producer I'm gonna call Terry Dollars. Terry was working with a singing group who had been recently signed to a major record label. He asked me if I'd be interested in writing for the group and helping them in the studio. I arranged to meet the girls at his home in Sherman Oaks.

The group was a trio of girls from Texas. I thought they were really cool girls. But it seemed like Terry Dollars could talk a good game more than actually have the ability to make the girls into stars. He just wanted me to write for them, and I agreed.

After I moved into his place to start working with the group, Terry and I ended up having sex a few times as well. It wasn't anything serious. It really happened because I was staying in his house and we were working in close proximity. He was cute; I can't deny that. But I definitely wasn't feeling him like that. He was just a convenient stress reliever to be honest.

One night, I went out with the girls in the singing group, Terry, and some of my old friends from the Oakwood, including Curtis. We went to the Hollywood Athletic Club, a well-known spot for hanging out and people-watching. As soon as we got settled inside, I saw Treach from the group Naughty by Nature. I knew Treach well. He was from my hometown, and we used to hang out together occasionally. He was very cool. Queen Latifah was a mutual friend; I was also cool with Treach's then-girlfriend Pepa, from the rap group Salt-N-Pepa.

We exchanged hugs and greetings, and I introduced Treach to my friends.

"Somebody here wants to meet you," Treach said.

"Who?" I asked. I was out in LA working, not performing, so most people didn't know I was in town.

"My boy Tupac wants to say what's up," Treach said, gesturing to a table behind him.

Before I go any farther, let me be absolutely clear on something. Many people have asked me why I wouldn't peel off in the opposite direction when I heard Tupac's name. And the answer is simple:

There was no need. I didn't know anything about what label 'Pac was signed to, whom he was cool with, whom he had beef with. I'd heard the rumors that 'Pac believed Big had been involved in the shooting at the studio the year before. But Big had brushed that off, saying he knew 'Pac knew better than to think that. No one told me anything had changed. And if he wanted to meet me—and he obviously knew I was Big's wife—I assumed there was no beef.

Just a few weeks later, I'd find out how wrong I was. But it's important to understand how quickly things spread. Being introduced by Treach to 'Pac was like a matchstick hitting a pile of dead leaves. And it was going to become an out-of-control wildfire in no time.

This was before the era of instant messaging, blogs, two-way pagers, and gossip Web sites that are constantly updated in real time. All I knew about 'Pac was that he'd just been released from prison.

Tupac approached me and we shook hands. He looked exactly like he did on television—bald head and thin, round face with heavy-lidded eyes.

Almost immediately after we were introduced, a photographer who had been trolling the club for celebrities came up to us and asked us to pose. In the picture, I'm not smiling, and I look high as hell. But although some people have said otherwise, that picture was taken literally seconds after we met.

After we exchanged a few pleasantries, Tupac began to compliment me. "I really like your music," he said. "When I was locked up, I listened to that album every day."

I thanked him and just continued surveying the crowd. Tupac made direct eye contact with me and looked very serious.

"I want to do a song with you. I love your sound and I feel like you the only person who can really do it."

I was flattered but not particularly excited about the prospect. Lots of people would approach me about writing or singing for them.

But many times, it didn't work out because of the money. Once I set my price and insisted on being paid immediately, these things often fell through.

"You'd have to get clearance from my label to put the song on your album," I said.

"That's not a problem," he said.

"It's not going to be cheap," I told him. "And I need my money up front."

"That's not a problem, either," he said. "How much?"

I thought about a conversation I'd recently had with Cheryl. I'd told her I was going to start charging people more. I felt like I wasn't getting what I was worth and I was determined to stand up for myself and do better when negotiating my terms. I could hear her in my head: *Now, Faith, you said you charging twenty-five thousand for the next one.* And *that's* not even a crazy amount!

"It's going to be twenty-five thousand dollars," I told Tupac.

"No problem," he said.

I still didn't really take it seriously. A lot of people will talk a big game about working together, and then it doesn't come through. But still, just to be on the safe side, a day or two later I spoke to Big and made sure to run it by him.

"I met 'Pac out here," I told him. "He wants me to do a song with him."

"Oh word?" Big said. "You gonna do it?"

"If the money comes through, yeah I'll do it."

We talked a bit more and that was it. If Big had said *Don't do the song with him* or if he had sounded the least bit concerned, all bets would have been off. Maybe Big wasn't concerned about Tupac just then. Honestly, I don't think anyone really knew just how buck wild Tupac was gearing up to be.

Soon after, I spoke to Mark Pitts and told him that 'Pac had asked me to work on a record with him. Mark was still on the road with Puff and everyone for the tour. He didn't say much about the opportunity, but he definitely didn't tell me that I shouldn't do it.

The next day, I got a page from 'Pac and called him back. We had some small talk for a minute. "So what are you working on out here?" he asked.

"I did a song on the *Waiting to Exhale* soundtrack," I told him. "I'm going to the release party for that."

"Yeah, I'm going to that, too," he said. "So you still down to do a song with me?"

"That's a possibility."

"I'm gonna get everything approved by my attorney," Tupac said.

The next night was the party for the release of the *Waiting to Exhale* soundtrack. There was a lot of buzz surrounding the movie and soundtrack, and I was looking forward to supporting the album with my appearance.

I took a limo to the party with my friend Nicci, a singer in the group Brownstone. As soon as we pulled up to where the cars were dropping off artists to walk the red carpet, my cell phone rang.

"What up, Faith. Where you at?" It was Tupac. I told him I was at a party for the soundtrack.

"Word?" he said. "I'm here, too! Where are you?"

I looked out the car window, and there he was. He made a bee-line for the car, opened up the door, and jumped in the backseat with us. We were already very close to the drop-off spot for the red carpet; we would only be in the car for another minute or two. But I was still very uncomfortable. I wasn't planning on hanging out with 'Pac. I introduced him to my friend Nicci, and we chatted until it was time to hit the red carpet. When we exited the car, flash-bulbs started going off and people in the crowd craned their necks to see who was coming. Tupac was smiling and waving at folks as we walked into the venue. I wasn't quite as energetic. I wanted to walk up to each person and tell them: *I'm not actually with Tupac. He just jumped into my car a few minutes ago. And I met him for the first time yesterday.*

When we got inside the venue, I found my table and sat down. I was just starting to get comfortable when Tupac slid into a chair next to me and Nicci. He was grinning ear-to-ear and settled back like he was going to sit there for the rest of the night.

Now, Tupac seemed cool to me. There was nothing about him, personally, that made me feel uncomfortable. But I was conscious of perception. I was still married to Big. And no matter what we were going through, I was very aware of how I carried myself.

So, as 'Pac was sitting in my row, all chummy and friendly, I was very self-conscious, the way I would have been with anyone I'd just met. He didn't try to kick it to me or make any kind of moves. It was just the way it all *looked*. I saw Whitney Houston from across the room, and she gave me a look that said *Oh word? You're with him?* And my heart sank.

At one point, Clive Davis addressed the crowd, introducing the various celebrities who were in attendance. I was subdued and quiet, uncomfortable and uneasy because of Tupac's presence.

"Ladies and gentleman," said Clive Davis into the microphone. "We have a special guest here tonight—Tupac Shakur!"

The crowd cheered and clapped. I was just ready to get out of there. I didn't like the vibe and I was relieved when the night was over. Until I saw Tupac standing near our limousine at the end of the night.

"Where y'all going now?" he asked with a bright smile on his face.

"We're leaving," I said quickly. "We're going to a party."

"Where?" he asked.

"The Peninsula," I said.

"That's where I'm staying!" he said. "I'll catch a ride over there with y'all."

Tupac jumped in the limo and stretched out, making himself comfortable. Now I was definitely feeling weird. Everything in me wanted to say: *You don't belong in this car! This is not right!*

But I didn't have any real basis to say that. And it would have been weird if I'd told him to get out. I just didn't like how it looked on the outside.

After the party at the hotel, we hung out a bit more with Tupac and his friends, shared a blunt, and discussed the specifics of my guest appearance. I confirmed with him that he was sending a car for me a few days later to go to the studio. Then I went back to the producer's house.

Right on time a few days later, a car came to Terry Dollars's house to pick me up. But instead of a livery service and a driver, it was Tupac himself, driving a black convertible Mercedes-Benz with the top down. I was stunned. Why the hell would he pick me up himself—in a convertible no less? At this time, Tupac had enough fame and notoriety that he did not need to be driving around Los Angeles in a top-down convertible. At that moment, I wanted to tell him that I would drive to the studio myself in my rental car. But I didn't. I just got in the car, and we pulled off. I noticed immediately that a black Town Car was following us. From the look of the beefy guys in the backseat, they were security guards.

The ride to the studio was about fifteen minutes long. We didn't talk much. I didn't like any of it: the convertible, the security behind us, none of it felt right. I decided I would go in, do my part and haul ass out of the studio as soon as possible.

We pulled up to a nondescript parking lot in nearby Tarzana, California. I followed Tupac through the doors of an office building. As soon as the doors opened, I saw blood-red carpeting throughout the hallway entrance and a lighted sign that said DEATH ROW RECORDS.

I felt the blood rush from my face and I thought I was going to pass out.

Chapter Seventeen

Live from Death Row

Until that very moment, I had no idea that Tupac had signed to Death Row Records after he was released from prison. He had only been out of jail a few days when we met at the Hollywood Athletic Club.

I hadn't yet heard that Suge Knight had bailed him out of prison in return for signing to the label and immediately recording an album. If I had known that Suge Knight had anything whatsoever to do with Tupac and hiring me as a vocalist, I would never in a million years have agreed to it.

It was Suge Knight, not Tupac, who had the reputation at this time. Years ago, I'd heard that he roughed up Andre Harrell during his tenure at Uptown, I'd also heard something about Suge making some guys drink urine. And there was a rumor about him shaking down Vanilla Ice.

One thing I did know was that he didn't like Puff one bit. I remembered all those slick things he'd said at The Source Awards the year before. I knew Suge Knight was someone I didn't want to do business with. But I didn't know Tupac was now affiliated with him.

I went from concerned to cautious to downright petrified. We walked into the main room of the studio and I saw several Death Row artists, including the rapper Kurupt and his pregnant girlfriend and a female singing group called YNV.

In my mind, I was screaming: *I don't belong here!* But I had to remain calm. I hated the fact that I hadn't driven in my own car. I was stuck there and didn't have the guts to scrap the whole plan and call someone to pick me up. I just stayed focused on the plan: I was going to sing my song, collect my twenty-five grand, and be out of there.

I got a Budweiser and Tupac rolled a blunt. I chilled out, waiting for the session to begin. Before long, Suge Knight came in and made a beeline to where I was sitting.

"It's nice to meet you, Faith," he said with a smile.

I smiled back and shook his hand.

"I've heard a lot of nice things about you," he said.

I just smiled and nodded.

In that moment, I just wanted to sing the song and leave. I waited for hours as Tupac finished up other songs. I moved around the studio, trying to be sociable. But inside, I felt very self-conscious. Everyone there was from LA and on Death Row and here I am, from the East Coast, an artist signed to Bad Boy? I know people must have been looking at me like I was crazy, considering how Suge felt about Puffy at the time.

Three hours passed before Tupac finally called me into the studio. It was crammed with people. I asked him to roll me a blunt and smoked it just to get over the nervousness. I knew I would be able to get into the booth and do whatever I needed to do. They played the song for me. And the title was: "Wonder Why They Call U Bitch."

If I could have felt any more uncomfortable at that point, I did when I heard the title. And then, on top of everything else, the song just wasn't really that good.

Let's recap how bad this situation is. I'm in LA, writing and recording, instead of on tour with my husband and the rest of the

Bad Boy label. I've met Tupac in a club and had my picture taken with him (while I am coincidentally wearing a red suit).

Then it looks like we arrive and leave together from a soundtrack party. He picks me up in a freaking convertible and drives me to the Can Am Studios, home of Death Row Records. Suge Knight, Puff's archnemesis, is there. And I am there to sing a song called "Wonder Why They Call U Bitch."

I'm surprised I didn't just implode right there in the vocal booth. But I didn't. Somehow, I held it together and sang the one or two lines they wanted me to do. In less than an hour, I was done. A few hours later, Tupac was done with his session, and he led me to a waiting limo in the parking lot.

"Where's my check?" I asked.

"My manager is bringing it to my hotel right now," he said. "I can bring it to you later on this evening. Or we can swing by there right now and pick it up."

I had plenty of experience with people saying they would bring money by at some later time. I wasn't having that. I wanted my check immediately. I agreed to ride with him to the Peninsula Hotel where he was staying.

And of course, when we got there, no manager was in sight. There were two dudes in 'Pac's room, smoking, drinking, and listening to music. After an hour of waiting for the manager, I was ready to leave.

"I'll just come back and get the check tomorrow," I said.

"Nah, just wait a minute. He's on his way," Tupac said.

His two friends left. We were now in his hotel room—alone. And it seemed I had been there forever. I was a little uncomfortable and a bit leery. I wanted my money. And then I wouldn't care if I never saw Tupac Shakur again.

As soon as the door closed behind his friends, Tupac turned to me. His face was completely different. His teeth were clenched, his nostrils were flared, and his eyes were narrow.

"You know, I love New York," he said. "But I'm not fucking with New York right now."

The air in the room seemed to get really thick all of a sudden. His demeanor had changed so quickly that I was truly afraid.

"Really?" I asked. "Why is that?"

"'Cause niggas set me up that night. You know that, right?"

I swallowed hard and took a deep breath. He was staring at me like he thought I was the one who set him up.

"You don't really believe that bullshit," I said.

"I'm telling you . . . niggas set me up," he said in a low voice.

"Look. 'Pac. I just need to get my check and then I have to go . . ."

"The situation with the money is like this," he said. "If I give it to you, then you my bitch."

"Your *what*," I said. I felt a chill go up my back.

"You heard me. You gotta be my bitch."

I got up and moved farther away from where he was standing.

"I'm not anybody's bitch," I said, trying to keep my voice even and steady.

"You Biggie's bitch."

I thought about how people always got shit wrong. He was probably thinking about the song "Me & My Bitch." And I wasn't with Big when he made that record.

"I'm his *wife*."

"I thought y'all broke up?" he asked.

"We still married."

"Whatever."

"Look," I said. "You hired me to do a song. I did it. I want my money and that's it."

"Oh word, it's like that? You just want your money?"

"You told me it wouldn't be a problem," I said. "The only reason why I came up here is because you said—"

Big and CJ at my apartment in Manhattan (© Faith Evans)

Chyna
(© Faith Evans)

CJ (© Faith Evans)

Joshua (© Faith Evans)

Me and Puff at my twenty-fifth birthday party (© Faith Evans)

CJ and T'yanna at the 2005 Hip Hop Honors: Honoring the Notorious B.I.G.
(© Faith Evans)

Joshua, CJ, and Chyna on Easter Sunday 2001 (© Faith Evans)

At the *Waiting to Exhale* listening party (© Faith Evans)

George Jenkins, Sampson Davis, Rameck Hunt (The 3 Doctors) and me at the Essence Awards (© Faith Evans)

Me and Todd on the way to the 2002 Grammy Awards (© Faith Evans)

My sons, CJ, Ryder, and Josh, at our home in 2008 (© Faith Evans)

My youngest son, Ryder, at eleven months (© Faith Evans)

T'yanna and CJ at a photo shoot (© Faith Evans)

Me and my crew on Chyna's birthday (© Faith Evans)

Me and Todd in our kitchen in Georgia on our fifth anniversary
(© Faith Evans)

"So you not trying to suck my dick?"

"What!" I screamed. "What are you talking about?"

Tupac raised his voice. "You know you want to suck my dick, bitch! Don't fucking lie." I burst into tears and grabbed my purse. "I have to get out of here."

Tupac kept going. He was making no sense, cursing and yelling. He said something about Big and the East Coast.

"But...but...I...thought y'all was friends," I said. At this point, I could barely speak clearly because I was crying so hard.

"Whatever. You know you wanna be *my* bitch," he said, before going into the bedroom area and slamming the door.

As soon as I got my things together to leave, Tupac came back out to the common area.

"Where the fuck you going?" he asked.

"I don't know what you thought," I said. "I really don't. But it's not like that."

Tupac just nodded slowly, staring at me intently. He wasn't ranting and screaming anymore. But he had this very sinister smile on his face. I kept looking around the room because I felt like something was about to happen to me. I wasn't sure if those guys were coming back or what. But something was wrong.

"It's not like that?" he kept saying over and over and nodding. "Well, ai-ight then, fucking *bitch*. You want to leave? Tell the driver to take you home. The limo is still out there. Get the fuck out."

I dashed down to the lobby and called my friend Toni. I was crying and told her I was on my way to her house and that I would explain everything when I got there. I got into the limo and cried even harder. And I cried all the way to Toni's house. I told her everything that had happened.

"What are you going to do now?" she asked me.

"I have no idea," I said. "But I know I gotta get that check."

"Just forget about it!" she said. "That dude is nuts."

"Are you crazy?" I yelled. "I gotta get that check. Especially after this bullshit. I can't let them know I went into the studio with this dude and didn't even get paid!"

"So what are you going to do?" she asked me.

"I don't know," I said. "I just know I have to get that check."

I spent the night at Toni's house. And the next morning, I went back to the producer's house in Sherman Oaks. I was sick with worry. I did not want Puff or Mark or Big to know that I'd worked in the studio with Tupac and not gotten my money. And my mind was reeling over how 'Pac had flipped on me. I decided I would call 'Pac and let him know I was not going to just forget about the money. Even though I had no idea that no dollar amount would change the drama that was about to come.

That day, I called him up.

"I want my money," I said. "I did what I was hired to do. And I want to be paid."

"No problem," Tupac said. "I got that." His voice was very flat and even.

"I need to get the money *today*," I said.

"Cool. Come by the hotel."

"I'll be in the hotel lobby at six," I said.

I got my friend Curtis to drive me to the hotel. He dropped me off and told me he would be back to pick me up in thirty minutes. I called Tupac's room from the lobby and told him I was at the bar. Twenty minutes later, still no Tupac. I called again and he answered.

"Oh, so you trying to be funny?" I said. I felt bold enough to tell him how I really felt since I was on the phone and not in person. "I did the song. And now you not trying to pay me? What are you doing? Why are you doing this?"

Tupac didn't say much. He sounded very vague and distracted. I think he was surprised that I actually came back to get the money. I think he thought he'd scared me enough that I wouldn't dare try to get my money back.

"I'm still down here," I said. "And I want my money."

He never came down. My boy Curtis pulled up to the front of the hotel, where I stood crying. I got in the car and we left. I was going to have to take that on the chin. I was hurt, embarrassed, angry, and ashamed. Now this song that I'd worked on was out there. He could use it for anything. And I wouldn't even have the benefit of a check to justify why the hell I would work with Tupac.

I realized at that point that Tupac had played me out. But I had no idea how far he would take our brief interactions and what lengths he would go to in an effort to make me look bad.

I knew it was time to get out of LA. I felt a deep foreboding sense that things were about to get really complicated. Things were about to explode in my face. Tupac was on some bullshit, and if he was capable of flipping on me like that, there was no telling what else he had planned. I was going to have to get ready to defend myself. And the first thing I had to do was talk to my husband.

Chapter Eighteen

The Seed

I told the producer guy that I was going to be finishing up and needed to be paid for my work. He kept stalling me, and I couldn't wait. I left for New York and decided I would deal with him and getting my money later.

Soon after I got back to New York, I got a call from a girl named Jennifer, who worked at Bad Boy.

"Yo. Have you heard? Big is pissed *off*. Him and Puff are wilding out right now."

"Wait a second," I said. "Why is Big mad?"

"Someone told him that people were saying you were messing with 'Pac."

I took a deep breath. "But I wasn't! Who told him that?"

"Look, I just wanted you to know you'll probably be hearing from Big soon," she said before hanging up. I had checked into a hotel, so I wasn't sure if Big knew how to reach me if he did have something to say.

Within hours, he called my hotel room. "What the fuck is going on?" he screamed.

"Listen, I don't know what you heard but—"

"You fucking with Tupac?"

"Hell no," I yelled. "I told you I did a song with him."

"And then what happened?" he asked.

"Nothing! I swear to God nothing happened."

"Faye! Don't fucking lie to me! Why are people saying this shit?"

"I don't know, Big. But you know I would never—"

Big hung up on me. I paced the hotel room for a while, trying to gather my thoughts. I had to think of how I would reassure Big that nothing happened with 'Pac. I hadn't been completely innocent. While I was in Los Angeles, I'd had sex occasionally with Terry Dollars. And I'd even seen Roger, the NBA player, a few times when he was in town. So technically, I had cheated on Big. But *not* with Tupac.

I had no idea what he had heard and from whom. I just knew that he was very angry. I took a shower to clear my head. I got out, wrapped myself in a towel, and was about to get dressed when I heard banging at my door. I knew it was Big. As soon as I opened up the door a tiny crack, he barreled through. Big grabbed me by my shoulders and shook me.

"What the fuck is wrong with you? You fucked Tupac?"

I tried to break free from him and started crying. "Hell no!" I said. "You have to believe me!"

Big's friend Damion had come with him. He was standing in a corner of the room.

"Damion," I screamed. "Please tell me what's going on."

Damion didn't say anything. But I knew from the look on his face that he knew I didn't deserve this.

"So why is this nigga saying this shit? Huh, Faye? Why?"

Big pushed me to the floor, and I covered my head with my arms while he continued to scream and curse at me. After ten minutes, it was over. He stormed out, leaving me on the floor sobbing and hysterical.

A few days later, I saw what had made Big so angry. Suge Knight was on the cover of the *New York Times Magazine.* In the story, Suge urges 'Pac to tell the reporter the name of the person who bought the outfit he's wearing.

> *"The wife of a top rapper bought this for him," Suge says, razzing Tupac. "Who's that?" Tupac smiles. "His name is an acronym." Suge smiles. "Notorious B.I.G.'s wife, Faith Evans."*

I read this line and almost screamed in frustration. It was a straight-up bald-faced lie. I hadn't gone anywhere with Tupac. I met him at the club and then saw him at the afterparty for the *Waiting to Exhale* soundtrack. I worked with him in the studio and tried to get my money back at the Peninsula Hotel. Everything else was bullshit. I continued to read in a blind rage.

> *"She bought him this and a suit and some other stuff," Suge says. "And how did you thank her, Tupac?" Tupac pauses. "I did enough," he says, rather salaciously.*

I could not believe what I was reading. I had never been lied on so openly before in my life. I thought I had developed a pretty thick skin at that point. I'd been called a gold digger by people who thought I married Big because of who he was. There was all the chatter about whether or not me and Mary had beef or whether or not I had beef with Lil' Kim.

But nothing made me more enraged than reading the lies Tupac and Suge were saying about me. I was more than angry. I was afraid, too. I heard that people in the Bad Boy family were being threatened. Anonymous people were calling Big's house in Teaneck and saying stuff about Tupac and then hanging up on Big.

The more people talked about Tupac alluding to having sex

with me, the more I feared that his taunting would lead to violence between the two camps. Looking back, that's why he'd wanted me on the song in the first place. And I'd been clueless enough to walk right into the trap. Everything was on fire now: DJs on radio stations, the hip-hop media, mainstream outlets. Everyone was talking about what 'Pac was saying about me and wondering whether or not it was true.

I could not understand how 'Pac was getting away with this. How could he just lie on me to journalists? Wasn't this against the law? I went to see Stuart Levy, my longtime attorney, and told him I wanted to sue Tupac for libel and defamation of character.

"You know," he told me, "they say any publicity is good publicity."

"Not in this case," I said. "This could cause some serious shit to go down. I need him to stop talking about me."

"Do you really want to spend your money on this?" he asked. "It will be very expensive."

"I don't care. I want to do it."

"Keep in mind," he said, "this will take a lot of time and money. And you'll have to speak on everything you said and heard while you were out there."

I had to just leave it alone. By suing them, I'd only ended up opening myself and everyone else to more scrutiny.

I called Big after giving him some time to cool off and think rationally.

"I swear on my life that nothing happened with that nigga," I told Big.

"I don't understand why he would be saying this shit, Faye," Big said.

"I didn't even know 'Pac was on Death Row until I got to the studio."

Big listened to me. But I could tell he was still angry and wasn't sure what to believe.

I refused to go into hiding although part of me wanted to. I didn't do any interviews, but I was still doing studio sessions and writing songs. I knew everyone in the music industry was talking about me, and I wasn't dealing with any of that bullshit.

The one thing that really hurt me during this time was the idea that Big might really believe 'Pac's lies. At this point, Big and I were pretty much over. Although we lived separately, he still referred to me as his wife, and we always stayed in touch. We even had our occasional hookups. I still felt very strongly for him, and it would kill me if he thought for even one second that I would betray him like that.

But then in some ways, I was confused about why no one warned me about 'Pac. Before I was in LA, something was brewing. I didn't know that 'Pac was signed to Death Row and was running with Suge. And no one told me. If I'd had any suspicions, things would have turned out differently.

The year 1995 ended with me doing a New Year's Eve show at the Apollo. D'Angelo and Monica opened for me, and the show was a rousing success. I spent a lot of time at my apartment on West End Avenue, keeping a low profile. I still went out on tour dates and it would be me, Cheryl, my friend Roz, and Chyna. But after all the drama, I'd hired security to travel with us.

On one trip for a show, we were short a background singer. We knew that Missy could sing, so I hired her to fill in at the show. Missy and I were becoming very cool, and I was enjoying watching her make some moves in the industry. She was still back and forth to Virginia a lot. And I told her that anytime she needed a place to say, she could stay with me. I thought what Missy was doing was really fresh and innovative. Her lyrical style was energetic and brash, and her production was futuristic and fun. I was proud of her and made sure to tell her so.

"Your shit is hot," I'd say.

"Thanks, Faith," she would reply. "I'm just trying to do it big."

"You will," I told her. "There's no question about that."

I talked to Missy quite a bit about the things I was going through with Big and our marriage and the rumors and the shady music industry. I didn't know much about her past, but I knew she'd been through a lot and could relate.

I also told her about how I still owed Lil' Kim an ass-beating.

"She needs to keep my name out of her mouth," I told her.

"Faith, you crazy!" Missy said with a laugh.

"No, I'm serious," I said. "I will beat her ass."

By the start of the new year, Missy was staying with me regularly as she continued to try to snag work as a songwriter. My apartment wasn't that big, but I was out of town so often that most of the time we weren't there at the same time anyway.

I was becoming more and more of a loner. And I didn't hear from Big as much as I had been. I started to believe that maybe it was really over. I wasn't sure. But it was definitely starting to feel that way.

And every morning, when I looked in the mirror, I saw that tribute to Big on my chest. That tattoo had come to symbolize how hard-core my love was for him. But as time wore on, I wondered if it was time for it to be modified.

The next time I went back to Jersey to check on my grandparents, I went to Elizabeth to my favorite tattoo parlor. I had the letters FAYE tattooed right under the word BIG so that it read BIG FAYE. When the tattoo was done, it looked seamless, as if I'd never meant to tattoo his name at all and that it had always read BIG FAYE.

I didn't seek Big out to show him. I figured he'd see it eventually. A few weeks after I got my new tattoo, I did a show at a nightclub on the Upper West Side. The night of the show, I got a call from Big. He was coming to the show with Cease and D-Roc.

Big liked to watch me perform. Whether we were together or not,

I would step on stage many times and see Big and his boys sitting front and center, catcalling and cheering me on as loud as humanly possible.

After my show, I came out to the front of the stage and down the steps on the side leading into the seating area. Big was about twenty feet away, talking to his friends. I walked slowly up the aisle to where he stood and then waited for him to see me.

He turned to face me and immediately looked down at my chest and noticed the new tattoo. His face fell and he looked me in my eyes. He seemed equal parts disappointed, hurt, and angry.

"Oh. It's like that?" he said, gesturing toward my chest.

"It is what it is," I said, holding my head up defiantly.

Big's eyes were stormy. He looked like he was about to say something else to me, but he didn't.

"You had a good show tonight."

"Thank you."

"I'ma holla at you later," he said.

He kissed me on the cheek and walked away without saying anything else. I'd made my point. Big knew I still loved him. But I was also going to assert my independence and let him know that if he was moving on, I could, too. I'll admit that part of me wanted to get a rise out of him. If he really believed Tupac's lies, would he even care if I covered up the tattoo? Would he still want me to be branded with his name if he thought the whole world knew I'd been disloyal? From the look on his face before he walked away, I thought I had my answers.

In February, I was on a rare break between tour dates. Valentine's Day had just passed and I got a call from Big. I assumed he was just calling to check in. He was in New Orleans for a show.

"I want to see you," he said. And my heart skipped a beat.

"Really?" I asked.

"Yeah, you should fly down tonight."

"I'll see you tonight."

I was actually excited about seeing him. I didn't realize how much I'd missed him until I heard his voice. And after seeing how I'd covered up the tattoo, I wasn't sure if he was still feeling me at all. When he called and invited me down, I knew then that he didn't believe any of the lies that were swirling about me. If he did believe them, he would never have invited me.

When I got to his room in New Orleans, it was filled with all of the Junior M.A.F.I.A. guys. But Lil' Kim was conspicuously absent. I'd told Big on numerous occasions that I was gonna beat the shit out of her as soon as I saw her. So I assume he made sure she was nowhere nearby.

Big and I settled into our usual routine: sharing a blunt, a meal, and each other. I felt like there might be a possibility that we could get back together. He felt so familiar to me. And I felt safe around him. I wasn't going to ask him. I decided I'd let him come to me if that's what he wanted. I was just going to stay in the moment and enjoy the time we were sharing. But I did think it was a good sign that we were together. He wasn't with Kim. He wasn't with Tiffany. He was with me, his wife. And in some ways I thought that's how it should be. What neither of us knew was that spending that night together in New Orleans would end up connecting us forever.

A few weeks later, I sat in the bathroom of my apartment and stared at the little white stick with the dark blue line. I was pregnant. And I knew exactly when it had happened.

I couldn't believe it. Big and I rarely used protection and I'd only gotten pregnant once, early on in the relationship. I'd had a miscarriage before we could even think about what we were going to do about it. And because nothing had ever happened since, I thought it couldn't happen. In my mind, I went over the pros and cons of the situation. I'd had enough abortions in my life. I was getting a bit older and more stable. I decided I was keeping the baby. I called Big at his house in Teaneck and told him the news.

He didn't sound happy or sad. Just very noncommittal. "You keeping it?" he asked.

"Yeah. I am," I said.

It was quiet for a moment. "Are you sure?"

I wasn't sure what he meant by that. "Yes I'm sure..."

Big made a weary sound. "Homegirl got pregnant, too."

"What does that have to do with me?"

"I made her get an abortion," he said.

"So what are you saying?"

"You sure this is the right time?" he said.

"Look," I told him. "I wasn't prepared for this, either. I know we're not together. But now we're going to be parents. And we'll have to make it work. You can figure out how to relay all of that to your little girlfriend."

Big and I got off the phone abruptly. I knew it wasn't the best situation. But he was going to have to deal with it. We'd laid down together. And now we were going to be parents together. It was as simple as that.

On my next visit to the doctor, I got my first ultrasound. The doctor scanned my belly, looking for the fetal sac to make sure the baby was developing properly. He found the sac—and another one right next to it.

"Ms. Evans," the doctor said with a smile. "You're having twins."

My mom is a twin, and there are five sets of twins on her side of the family. I shouldn't have been surprised to hear that I was having twins. Knowing I had two lives growing inside me actually lifted my spirits. I was telling anyone who would listen that I was pregnant. Even people who didn't need to know.

I ran into Angie Martinez, a DJ on Hot 97, at a party.

"Hey Faith!" she said, giving me a hug. "How are you?"

"I'm good!" I said. "Me and Big are having a baby!"

Of course Angie announced it on her show the next day. I don't know what I was thinking. It's not like we were personal friends and she would keep that to herself.

I remember seeing Puff during this time. He said to me: "You can't be letting people into your business like that. Stop telling people things they don't need to know."

I told Ms. Wallace, and she seemed happy. She knew we were separated. And I knew that she often took T'yanna to Big's house in Teaneck for weekend visits, so I assumed she'd met Tiffany and her daughter. But Ms. Wallace never mentioned anything about any other women to me. So although Big was in another relationship, I didn't give it that much thought. If there was anything I needed to know — like he wanted a divorce — I was sure he'd tell me.

So when this Tiffany chick called my house in the early days of my pregnancy, I was not amused.

"You supposed to be having Big's baby?" she asked me.

I had to take the phone away from my ear and just look at it in utter shock. "Who the fuck is this?"

"This Tiffany. I want to know what's going on . . . you supposed to be having twins or something?"

"Are you out of your *mind*?" I asked. I had actually just found out that one of the eggs had failed to develop and that I was only carrying one baby. But that was none of her business. "Did Big tell you to call me?"

"No," she said. "I just wanted to know if —"

"Oh no no no . . . you got it *all* wrong. Don't you *ever* call my fucking house."

"Well, I don't know how Big gonna be supporting no new baby. He said he was gonna pay for my father's funeral!"

"I'm gonna say this one more time," I said. "That ain't got *shit* to do with me and *don't* call my house."

"Why y'all not divorced anyway? I studied law in school and I know it don't take that much to get a divorce."

I thought to myself: *Bitch, if you studied law, why don't you have a job?* But I just took a deep breath.

"You are talking to the wrong person right now," I said. "Don't make that mistake again."

I hung up. I was so mad I was shaking.

I had to collect myself and focus on what was important. I was not trying to fight this girl.

I'd promised myself that if Big wanted to go his own way, I'd let him.

A few nights later, I went to the Palladium with the singer Monica and my friend Cheryl. As soon as I got there, I heard whispers that Big was there — and Kim, too. I wasn't trying to get into it with any of them.

I didn't say anything to Big, and I didn't even see Kim. I left shortly after and ran into a girl named Tasha, who was dating my good friend Red at the time. We stood outside talking, and I saw Kim drive by in the passenger's seat of some girl's car. She was giving me a serious ice grill, like she was really trying to take it there. I just rolled my eyes. If she wanted to get out of the car, I'd be standing right there waiting for her.

She never did. She just drove around the block a few times, glaring at me. I remember Tasha telling me to stay put 'cause Kim wasn't really going to try to come for me. It was all juvenile and silly.

I tried to put it all off my mind and went home to start packing my bags for Los Angeles. I was on my way west for the annual Soul Train Awards. In the spring, everyone involved in the urban music industry goes out to these awards. Until the BET Awards, the Soul Train Awards show was always the biggest night in black music, and it wasn't to be missed.

I managed to avoid Big for my entire trip to LA. And keep in mind, we *performed* together! I stood on a riser high above the stage and sang the hook for "One More Chance," and Big did a few of his own songs and one with Junior M.A.F.I.A. I didn't speak to him after the performance or for the day or so that I was in Los Angeles.

Cheryl called me in my hotel the morning I was leaving to come back to New York. "Is everything okay out there?"

"Yeah. Why?"

"People in the office are talking about some guys from Death Row stepping to some guys from Bad Boy. I heard somebody pulled a gun."

"I came right here back to my hotel after the show," I told Cheryl. "I haven't been out like that."

"It's probably better that way," she said. "'Cause niggas are really starting to get carried away."

Hearing that there was a near-physical altercation between Bad Boy and Death Row worried me. When it was just words back and forth on the radio, on records, and in magazines, that was painful but manageable. But if the beef was moving to physical confrontations — I was very skittish about where that could lead.

A few days after we got back to New York, Big and Cease came by my apartment and I ended up giving them a ride to the studio. Big was his usual jovial self, cracking jokes and laughing with Cease.

"Faye, I got a new song I want you to hear," he said.

I pointed at the cassette player in my truck. Big dug a tape out of his pocket and slipped it in. His instantly recognizable raspy voice boomed out of my speakers.

As usual, Big's lyrics were amazingly vivid. The song went back and forth with verses from a new rapper named Jay-Z. The two of them were in character, trading lyrics on how gangster they could be. I liked the song and told Big so.

"That's gon' be on Jay-Z's new album," he told me. "That nigga is *nice*."

I didn't think about the song again until a few weeks later, when I got a call from Cheryl. "Have you heard Big's new song?" she asked me.

"Which one?"

"The one with Jay-Z."

"Yeah," I told Cheryl. "I heard it awhile ago...why?"

"You must not have heard this version," she said. "'Cause this nigga is wildin'."

I don't know what happened in the studio between the time Big played the song for me and when the album was released. But when I finally heard the song on the radio, my mouth dropped when I heard the last line of Big's verse.

> *If Faye have twins, she'll probably have two 'Pacs*
> *Get it? Tupac's...*

I called Cheryl after I heard the song. "Why would he do this?"

"I don't know," she said. "But that shit is fucked up."

Cheryl had always been right there when me and Big were going through something, and she usually would try to avoid choosing sides or getting in the middle. But this was too much, even for her.

"I can't believe Big would do this," she said. "It's just wrong."

Not only was the media having a field day with Tupac's allegations — now Big was publicly recording a song that speculated the same damn thing? I was so angry I couldn't even see straight. Big knew it was his baby. And he knew — at least I think he did — that I had not been intimate with Tupac. And this verse wasn't a freestyle or a remix. It was on an album that would be out there in the world forever. What did he think I was going to say to our child about this song when the time came? I thought it was selfish and immature, and it really pissed me off that he would say such a thing.

I didn't immediately try to reach out to Big to talk to him about it. And before I could even curse him out about it, I heard Tupac's latest single, a song called "Hit 'Em Up," which was released just a few weeks before Jay-Z's *Reasonable Doubt*.

The song used the same sample as Junior M.A.F.I.A.'s song "Get Money"—the track that people thought Big was using to dis me the year before. This time, it was Tupac fueling the flames. The opening line of the song is Tupac screaming. He taunted Big, claiming he slept with me, in very crude terms.

It's hard to describe just how deflated this made me feel. It was as if my life had been reduced to a punch line. And I did not deserve it. I tried to keep a stiff upper lip but it was so hard.

I was scheduled to perform at KMEL's annual Summer Jam concert in the summer of 1996. Both Tupac's song and Big's song were being played on the radio. And each song made me seem like something I wasn't. I was pregnant and trying to stay positive and healthy. And I wasn't about to just crawl under a rock and hide.

At this point, my first single was still on the charts. And I'd released two more, "Soon as I Get Home" and "Ain't Nobody," that were both doing very well. I was not going to waste this time in my life worrying about what people were saying about me. I knew I had fans who loved my music, and I was determined to keep working.

After the Summer Jam show, my friend Toni and I went to a nearby hotel to hang out with Queen Latifah, who'd invited us to stop by. Outside the hotel, a fan walked by and stopped when he saw me talking to Toni.

"Yo, Faith!"

I turned around, ready to give a smile or sign an autograph.

"Is that Big's baby or Tupac's baby?"

I cocked my head to the side and rolled my eyes. "You don't know me like that," I said. "Why would you even ask me some disrespectful shit like that?"

Things were getting really out of control. When random

strangers on the street felt like they could question the paternity of my unborn child, I knew things had gone way too far.

Even with all this, I still continued to travel between New York and Los Angeles for songwriting gigs and to do promotional appearances for my album. I just kept my head facing forward—literally and figuratively.

Now that I was pregnant and had a toddler, having friends who liked to entertain Chyna was very helpful. I needed to take care of business, taking meetings or going into the studio. And although Chyna was right on my hip 90 percent of the time, I didn't mind when Missy—who continued to stay with me off and on for that summer—asked me if she could spend time with my daughter.

The funny thing was, it seemed like every single time I sent Chyna to hang out with Missy for the day, Chyna would end up wetting herself and I'd have to leave whatever I was doing to bring a change of clothes to wherever Missy was. And if I sent a change of clothes, she'd have *two* accidents and I'd still have to bring clean clothes.

Once or twice, Missy had taken Chyna up to the office of Todd Russaw, one of the producers she was writing songs for. Todd was executive-producing an album by a new R&B trio called 702. And Missy was writing songs for their project. And as soon as Missy and Todd got involved in a business conversation, Chyna walked up to Missy and told her she'd had an accident.

"I was like *damn*!" Missy told me that night. "I'm trying to convince this dude to cut my check and here go Chyna talking about she peed on herself!"

I shook my head. "I told you take her to the bathroom every hour!"

Missy laughed. "You mean every *half* hour!"

The next night, Todd ended up coming by my apartment to bring some paperwork for Missy.

Todd had a medium build with a caramel complexion, close-cropped haircut, and neatly trimmed mustache and beard. And there was something about his Adam's apple that was very familiar to me. When he came into the apartment, I was in the kitchen preparing dinner.

"Your little girl is a cutie," he said. "Even though she peed on my couch!"

I laughed. "I am so sorry!"

"It's all good. Don't worry about it. She's a sweetheart."

"I just realized where I know you from—you worked with Mike Bivins…"

"Yeah, we were there when you recorded 'You Used to Love Me.' I went back to LA and told everyone how hot that shit was."

"Thanks. I appreciate that."

Missy came out, and she and Todd went over some paperwork; I went back to preparing dinner. I was conscious of the fact that Todd was cute. More than cute, actually; he was very handsome. But there I was, married and pregnant, though I was clearly not really with Big at all. I also wasn't in a position to like anyone else. It definitely wasn't a good time for new romance. It was going to have to be all about motherhood and career for a while.

The next day, Missy and Chyna went out again. And once again, Chyna had an accident. Missy and I arranged to meet at a Gap clothing store near the studio where I was working.

As Missy and I rummaged through the racks to find things in her size, Chyna walked up to me with a strange look on her face.

"I lost my nickel, Mommy," she said.

"Okay, Chyna," I said, going through the racks and only half paying attention. "I'll give you another nickel later."

Chyna started coughing. "Missy, I lost my nickel in here," she said, pointing to her throat. Missy and I spun around and looked at Chyna. We bent down to her level.

"What do you mean you lost it in there? Do you mean you *swallowed* it?" Chyna nodded and coughed again. She was breathing, but there was clearly something lodged there.

"Oh shit," Missy said. "We have to get her to a hospital right now."

Missy and I hauled ass with Chyna out of that store and to the nearest hospital. Chyna was fine. They had to stick an instrument down her throat to take the nickel out. I was petrified but after a while Missy and I were able to laugh about the insanity of it all.

Even though Chyna gave me a good scare, I had actually dialed things down quite a bit at that time. My crew of people I trusted was getting smaller and smaller because of all the drama going on. And I felt especially vulnerable because I was pregnant. So all my senses were heightened and I was really tense.

I was so tense, in, fact, that I have to admit I continued to smoke weed during this time. It was hard for me to stop with all the stresses going on in my life. I know it was risky, and I felt so guilty about it. I'm sure I'll be judged for making that choice. But I was doing the best I could to keep myself together.

I even talked to a few older Jamaican folks to find out what the real risks could be.

"You and dat baby gwan be fine!" I heard over and over again from other folks who'd occasionally smoked marijuana during their pregnancies.

I'm not advocating this to anyone. I'm just being honest about what I was going through during a very difficult time in my life. I felt like the whole world was talking about me, judging me. It was an awful feeling. Especially since I hadn't knowingly done anything to deserve it. And I wanted to defend myself publicly—but I knew that anything I said would be twisted around and probably just make things worse.

I was all about getting my money straight at this point. One person who owed me money was Terry Dollars, the producer in LA I'd worked with. When I left LA after all the Tupac rumors started flying, he'd been stalling me. But I reached out once or twice to remind him that he owed me for the work I'd done.

I'd never come up with an exact fee. But I'd written several songs for the group. And Terry Dollars had actually scored a production deal with a major record label based at least in part on the fact that he was working with me.

We both knew that he owed me at least fifteen to twenty thousand. And I expected to collect it. I had been burned by 'Pac and I was on a mission to not let that happen again.

Before I really started trying to collect money from him, I'd introduced him to Missy, and she began also flying out to LA to work with his R&B trio. I'd sent word through Missy to him about getting my money. One day, I asked Missy if *she'd* ever gotten paid from him. She said she had. And that's when I hit the roof. This nigga was trying to stall me on a year-old bill, crying that he was broke? But he was somehow finding money to pay Missy?

I happened to be in Los Angeles when I found out that the dude was really not trying to pay me. I drove right out to the studio on Lankershim and Burbank.

As soon as I spotted the dude in the hallway of the studio, I didn't hold anything back.

"You owe me some money, nigga," I said. "And I want my shit right fucking *now*!"

"I told you I was waiting on some things to come through—"

"Fuck that!" I screamed. "Ain't no more waiting for shit!"

Terry Dollars didn't have much to say. I kept screaming on him, cursing him out, making a scene and not giving a damn about it.

I made a few calls to some of my peoples in LA to try to get someone to come and beat the dude's ass.

"You about to get fucked up if you don't get my money together," I told him.

Suddenly some chick was in my face. She said something about being Terry Dollars's sister. "Oh it ain't gon' be none of *that*," she said.

"You want to get in this?" I asked. "I don't even know you."

Then I saw Todd Russaw, the producer who was cool with Missy. He came down the hallway and got between us and then led the girl away, telling her to chill out. I continued my rampage, screaming and cursing on the producer and daring someone to stop me.

After Todd got rid of the producer's sister, he came back over to me. "Can you come sit in my car and just relax for a minute?"

"Hell no. I ain't relaxing for shit."

"Just for a minute," he urged. "Let's just talk for a second."

Even though he was obviously cool with the producer and his sister, I still agreed to hear him out.

"I know you're pissed off," he said. "But you gotta chill—"

"That nigga paid Missy! I'm the one who introduced them! He gotta pay me something...," I said.

Todd tried to calm me down. We ended up talking for a while in the car.

"I haven't seen you since the last time I was in New York," he said. "How've you been?

I looked out the window of the car. "I've been better," I said.

Todd nodded. "I saw your show at the House of Blues. It was *hot*."

I smiled. "Thanks. I appreciate that."

"Why are you rolling by yourself up here anyway?" Todd asked. "You think you just gonna shake people down and get your money from mu'fuckas?"

"It's the principle of the thing," I told him. "That shit is not right."

"I feel you," he said. "You gotta handle your business. I gotta say, I'm kinda impressed."

"Why?"

Todd smiled. "I'm saying. You got a lot of heart. Rolling up on dude like that."

I felt myself stifling a smile.

"I mean, look at you," he said, pointing to my outfit. "You come up here wearing a white pantsuit and high-heeled pumps. Trying to beat somebody up!"

"You right about that shit," I said.

Todd and I discovered we had a few friends in common and that we had a lot of the same taste in music and movies.

It was cool to meet someone who made me laugh, especially when I'd been so close to fighting just a few minutes before. It had been a long time since I'd been intimate with anyone. But I couldn't really think about Todd in that way. I was pregnant, not speaking to my future baby daddy, and trying to get my money straight. And those were the main things on my mind.

I never got my money from that dude. I had to chalk it up to experience again. Although I never stopped being angry about it, I couldn't continue to waste my energy on it when there was so much other stuff going on.

CHAPTER NINETEEN

Keeping Promises

*A*rare bright spot came in early September: The nominees for the Soul Train Lady of Soul Awards had been announced, and I was listed in several categories. Considering everything else going on at the time, I was happy to be recognized for my musical talent.

By this point, I was eight months' pregnant. I hadn't gained an inordinate amount of weight, but I still had slowed down quite a bit. I was performing here and there but I was beginning to stick closer to home, keep up with my doctor's appointments, and just take it easy as much as I could.

I was still quite in demand to perform my hit singles. My album had been certified gold, having sold over half a million copies. With all of the Tupac rumors still flying and me and Big not really speaking, I wasn't in the best space personally. But professionally, things were going really well.

Missy, who was still part of my crew and staying with me when she needed to, was beginning to also have some success in the music business.

One night, she and I were in the apartment hanging out with my cousin Candy, who was visiting from New Jersey, when my phone rang. It was Puff.

"Yo, Faye. Is that girl over there? The songwriter who be with you?"

"Missy? Yeah, she's here." I waved one arm to get Missy's attention while still talking to Puff.

"Tell her to come down to the studio. I got a project I need her to work on."

"Aiight, I'll let her know."

"Tell her to come *now*."

I hung up and went into the living room. "That was Puff. He wants you to come down to Daddy's House right now."

Missy's eyes widened and she bit down on her bottom lip. "Word? To work on music?"

"Yeah, I think he has a new singer down there he's working with."

"Okay. Let me get ready."

"Hurry up!" I said. "Get dressed and get the hell out of here."

Missy got dressed and gathered her brown paper bag packed with candy and her money and keys.

"Call me and tell me what happens," I told her. "And good luck, girl. This is *big*!"

Missy smiled. "Thanks. I'll call you later..."

About an hour later, my phone rang.

"Yo, Faith." It was Missy.

"What up, girl?"

"I'm at the studio," she said. "Your girl Kim is here..."

"Oh *word*?"

I got off the phone with Missy and got dressed.

"Let's go, Candy," I told my cousin. "I been waiting a long time for this."

I grabbed my keys and a purse. I knew I didn't have much time. I had no idea how long she would be there so I had to act fast. Candy and I took a cab to Daddy's House, Puff's recording studio.

"You look in every room and then yell out when you see that bitch," I told her.

We went to the front desk, and I told the receptionist I was there to see Missy. I was an artist on the label and I was very pregnant, so she let me in without even considering that it might be a security breach. Candy and I split up. I eased through the hallways, peeking in every studio room, and saw nothing.

I met back up with Candy and gave her my bag to hold while I cased the studio one last time.

Finally, I peeked through the window of a room near the back and saw a tiny woman bent over a notepad and paper. At first, I didn't recognize her. She had on a lot of makeup and looked much lighter. And she was wearing a longer weave than usual with a red spandex outfit. But it was her, for sure.

I ran up in the room and just jumped her, swinging and punching blindly with a pent-up anger I'd been holding on to for months.

"Yeah, bitch!" I screamed. "I told you I was gonna fuck you up!"

Puffy, Stevie J., one of his producers, and D-dot came scrambling from across the room.

"Faye, stop it!" Puff said, trying to pull me off Kim.

I kept swinging. Stevie J also tried to separate us. "Oh shit!" he said. "Faith, you wildin'!"

After a few minutes, they were able to get me off her. She dashed to the other side of the room and picked up a metal folding chair that I guess she was planning to hit me with. But it was all over so fast. I don't know if I marked her up. Or if I even got in a good punch. I can't lie, though: It felt good to finally honor my word. Before we left the studio, Puff came to the lobby to talk to me.

"Faith, are you *crazy*?" he asked me.

"I told her," I said. "I told that bitch I was gon' beat her ass."

Puff couldn't do anything but shake his head.

A few hours after I got home, Lucius my doorman called upstairs to tell me there was a rowdy group of girls looking to get upstairs to my apartment. I knew immediately what was going on.

"Kim's downstairs," I told Missy, who had come back to my apartment.

I had no intentions of going down there. I lived in a quiet upscale neighborhood, and I always carried myself very dignified when I was at home. Now of course, when I wanted to wild out, I would. But not at my house. Kim could stand there until the next morning as far as I was concerned. She could have a rematch if she wanted one. But it wasn't going to be at my crib.

Somehow, Kim got my home number and started calling the house directly. I didn't answer it. But Missy kept picking it up. I could hear Kim hurling insults through the phone.

"That's why your pussy smells like shit!" she screamed.

I just rolled my eyes. Missy would tell her I wasn't coming downstairs and then hang up. And Kim would call right back. I told Missy not to bother answering but she kept picking it up. I got the sense that she sort of liked being in the middle of all the drama.

After a while, Kim gave up and left. A few hours later I got a phone call from Big.

"Are you crazy?" he asked me.

"I told you I was gonna beat her ass," I said calmly.

"Faye. You are *pregnant*."

"I don't care."

"Yo. Ma. Can you chill?" Big asked.

"It's over now." I said. "And besides, I ain't even really get at her."

But I knew it wasn't quite yet over with Kim. I wasn't completely sure I'd gotten my point across.

And then just like that, I was able to switch over to my other side: the sensible R&B singer who crooned love songs and remained polished and professional in public. After the Kim drama, I was really looking forward to attending the Soul Train Lady of Soul Awards. I didn't think I had any chance of winning the awards I was nominated for. I was up against Mariah Carey for Best Female R&B Album, and she'd been cleaning up at every awards ceremony that year.

But the date for the awards drew closer, and I still hadn't heard anything from my record label about traveling to LA. It's customary for your record label to pay for your travel and other expenses if you've been nominated for these kinds of awards. It's good publicity for the label if you win, and it helps to sell whatever product you have out at the time. But weeks went by and I wasn't hearing from anyone.

Finally, I got a call from Cheryl. "Jeff called me," she said, referring to the general manager of Bad Boy.

"What's going on?" I asked.

"He said it wasn't appropriate for you to be at the awards..."

"But I'm *nominated* for four awards!"

"I know," Cheryl said. "He said because you were pregnant or whatever..."

"I'm a grown woman! I can't have a baby?"

"He said they're not paying for you to go out there."

"I'm going anyway," I said.

"You really want to spend all that money going out there?"

"I have to!" I said. "I worked hard on my album. I'm being recognized for it and I'm going. Period."

I was eight months' pregnant and huge. It felt like the whole world was whispering about me. And I was still going out to Los Angeles on my own dime. If Bad Boy didn't want to support me, I'd have to support myself.

I thought it was really foul that my own record label didn't want to support me at the awards. I had an album out and I was being recognized for it. It just reinforced the alienation I'd been feeling ever since I moved from Brooklyn and refused to go on that promotional tour.

I felt like I was the First Lady of Bad Boy in name only. But before I was ever signed to Bad Boy, before I ever got married, before all of the music and the videos and the drama, I was a singer. And I was going to represent for my family at home in Newark, for my daughter, Chyna, for my unborn child, and for myself.

A few days before I left for Los Angeles, I got a call from B.I.G. "Yo, you heard?"

I was immediately on edge. Big sounded shaken up, and that was unusual for him.

"Heard what?" I asked. "What's wrong?"

"Tupac got shot out in Vegas."

I didn't know what to say. Of course I had nothing good to say about Tupac, though I knew he had once been a good friend of Big's. But Big seemed more worried about safety.

"You think something's gonna happen out there?" I asked.

"I don't know, Faye," he said. "But this shit is fucked up."

I could tell that Big was crying through the phone, and that shook me up even more. That wasn't Big's style. So I knew things were really getting serious. I turned on the television and watched the reports of 'Pac's shooting in Las Vegas. On every channel, the newscasters were saying the same thing: *The rapper is expected to survive.*

CHAPTER TWENTY

Jagged Edge

nd the winner is... Faith Evans!"

You know how people who win an award sometimes look like they're surprised and look around like, *Who me?*

Well, that was me on the night of September 9, 1996. I could not believe I'd beaten out Mariah Carey to win the award for best R&B album. I couldn't even hear the applause around me because I was so pent up with emotion.

I felt like after everything I'd gone through, I was at least finally being recognized for what really mattered—my talent. I waddled my pregnant self onto the stage and didn't know what to say.

"I...I want to thank my daughter Chyna and thank you everybody!"

I don't even remember what else I said. But I know it probably made no sense. And then, just a few minutes later, my name was called again, when it was announced that I'd won for Best New Artist.

When I took the stage to accept my second award, I saw a familiar face in the crowd grinning at me from ear to ear. It was Todd, standing in the middle of the aisle. I'd seen him here and there occasionally since the day in Los Angeles when I'd confronted the producer who owed me money. He was always really cool. He always had weed and he was just laid-back and cool. At a time when there was all of this bicoastal tension, he didn't seem like he was tripping off that shit at all. He was a loyal West Coast dude. But he seemed just as comfortable around the grimiest Brooklyn dudes or a Jersey girl like me.

Winning at the Soul Train Lady of Soul Awards should have been a celebratory, triumphant moment for me. But after the show, I still kept a low profile. I hadn't walked the red carpet at the start of the ceremony, and I didn't do any press afterward. I knew no one would congratulate me on my awards. They would only ask me about the so-called East Coast–West Coast rivalry, my husband, and my baby. I wasn't trying to answer any of it.

There was an afterparty in an airplane hangar in Santa Monica. I went with Toni but didn't mingle much with anyone else. There was thick tension in the air. All the talk was about Tupac being shot just a few days before and whether or not he was going to make it. And I know people were talking about how I was connected to the whole mess.

As I stood with Toni apart from the rest of the crowd, I saw Todd. When he spotted me, he came over to where we were standing. "Congratulations!" he said, giving me a hug. "How you feeling?"

"I'm hanging in there," I said.

Todd and I, along with Toni and one of Todd's friends, ended up sitting on a fire escape at the hangar, talking, laughing, and smoking weed for a long time. It was a nice but all-too-brief break from the craziness.

Something clicked inside me as I stood with Todd that night. I wasn't sure if I was ready to admit it. But I liked him. He made me laugh when everything else in my life was super-serious. He made me feel safe in a place like Los Angeles, when things were tense there. And he never hesitated to let me know that he appreciated my work.

But just as I was ready to tell Todd that I was starting to feel him, I came home from Los Angeles and heard the news that rocked everyone to the core.

Tupac was dead. I was shocked like everyone else. All the reports had kept saying he was expected to live. And he didn't.

At this point, everyone started freaking out. Who killed 'Pac? No one knew. Or no one was saying anything. Why was he killed? Collectively, the entire West Coast whipped their necks and started pointing fingers at the East. Big and Puff were beefing with Tupac when he was killed. There were all kinds of rumors about me having a relationship with 'Pac, which some people were saying would give someone a motive. It was just an awful mess.

I can't say I was mourning Tupac's death. I knew it was an unfortunate thing. But this was someone who'd lied on me publicly and had so many people looking at me crazy. It was hard for me to feel what everyone else was feeling.

I did feel for Big. He seemed shell-shocked about the whole thing.

"Something ain't right, Faye," Big told me.

"I know. What's going to happen?"

"I don't know all that," he said. His voice was low and small. "But something is not right, Faye. That was my nigga right there. Shit got fucked up somewhere along the way. But that was my nigga."

I started to feel really paranoid. I was only a month away from my due date and I began to tighten up my circle of friends even more; I didn't travel far without security. Every time the phone rang, I felt anxious. On the Tuesday after Tupac died, I happened to call Mark Pitts, Big's manager, to get some information about a tour date.

"You heard about Big?" Mark asked. "He was in an accident."

"What! What kind of accident? Is he okay?"

"It was a car accident," Mark said. "He's in the hospital."

"When? Where?"

Mark seemed to hesitate just a bit. "Last night," he said. "He was on his way home. Cease was driving."

"Is he okay?"

"He will be. Tiffany was with him, too. She's hurt..."

I fought the urge to go straight to the hospital. I knew there would probably be a ton of people there. And since Tiffany had been there, I just thought it would be best if I stayed put. I told Mark to keep me posted on Big's progress and to tell me when I could visit him.

When Big was transferred to the Kessler Rehabilitation Center in New Jersey, I went to see him. He was laid up in the bed looking vulnerable but not necessarily in pain. He'd broken his leg in two places and couldn't walk. All the extra weight he had was making it harder for him to heal.

"What's up, Few," he said. "Finally came to see your husband..." I looked at the wall next to his bed, where there were cards signed by Tiffany on the bedside table.

"You've been doing okay," I said. "Looks like you ain't been lonely."

"You ready to have this baby?"

"Are you?"

"Hell yeah, I'm ready..."

A nurse came in to give him some medication. Big pointed at me.

"This my wife right here," he said with pride. "'Bout to have my baby."

The nurse looked very confused. I guess she'd seen Tiffany up there visiting and was a bit perplexed to see a different woman—and a pregnant one at that—being introduced as his wife.

The car accident forced Big to slow down at the same time that I had to slow down, too. I didn't visit him often because I wasn't trying to run into Tiffany. But I called to check up on him and kept in touch with his peoples, too.

Big and I weren't together anymore and I was getting more and more signs that he'd moved on with Tiffany. I saw them in pictures together in the press. I heard that he'd dubbed her Charli Baltimore and planned to get her rap career off the ground. I'll admit that it stung a bit to know that he was moving on — publicly. I heard that she had practically moved into the house in Teaneck. I guess he was really feeling her. Still, I understood the need to move on because I was trying to do the same.

By this time, I realized that I liked Todd. And we were talking on the phone and hanging out occasionally.

We'd both been playing it cool. Until one night, right after I visited Big in the hospital. I was in my bedroom after putting Chyna to sleep, watching television and drifting off to sleep. The telephone rang, and I rolled over to check the caller ID. I recognized the Los Angeles number and picked up on the next ring.

"Hey, Faith. This is Todd."

I could hear a lot of commotion in the background. "Where are you?"

"We just left the club," he shouted, talking over what sounded like a large crowd.

"It's four o'clock in the morning here…"

"I know," said Todd. "But I gotta tell you something."

"I'm listening."

"I'm really feeling you. I know you got a lot going on right now. But I just needed you to know that."

"I feel the same way."

"I mean, you might feel like you can't go there right now…"

"I don't know what I'm doing right now."

"I just wanted you to know how I felt," said Todd.

I'd known for several months that I was feeling Todd. And I was thrilled to hear that he felt the same. Now, of course I knew he was calling me from the club after a late night. But it was still all good. I knew it was sincere. Even if he needed a drink or three to get up the nerve to tell me how he really felt.

We talked for a few minutes and then we promised to talk more when I had free time. I was a bit overwhelmed. I liked Todd so much and I was conflicted about how to handle things. Finding yourself falling in love when you're just about ready to deliver a baby isn't the ideal. I hoped that Todd was patient. Because I had to get ready for my newest arrival, and that would take all the energy I had.

A few weeks after Big was released from the hospital, I was at the hospital preparing to have my baby. I'd gone for a checkup, and the doctor told me I was leaking amniotic fluid. He told me to go home to pack a bag and then come right back. I called Big and asked him to meet me there.

"What are we going to name this baby?" I asked Big after I was settled into my room, waiting for the drugs they'd given me to induce labor to kick in.

"I don't know...," Big said. "Give me some ideas."

"Well, if it's a boy, I think we should name him after you."

Big made a face. "Christopher George Letore Wallace? That's too long. Plus I ain't naming my son after some father I ain't even know."

"Call your mom," I said. "See what she says."

Big reached for the phone and called his mom in Brooklyn. "Ma, we need a name for this baby."

Then I saw him nodding. He covered the mouthpiece. "She said what about Charles?"

"Charles? Um... What do you think?"

Big shook his head and went back to the phone.

"Nah, Ma. Not Charles. What else?"

Big got off the phone after a few minutes.

"She said she likes Christopher," he said, shrugging.

"I like it, too," I told Big. "We don't have to add all the middle names."

"Christopher is cool," Big said. "But we definitely need something else for the middle name. Something hot..."

We tossed around a few middle names and nothing seemed to

work. Big wanted something strong. Something that represented someone he respected.

"Jordan." he finally said. "Then we can call him CJ."

A few hours later, my labor began. After the horrors I endured having Chyna, I told the doctor I wanted a real epidural, and he promised me I could even have two if I felt it wear off.

Just about everyone from Junior M.A.F.I.A. was out in the waiting room, in addition to my friend Cheryl, my mom, and several of our friends. It was insane how loud and raucous it was. I thought for sure they were going to kick some of our people out. When it was time for me to start pushing, the doctors said I could only have one other person in the room with me. My mom said she really wanted to be there. I asked Big what he wanted to do.

"Sorry," Big said, shaking his head. "Your moms gotta go. I can't miss this."

I knew my mom would be disappointed but she'd have to understand. My husband took his place right next to me, still in his wheelchair, and watched as I pushed our child into the world.

"It's a boy!" I heard the doctor say.

I was weak and worn out. And I heard all the commotion surrounding me as they cleaned up the baby and they brought him to me.

When I took my first look at my little boy, I could not believe how much he looked like his father. He even had what looked like a lazy eye! And his face was like a half grimace and half scowl that was also pure Big. The only difference was that he was much lighter. Other than that, he was a dead ringer for his dad. Big held CJ in his lap, and the three of us shared a quiet moment together before all of our friends and family began to file in to get a look at our new child.

"He looks like a Puerto Rican Biggie!" Cease said. And everyone in the crowded room began to laugh.

After I returned home to my apartment on West End Avenue, I just wanted to stay put for a while. I'd been on the road, traveling and working, for almost two straight years. It was time for me to take stock of my life and determine how I was going to live it.

Several people in the industry sent flowers and gifts, which I thought was nice. And there was a constant stream of visitors through the apartment to see CJ. Looking back, I realize most of them were just trying to be nosy. Some of them were sincere. But others just wanted to see if CJ looked like Big.

I was between cars at the time that CJ was born. So I ended up taking the train out to Brooklyn to visit with Ms. Wallace, who was in love with her new grandson. She thought he was adorable. Honestly, I thought he was kind of mean looking. Although as the days wore on, he started to lose the lazy eye.

Big and I settled into a routine that felt like it was working for us. We lived separately and avoided the prospect of divorce. In one of our heated discussions, probably after I found out about Kim, I might have thrown out the word *divorce*. But it was never a serious discussion. And we began to have standing family time on Friday nights. Whenever Big was in town, he'd come over with Cease and a bunch of other folks. I would cook fried chicken or pork chops and macaroni and cheese or my famous lasagna. No one can really get with my lasagna. It's that good. I'd make a pan of it sometimes and bring it to whatever studio Big was working out of and people would go crazy for it. I learned the recipe by watching my mom make it.

Big was basically living with Tiffany at his house in Teaneck. And I was pretty sure he was still messing with Kim, too. I wasn't necessarily happy about the way things were falling into place, but I was beginning to accept it. A few times, after dinner was over on Friday night, all of the guys would leave and Big would stick around.

The first time or two this happened, we ended up having sex. It was so easy to fall into that routine because we knew each other so well. But at some point, I felt like I needed to move on. I wanted to live my own life, too, and that would include dating.

After I had CJ, Todd and I continued talking on the phone and seeing each other whenever he was in New York. I can't say that I was sneaking around. But I will say I wasn't trying to let Big know that there was someone else on the horizon. I knew that would not sit well with him. When he just saw me talking to my friend Dave, that poor guy ended up getting beat up in the middle of the street. I didn't want to expose Todd to that kind of drama.

Todd and I talked about the situation occasionally but didn't dwell on it. When we got a chance to be together, which wasn't as often as I would have liked, we just enjoyed each other's company. Very soon after CJ was born, Todd and I took that first step and made love one night in his hotel room when he was in town on business.

Now, this was not the first time I'd had sex with someone else since me and Big had gotten married. There had been the NBA guy and the producer in LA. And I'd had a brief encounter with a singer in a group who shall remain nameless.

But this was the first time it felt like it was someone I could really bond with. Which was kind of scary. Because Big was still a looming force in my life and I could tell that he wasn't going to just let me go easily—even if he was ready to move on.

One night, after our weekly Friday-night dinner, Big moved in close to me. Chyna and CJ were asleep in their bedroom. But still, I wasn't going to let Big take me down that path. Todd was in town and I was actually planning on visiting his hotel that night or having him come over.

"Isn't it time for you to get home?" I asked.

"Nah, I'm good...," he said.

"Seriously, Big. I'm not going there with you," I said, moving away.

"Word? Aiight. That's cool, Faye."

Even though I was strong enough to stop sleeping with him, I wasn't yet bold enough to truly move on with someone else and let him know about it. That wasn't going to be easy. Big definitely held me to a different standard. He never came right out and said I couldn't date anyone else. But I just knew he wasn't trying to hear that. And then, because of the whole Tupac mess, I was self-conscious about being connected to any other guy. There was so much being said about me that although I had every right to date, I felt like I had to choose my moves very carefully.

Big and I were doing this weird dance. He was out there doing whatever. I was trying to move on but I felt like he didn't really want me to. A few weeks after I rebuffed Big's advances, Todd came to town again and I insisted on going by to see him at his hotel on 49th and Broadway. I left my apartment and jumped in a cab.

As soon as I walked into Todd's room, my cell phone rang.

"Yo," said Big. "Where you *at*, Faye?"

I stopped dead in my tracks. "I had to um, run out...to the store," I said quickly.

"Aiight, Faye," he said. "I'm at your house...waiting for you..."

"I'm on my way," I said.

I had to cut my visit with Todd very short and get my ass back home. I could've told Big the truth. But I guess I just wasn't ready to have that conversation.

This is when I noticed a big change in Big's personality. It had happened very gradually over the two years or so I'd known him. Sometimes when he came by the house, I had to just shake my head.

The Big I met, the grimy, Timberland-wearing dude who was nervous about rocking the silk short-sleeved shirt I once bought him, had completely transformed. This was a guy who used to have to cut the backs out of his shoes so they could fit. The guy I used to buy clothes for all the time. And now he was wearing custom-made suits and a five-thousand-dollar watch. This was the man who refused to go more than a few miles from Brooklyn. Now he was traveling the world.

Sometimes, I'd even catch him checking out that watch a little too closely. "Nigga, you need to stop," I'd have to tell him. He was truly moving from "ashy to classy," and it was kind of funny to see the transformation.

I was transforming, too. My entire pregnancy had been full of stress. And I felt like no one really had my back in the music industry. From my husband to my record label, I was alone. I had taken the brunt of all the Tupac stuff and I felt like there was much more going on back then that no one told me to be careful about.

One Friday night, after our family dinner, I decided I really needed to know once and for all why Big would make a song like "Brooklyn's Finest" and pile onto the rumors about me and Tupac.

I was washing the dishes and Big was nursing a glass of Hennessy and Coke in my living room.

"What you thinking about, Few?" Big said.

I looked up from the kitchen. "Nothing."

"You lying," he said. His voice was a bit slurred from the cognac. "I know when you thinking about something..."

I finished drying the dishes and then came out into the living room. I sat on the sofa across from Big, folded my hands, and put them in my lap.

"Big, that song you did on Jay-Z's album..."

Big threw his head back on the sofa and put his hand over his face. "Awww, Faye, come on. That's over."

I shook my head. "As long as I can go into a record store and buy that album and listen to that song, it's not over." I gestured toward CJ and Chyna's room. "As long as CJ can turn on the radio and hear that song, it's not over."

Big kept his head back on the sofa. "I feel you, Ma."

"So why? Why would you play me out like that?"

Big finally lifted his head and looked straight at me. His eyes were heavy-lidded and glassy. I couldn't tell if he looked so pained because of the alcohol or the subject matter — or both.

"Yo, Ma. That was fucked up on my part. I ain't even gon' lie," he said.

I looked down at my hands and let out a sigh of relief. I really needed to hear that.

"That night, I was drunk as hell. I was under pressure. Niggas was talking shit in the streets…"

I nodded. Big continued talking. His voice actually started to crack and a few tears came out of his eyes.

"I'm sorry, Faye. That shit was wrong. I'm real sorry about that. For real."

I went over to Big and nestled my head into his shoulder. I was still upset that this song would be out there forever. But I did appreciate that he was man enough to admit that it was wrong.

While I enjoyed having Big coming over to my apartment in Manhattan, I began looking for a house to buy in New Jersey. The apartment on West End had served me well. But I was ready to get out of Manhattan. Now that I was a mother of two, I wanted a calmer atmosphere and space for the children to spread out. I knew that I was going to always make family a priority. And it was going to be up to me to make that happen.

As much as I wanted to live a normal life, trouble still seemed to find me no matter where I was.

Shortly after CJ was born, I flew down to Atlanta. Puff was celebrating his birthday by having a big celebration at a club. I was just starting to recover from giving birth and I needed a break. I went with Cheryl and of course took security with me. I checked into the Hyatt hotel and immediately exhaled. I was looking forward to a few days of just decompressing and de-stressing. I knew Big would be at the party, too. But I came with Cheryl and planned to just chill with her and not get wrapped into whatever Big was into. If I saw him, cool. If not, that was cool, too. I wasn't going to go looking for him.

As soon as I was settled into the room, I got a phone call on my cell from Todd.

"I was just checking in on you," he said. "How are you?"

"I'm doing good! But I'm out of town."

"Really? Me, too," he said. "I'm in Atlanta."

"So am I."

"Word? Where are you staying?"

"I'm at the Hyatt. Where are you?"

Todd laughed out loud. "I'm at the Hyatt, too. What floor?"

"I'm on the third floor," I said.

He laughed again. "Open your door," he said.

I went to my door, opened, it and peeked outside. And there was Todd, down the hallway, with his head sticking out of his own room. We laughed and talked for a few minutes, marveling at the coincidence, and then made plans to hang out at Puff's party later that evening.

I went with Cheryl and a security guard to the party. I had a new outfit—a beige DKNY skirt suit and a pair of chocolate-brown Gucci pumps. I looked more like a record executive than an artist. Before I'd left New York, I experimented with a new hair color. It was in a dark bob with blond streaks. I felt good and confident and ready to have a fun evening.

As soon as we got to the party, we saw Damion and his friend Lisa, whom we all called "the Mall" because she was known to be an expert shoplifter. We were all ushered to the VIP area upstairs. I wasn't really trying to sit up in VIP. But before I could protest, I found myself face-to-face with Big, who was sitting at a table looking like some kind of king, surrounded by a court of supporters.

"What up, Few?" he asked, with a smile on his face.

"Hey, Big…"

He patted the seat next to him. "Have a seat, Few…"

"You sure? I was gonna walk around for a minute and maybe—"

"I said have a *seat,* Few."

Big was smiling. But it was clear that for whatever reason, he wasn't going to take no for an answer and he wanted me sitting right next to him. So I sat.

Soon various celebrities and fans started packing the club. A line of folks snaked past Big's table, giving him handshakes and pounds and shout-outs.

It was like me and Big were a king and queen on a royal throne, greeting our subjects on an official receiving line. Except I wasn't quite sure why he wanted me there. I hadn't felt like his queen in a long time. But that night, he really seemed like he wanted to show me off. I just kept a glass of champagne in my hand and got tipsy as quickly as I could.

Big couldn't walk around because he was still using a cane from the car accident. And he wasn't letting me walk around, either. I felt some sense of pride. After everything we'd been through, Big still loved me and wanted everyone at this club to know it. He kept his arm around me and would lean in close to talk to me here and there.

At one point, Lil' Kim came walking toward the table. I hadn't seen her since the fight at the studio. She walked up to us and just gave Big a sharp look. Her face was tight, and she was definitely about to say something.

"Is there a problem?" Big asked her.

Kim didn't say anything.

"Well, move it along," he said.

Kim walked by and then looked at me. I just gave her a tiny smile as she left.

A few minutes later, another group of folks began to walk by Big's table. I looked up and found myself face-to-face with Todd.

Big still had his arm draped across my shoulders and I sat frozen in my seat. I opened my mouth to speak but didn't say anything. Todd looked a bit confused. I'd just seen him at the hotel, and I don't think he expected to see me hugged up with Big. I know he knew we were still married. But I'd told him we weren't together and now there we were...together. It was all so awkward. I didn't say anything, although I wanted to, and I just hoped I'd have an opportunity to explain at some point.

The next night, I went to Club 112 for another event. There was a long line when I pulled up to the entrance. We told the driver to let me and my friend Coco out at the corner. We went over to a restaurant near the club entrance in order to not draw attention to ourselves while we tried to decide if we were going into the club or not. As we stood there, a police officer approached us.

"You need to move," he said.

"I will," I said. "I'm just waiting—"

"You don't need to wait for anything. You need to move right *now*."

I opened my mouth to explain why I couldn't just wait on line with everyone else but before I could say another word, the cop was on me, twisting my arms around my back to forcibly remove me from the area.

Immediately, I felt the intense pain from having my arm twisted and I screamed out in pain. "Let me go!" I pleaded.

The officer continued to push me and the next thing I knew, I was falling backward through the plate glass of the restaurant I'd been standing in front of. I felt an intense, stabbing pain as the glass broke and shards of it stabbed me in my back.

To add insult to injury, the officer just grabbed me up and continued marching me down the street and through the entrance to the club while my back bled profusely.

"I am hurt!" I kept screaming over and over. "Please don't let me die." I was in so much pain. I didn't know where exactly I was wounded, and I really feared that I might have life-threatening injuries. I had just had two epidurals in my back when I delivered CJ, so that area was already sensitive.

I was arrested and charged with battery. The officer claimed that I attacked him and resisted arrest. I was taken to Grady Memorial Hospital in Atlanta—known to the residents as Shady Grady's because of their spotty treatment.

And there I was, handcuffed to a bed at Shady Grady's with shards of glass in my back, just weeks after giving birth. I couldn't do anything but cry. After the surgeons removed the shards from my back and stitched me up, I was taken to a holding cell in jail. Puff sent someone to bail me out, and I went to Big's hotel room. By this time, people had been hearing about the incident and began calling Big's room to find out if I was okay.

"She up here smoking a blunt," Big told someone who called. "She aiight."

I was okay on the surface. But deep inside, I was in a daze. I'd come down to Atlanta to relax. And I ended up seriously injured. And in jail. If trouble were money, I'd be a millionaire.

I went back home to recuperate from my injuries. And over the next few weeks, I continued to have horrible pains. I normally heal very quickly, and it was very disturbing to continue feeling so much pressure and poking in my lower back. Three weeks after I returned from Atlanta, Cheryl came by my place to check my wounds. She'd been coming over almost every day to change the dressings and see if things were healing. And they weren't.

At that time, I'd met a massage therapist from Georgia named Stephanie. She'd become a good friend and she ended up massaging my back and easing out tiny bits of glass that had been left behind. Stephanie and I had not known each other very long at that point. But she would become a lifelong friend that I'm still very close with today. I just spoke to Stephanie recently and she reminded me that when I was in the hospital that night, I wasn't allowed to have any visitors since I was under arrest—so she lied and said she was my sister. She also told me something I didn't know: Puff had come to the hospital as soon as he heard what happened and was in the waiting room with everyone else, to hear how I was doing.

Weeks later, Cheryl ended up driving me to the emergency room at a hospital in Hackensack, New Jersey, because I was still in a lot of pain. Sure enough, the doctors at Shady Grady's had left several pieces of glass in my back; I had to have surgery *again* to get them removed. So I had a second set of stitches underneath the first.

I got a keepsake from my surgery: a jar with all the glass inside. It served as an interesting reminder of how jagged my life had become.

CHAPTER TWENTY-ONE

The Beginning of the End

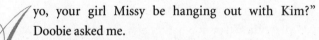yo, your girl Missy be hanging out with Kim?" Doobie asked me.

"Nah. They not cool," I told him.

"I don't know, Faye. I think she be hanging with her. My boy told me he saw them popping bottles at some club."

I thought about it. Missy had really become part of my inner circle. I had named her CJ's godmother, and she hung out with Chyna all the time. She had practically lived at my place before she started living mostly out of hotels when she really begin working steadily. Would she be hanging with one of the few people I didn't fuck with? I couldn't see it.

"Nah, they ain't cool," I said.

Doobie shrugged. "I don't know, Faye. Think you better double-check that."

The next time Missy called the apartment, I asked her flat-out. "You be hanging out with Kim?"

"Hell no," she said. "You know I ain't friends with her. I am trying to do a song with her, though..."

I nodded. My friend Doobie had probably heard about them in

the studio together and thought they were friends. I didn't mind at all if Missy was trying to work with Kim professionally. But it would have been kind of weird if she was hanging out with her socially, too.

About a week after that phone call, Missy called me again and asked me to bring Chyna and CJ to the Rihga Royal Hotel, where she was staying. It was early in the morning and I hadn't gotten the kids officially ready yet. But she begged me to just bring them anyway. My friend Rufus, who had originally introduced me to Missy, was at my apartment and helped me get the kids packed up then went with me to Missy's hotel room. When we arrived, she was on the phone.

We got the kids settled in the living area of the hotel and waited for Missy to finish her call.

"Yeah, I can be there at six," Missy was saying to someone. "But wait. Hold on. I have another call."

Missy clicked over to her other line and began talking and laughing with someone. Then she went back to her original call.

"Yeah, I'm back," she said. "That was Lil' Kim ... she'll be there, too."

Me and Rufus exchanged a look but didn't say anything. Missy got off the phone, and we all talked briefly. I showed her where all of CJ and Chyna's things were and then left her hotel room with Rufus.

"Did you hear what she said on the phone?" Rufus asked. "She was talking to Lil' Kim."

I thought about what Doobie said about seeing Missy and Kim together in the clubs.

"I asked Missy if she was cool with her and she said no."

"Maybe it was something work-related?" Rufus asked.

"Maybe..."

I had to run a few errands and Rufus was planning to go to the studio, so we said our good-byes. Rufus ended up in the studio with Missy. He called me up later that evening, very upset.

"I think something funny is going on with Missy," he said.

"What's wrong?"

"I think she was talking crazy about you, something about Chyna's hair."

"But she's the one who told me to bring them over first thing in the morning. I didn't have time to do her hair."

"I'm just saying. I'm the one who introduced her to you. I would hate for her to try to play you out."

"Why is she tripping?" I asked Rufus.

"I don't know. But you need to start thinking about who she might have around Chyna and CJ."

I knew that Missy had to be immediately dismissed from my circle. I didn't call her and tell her anything. She was just cut off in my mind.

And honestly, I didn't even plan to hold a grudge. Some friendships can be fleeting. I was going to have to tighten my circle — again.

Big and I were on the phone occasionally. Friday nights he still came over for dinner. And a few times he made it clear that he wanted to spend the night, and I had to send him home instead.

I still loved him. But I wasn't sure how he felt about me and what he wanted to do. Or if I should just move on.

As Christmas 1996 neared, Big was calling and visiting more often. "I want you and the kids to come spend Christmas with me," he said.

"We'll be there," I told him.

Big had been sending off vibes to me that I couldn't really pick up on. I was feeling like he really wanted me back but I wasn't sure. He was inviting me over to spend the holidays but was that just for the kids? He told me to make sure I was there on Christmas morning.

"Oh. You gonna have your other women outta there by then?" I asked.

"Whatever," he said. "Stop playing. Just be here."

"I'll be there," I said.

I was very curious. I knew he had just left the studio that night with Kim. I assumed Tiffany was at his house. I wondered how he was going to maneuver all that.

I don't know what got into my head. But I decided that I needed to know once and for all what Big was really trying to do. On that night before Christmas, I drove to Big's house on a mission to find out where I really stood.

The security guard at the gate just waved me in when I pulled up. It was Christmas Eve and she'd seen me come into the complex with the kids, so I guess she didn't think anything of it.

I parked in the rear of Big's town house and walked up to the garage. It was locked. I hadn't been over to Big's house a whole lot but I did know that you could jiggle the garage door a certain way and unlock it.

I got into the garage, where there was an elevator that would take me to both floors of Big's duplex. There I was, rocking a black skully cap and a heavy goose-down jacket, tiptoeing into the elevator and pressing the button to go up to the second floor, where his bedroom was located.

I can't believe how bold I was. I knew all his boys were probably there. And anyone in there could have shot me on sight, thinking I was an intruder. I moved slowly, tiptoeing through the house silently.

I got to Big's bedroom door, turned the knob, and went inside. As soon as I saw a small lump next to Big's large frame, I flew into a rage, ran over to the side of the bed, and pulled back the covers. I grabbed some chick out of the bed and started beating her ass. At some point, the chick's wig came off in my hand: It was a short, cropped wig. I stopped throwing punches for a minute to get a good look at the chick I was beating up. It *was* Lil' Kim.

She was completely butt-naked, yelling as I pushed her around the room.

"So you not fucking her, right?" I screamed at Big. "Yeah, you not messing with her anymore, right?"

When they heard all the commotion, Cease, D-Roc, and Gutter came running into the room.

"Oh shit!" they yelled in unison. "It's Faye! How the hell she get in here?"

Big sat up in bed and pointed at Kim, who was standing in a corner of the room, trying to cover her naked body with her hands while I was still yelling at Big.

"Yo, get her outta here," Big said. They led Kim out of the room, and she screamed and cursed the whole way.

It was absolutely crazy in that house. Kim was naked and being led somewhere to get dressed. I was still screaming on Big. Damion, Cease, and Gutter were laughing in amazement that I would be so bold. And Big looked like he was just too through with all of us.

He sat up in bed, shaking his head. Kim left the house and I stayed, talking to Big about why he couldn't be honest with me about her.

"I thought it was all about Tiffany?" I asked. "You still messing with Kim, too?" Big had nothing to say.

I have to say I actually felt some pity for Kim. Big had a wife, and she settled for messing with him. Then he started dating Tiffany and Big had a wife *and* a mistress. And Kim still settled for being the *other* other woman. It seemed pretty sad to settle for that.

When I left a few hours later to get the kids, I noticed that Kim had taken a key to my Land Cruiser and scratched up my entire car, from the hood to the back bumper.

Even though we ended up having sex that day, at that point I decided I was 100 percent through. I was not going to be a ride-or-die chick, always going to any lengths to show Big how I felt. I was the mother of his child and his wife. But I was going to have to let go emotionally if I wanted to move on and live my life. I couldn't be running around after him, continually kicking ass and taking names. I had to carry myself like a grown woman.

I started over the very next day. It was Christmas morning and I went back to Big's house like nothing had happened. I brought CJ and Chyna, and Ms. Wallace came with T'yanna, and we all had a wonderful family day. Chyna and T'yanna couldn't get enough of hanging all over Big, begging him to throw them in the air or smothering him with hugs. CJ, only two months old, watched everything going on like he was in awe.

It was actually a great day—considering all the drama from the night before. I loved seeing Big with the kids. His bond with T'yanna was very strong. She had him wrapped around her little finger. Although Chyna was not his biological child, she called him Daddy, and he treated her like a princess. And while CJ was too young to really understand the concept of a father, Big kept the baby in his lap whenever he could.

As I watched Big interacting with the kids, I thought about how we were going to move forward, raising children together, even if we weren't a couple. I thought about how I was in the process of moving to my own house in New Jersey; I was sure that was going to help. I would be far enough away to have my own space, but still able to get into the city when I needed to.

Moving was going to be a good opportunity for me to cut deadweight and once again tighten my inner circle of friends to just the people who were loyal to me and vice versa.

I wanted to turn over a new leaf and shed the drama. But before I started fresh, I did slash two tires on Lil' Kim's brand-new Lexus truck when I saw it parked outside the Bad Boy offices a few weeks after she keyed my car. I felt like she had that one coming.

Soon after I moved into my new house, my girl Toni was visiting from Los Angeles and helping me to get unpacked and organized. She answered the phone for me when it rang.

"It's Missy," she said.

I closed my eyes, shook my head, and didn't open my mouth. I did not hold anything against Missy—I really didn't. But it felt like she was trying to play both sides of the fence. She wanted to be cool with me and with Kim. Which would be fine—if she'd been honest about it. She was the one who had let me know Kim was at the studio so I could confront her! And then weeks later, they're painting the town red? It just didn't sit well with me. What would be next? I let her take my children out. Would she have them around Kim, too? That kind of thing just made me shut it down.

"Um, hey, Missy," I heard Toni saying. "I don't think she's here right now..."

I sucked my teeth and continued unwrapping my dishes from one of the boxes. "You ain't gotta lie," I said. "I'm sitting right here. But I don't talk to phony people."

"Missy...I'll tell her you called. Right. I understand...Hold on a second..."

Toni held the phone out to me.

"She sounds like she's about to cry. She said she really wants to talk to you."

I shook my head. "No thank you. I'm busy..."

Toni got Missy off the phone and came into my kitchen, where I was putting away my dishes in the new cabinets.

"She sounded really upset," Toni said. "She knows that you're upset about the Kim stuff."

"I don't even have the time or energy to deal with that," I said. "I've got to get my own act together. I'm not fucking with just anyone for the sake of having a friend. I got enough friends."

"Speaking of friends," Toni said. "Where's your husband?"

"In Los Angeles..."

"Is that safe? Since 'Pac died, it's been crazy," she said.

"I know."

Around the same time that I moved, Big finished recording his sophomore album, *Life After Death,* and went out to LA to add some finishing touches and do some press and promotion.

Big should not have been in LA for any extended period of time. I have to just put that out there. If he had business to take care of, he should have done it and come back to New York. It wasn't a safe place to be at that time. And this is not something I'm saying in hindsight. I felt like that then.

When Big would call to check on me and the kids, I'd constantly ask him when he was coming back to New York.

"I don't know," he would say. "I got stuff to do out here..."

"But you've been out there for over a month," I'd say.

"I know...I'm ready to come home."

"Then you should," I said.

Big just sighed. "You coming out here for the Soul Train Awards?" he asked me.

"I might be out there for work," I said. "But I don't know when."

As I prepared to come out to Los Angeles, I still spoke to Big here and there. But then I heard that Tiffany was out there, too, and that they were still seeing each other. I wanted to communicate with him when I needed to without getting caught up in his drama again. I wanted to raise a family with Big without being a member of his harem. But none of that stopped me from being very concerned about his extended stay in Los Angeles. It did not give me a good feeling at all.

Right before I came out to LA, Big and I spoke again. Somehow, we ended up arguing over something silly. That was always the way with Big. We could escalate from zero to sixty in no time and go from a casual conversation to a screaming match. And then make up just as quick.

"I'm coming out there tomorrow," I reminded him. "You better let all your little girlfriends know ahead of time."

I wasn't even planning on spending time with him. But I wanted him to know: *You can do what you want. But don't let me see you.*

"Why you gotta act like that?" he asked. "I ain't even dealing with this shit."

"Whatever, Big," I said. "You ain't gotta deal with nothing."

We hung up on each other. It was easy to do. I was on my way to LA anyway. So of course, our paths would cross and we'd be cool again.

But I never spoke to Big again.

The Beginning of the End

CHAPTER TWENTY-TWO

Til Death Do Us Part

I flew out to Los Angeles on March 5, 1997. On my flight, I saw Lisa, a friend of D-Roc's. We were friendly, too, and she'd become an occasional liaison between me and Big.

Bad Boy didn't send me to the Soul Train Awards, so technically I didn't need to be there. I hadn't been nominated for any awards, and I'd released three singles and videos for my album so there wasn't much more promotion to do. But I still wanted my presence felt. I knew how important it would be to keep my name out there.

Since CJ was four months old and I was able to start traveling again, I felt like going out to Soul Train was the equivalent of finishing up maternity leave. I did not plan to attend the actual awards, but I knew there would be other opportunities to connect with my supporters and perhaps secure songwriting work. I had started recording my second album and had a few songs under my belt already.

When our flight landed, I walked out with Lisa and waited for my car service to arrive. It was a typical sunny and warm Los Angeles afternoon, and I sat with CJ on my lap on a hard tiny stool outside the sliding glass doors near the luggage claim section. CJ was a little bit fidgety from the long flight, so I had to bounce him on my knee to keep him settled down.

I had my head down, kissing CJ on the cheek, when I saw a black Suburban pull up about twenty feet away from me. Someone had come down to pick up Lisa from the airport, and Big was in the front seat. I knew he was there but I purposely didn't look his way. I was waiting for him to acknowledge me.

Lisa went over to Big's car and put her luggage in the backseat. I saw her talk to Big briefly and then walk over to me.

"Big wanna see the baby," she said. "Can I take him over there?"

I didn't say anything. I just handed CJ over to her and turned my head away from Big's direction. I glanced over briefly and saw Lisa holding the baby up to Big's window. He took the baby in his arms and brought him up to his lips for a kiss. I could see him bouncing CJ on his lap and tickling him under his chin. After a few minutes, he handed the baby over to Lisa, who brought him back to me.

"Maybe I can come by your hotel this weekend and get the baby?" she asked. She gestured toward the car. "I think Big might want to see him."

My car pulled up and I stood. "We'll see," I said. "He can call me."

I stayed at the Universal Hilton. I could have stayed at the Mondrian or the Standard, right in the center of where every-thing would be going on. But something told me to stay somewhere on the outskirts of town. I was already figuratively in the cen-ter of everything. I didn't need to be literally in the middle of the festivities.

The day I came to town, I got a call from a DJ at a local radio station. He wanted me to come on for a brief interview.

"Faith," he said. "You're not afraid to be out here in LA while all this tension is in the air?"

"I've always had love for Los Angeles," I said into the microphone.

"I've been coming out here since long before I had a record deal. I hope the people here still have love for me, too."

The phones began to light up. The callers were so supportive that it made me feel better—at least temporarily.

I still hadn't decided when or how I was going to deal with Big. I knew I wouldn't be able to avoid him for the entire weekend. I did want to see him. But I wanted him to reach out to *me*. I was also hoping I could spend some time with Todd, so I wasn't completely focused on just seeing Big.

On my second night in town, I went out with Speedy, a friend of Big's from Harlem whom I was cool with, too. I was hanging out with him and his friend Jay-Jay, driving around, talking shit, and smoking weed. As we pulled up to a light at Sunset and Laurel Canyon, I saw the Suburban that Big had come to the airport in. I was sitting in the backseat, behind Speedy, who was driving.

"Is that Big in that car?" I asked.

Speedy looked over. "Yeah," he said. "That's him."

"Damn," I said. "I ain't in here."

As soon as we pulled right up to the car, I dipped down to the backseat to hide. I brought my face up just enough to peek out of the window. I saw Big roll down his window, and I put my head down again. It wasn't a big deal to be in a car with Speedy and Jay-Jay. I just didn't want this to be the first time I spoke to Big. I was hoping to talk to him one-on-one, not bump into each other randomly.

"What up, Big? What's good!" I could hear Speedy saying.

"I'm chillin'. I'm chillin'," Big said.

"Word. We just trying to find something to get into tonight...," said Speedy.

The light turned green but Big's car didn't move, so Speedy didn't, either.

"Yo." Big said. "I got a question for you."

I could tell by the sound of his voice that he was leaning out of the window a little.

"Any of y'all seen my wife?"

My heart stopped in my chest. There was a hint of playfulness in his voice. I wasn't sure if he knew I was hiding in the backseat and was trying to let me know or if he just wanted to get the message to me that he was looking for me. Either way, I figured it was just a matter of time before I just had to deal with Big. He was going to find me. He always did.

The next day, I went to a celebrity basketball game. I was with my old friends from the early days—Toni and Curtis. And Roz, my good friend from home, was in town as well. Even though we were happy to be together, I can't say we were all-out excited and celebratory. It was more of a low-key, chilled-out vibe. I was very conscious of the fact that I wasn't on my home turf. I was keeping a low profile.

"We going to the *Vibe* party tonight?" Toni asked.

"I'm going," I said. "You coming with me?"

"Of course."

"Do you think your mom would watch CJ for me?"

"I'm sure she would," Toni said. "I'll ask her."

"I want to go early," I said.

"I hear you," Toni said. "Now, you know Big is gonna be there…"

"Yeah," I said, nodding. "I know."

"Are you gonna talk to him?"

"I might…"

On the night of March 8, I was at my hotel, getting ready to go to the *Vibe* afterparty at the Petersen Automotive Museum. My hair was pulled back in a simple ponytail. I did wear my jewelry, a pair of gold hoops and a thin gold chain. I stood in front of the mirror, making sure my hair was neat. And then I slipped on my rings. I had several gold rings in different designs. Some were simple, and some were jeweled. I put them on, one on nearly every finger, and then looked at a final reflection of myself in the mirror.

We had our security drive us to the venue. I was in the front seat. Toni and Roz were in the back with CJ. We took the baby to Toni's mother's house first and got him settled in for the night.

Then we made our way to Wilshire Boulevard. We got there a little bit before midnight. And it wasn't crowded at all. Which is exactly what I wanted. My plan was to case the place first, finding the right spot to chill and stay put.

"Let's go right to the bar," Toni said.

"I'm right behind you."

Toni, Roz, and I posted up near the bar and ordered screwdrivers. I sipped my drink slowly, taking in the scene. Someone walked up behind me and leaned down to speak.

"Well, if it isn't Miss Faith..."

It was the singer Christopher Williams.

"Hey, Grandpa!" I said as I hugged him.

It had been so long since I would tag along to the studio with Kiy when he was working with him. Even before I got pregnant with Chyna. In a way, my career had jumped off because of Christopher Williams and the way life brought us together. He had encouraged me quite a bit in those early days, which made me more confident when I started working with Al B. Sure. It was good to see someone like Christopher, someone who knew me way back when. Who understood my true character and what I was really about—underneath it all.

"I'm proud of you, Faith," Christopher said. "You've come a long way."

I smiled and held up my drink for a quick toast.

"Thanks, Christopher."

We clinked our glasses and spoke for another quick minute before he moved on to work the room. I stayed put, with Toni and Roz on either side of me, swaying to the loud music and keeping my glass full.

A few minutes after Christopher left, Heavy D came to the bar to get a drink and saw me sitting there.

"Faith Evans is in the house!" he said in a loud voice.

We hugged, and he kissed me on the cheek. It was always great to see Heavy. He was gregarious and jovial and never failed to make me smile. A few months before, I'd done some writing for two of the acts on his label, Soul for Real and Monifah, and he'd been very supportive of my efforts to do more songwriting for outside acts. Heavy is one of the coolest guys in the music business. Just laid-back and fun loving. And when you see him at a party, you know you're going to have a good time.

"What up, Hev!"

He grabbed my hands and made me do a little dance with him right at the bar. I laughed out loud and tried to wave him off.

"Nah, girl," he said. "We partying tonight! You know how we do!"

I knew just what Hev meant. I was never the type to get ushered into VIP at a party. I wanted to dance and have a good time. That's what I had loved about hanging with Mary in those early days of being signed to Bad Boy.

"I'm coming back," Heavy said, pointing at me as he got his drink and walked away. "And I *will* have you out on that dance floor."

Other folks came and greeted me warmly. Within an hour, the club had become packed, shoulder-to-shoulder. Toni and Roz and I were squeezed tighter and had to constantly move one way or the other to let people get to the bar.

When I had my back to the bar, I had a pretty good vantage point of the entire venue. But as the space began to fill up, it became harder to see who was coming in and going out.

Toni nudged me in the ribs with her elbow. "There go Big and them," she said. She jutted her chin out and nodded toward the entrance.

I leaned back at the bar and sipped on my drink. "I see 'em," I said calmly.

I couldn't make out each member of the crew. And I wasn't looking at them directly. But out of the corner of my eye, I could see the outline of Big's heavy frame, limping with his cane. I was able to make out Damion, Cease, and Gutter as they came in with him. And then I saw Puff with his security guards Wolf and Paul.

If they had all come in earlier, when it wasn't so crowded, I may have walked over and said hello. But as it was, I was not going to maneuver my way through the crowd just to say hello. I had a little too much pride for that.

Through the crowd, I saw a familiar round face. It was Cease, and he was inching through the crowd in my direction. I'd known Cease for just as long as I'd known Big—he was standing right there the first time I met Big. In the glory days of our marriage, I'd spent nearly as much time with him as I had with Big.

"What up, Faye," he said, smiling.

I gave him a tiny smile but kept an aloof look on my face. I knew he was there as Big's representative.

"What you doing over here?" he asked, rolling a blunt.

"Chillin'," I said.

"You saw Big?" he asked.

"I know he over there," I said, turning my head in the opposite direction.

"You coming over to where we at?"

"I'll be over there...," I said.

Cease and I smoked together for a minute and then he was gone. Absorbed back into the thick crowd between where I stood and a small alcove that Big and his entourage were tucked into.

It was clear that Big had sent Cease over to scope me out. But I was trying to play it ultra-super-cool. I didn't want to cramp his style and look like I needed to be in his space. It was Big's night. The DJ was playing Big's new song on repeat. It was "Hypnotize," a simmering track with a rich bass line and an infectious hook. Every time the song came on, everyone in the venue just starting nodding and singing along to the chorus.

It seemed like the crowd really was hypnotized. The song has a mellow groove, and everyone seemed to absorb it.

And then it was suddenly like someone had scratched the needle across the record. I could only hear snatches of random conversations as people started to move in one direction.

...overcrowded...police...shut down...fire department...

"We gotta go," Toni said. "They're shutting it down because it's too crowded."

Toni, Roz, and I began following everyone else out through the exits and toward the underground parking structure.

When we got outside, it was just crawling with people. Not any large groups, just a lot of people fanning out everywhere. As we continued to make our way to the car, we heard a series of loud pops. *Pop! Pop! Pop!*

It wasn't loud enough for us to duck. But it was enough for us to stop and wonder where it was coming from.

"What the hell was that?" I asked, craning my neck to see something.

"I have no idea," Toni said.

Next to us, a group of people who worked at one of the record labels began getting into their SUV.

"Y'all going to Andre's party?" one guy asked.

"Where is it?" I asked.

"Up in the Hollywood Hills," he said. "Y'all can follow us."

I told the driver to follow the car, and we began to file out of the parking structure and up to the hills.

It only takes a split second for your life to be irrevocably changed—even if you have no idea that it's happening at the time.

That night I was twenty-three years old. And as our car left the parking lot of the museum, my life, as I'd known it, was over.

As our car climbed the Hollywood Hills, I laughed and joked with my girls, not knowing that my world would never be quite the same again. And it wasn't just my world—my daughter, four years old, was three thousand miles away with my family, while my son, just four months old, was a few miles away with Toni's mom. Their lives were changed forever at that moment, too.

And it wasn't just our lives that had changed. Hip-hop music had been forever altered in that moment. The music industry would never be the same. Violence and hip-hop were about to be linked together in a massive media event that would have reverberations for years.

A violent crime had been committed as our car climbed those hills. One that would not be solved immediately. As you read these words, I am *still* trying to piece together what happened that night and find out who was responsible. And I am still trying to bring those people to justice.

There's so much I wish I could tell that younger version of myself: the young mother of two driving with her friends to an after-afterparty. She had no idea that at that moment, her husband's chest had been cut open, his heart was being massaged in an effort to get it beating again. As she sat in the front seat, watching the scene rush past her window, she didn't know that her son was in the process of losing his father and that her daughter was losing a stepdad she loved. And she was about to be thrust into the spotlight to handle things the best way she could. She had no idea what kind of grief awaited her.

CHAPTER TWENTY-THREE

Walk with Me

I was numb. I sat on the small hard chair in an antiseptic waiting room at Cedars-Sinai and cried my eyes out, the rings that I'd torn off my fingers in a panic scattered on the floor around me.

"Who brought you here?" Puff asked me in a soft voice.

"Roz," I told him.

Puff left to find her and brought her into the waiting room. She came over to where I sat and helped me stand up.

"Roz...They won't let me see him..."

"I know, Faye," Roz said, hugging me tight. "Come on. We have to get out of here."

"Roz, I *can't* leave. I can't leave Big here...Why can't I just see him?"

"C'mon, Faye," she urged.

I let her lead me out of the hospital, right through the same doors I'd come in. The crowd had gotten larger, and there were a lot of familiar faces in it.

"Where is everybody?" I asked. "What do I do now?" Roz led me to a waiting car and driver. "We're going back to your hotel."

We got in the car and drove to the Universal Hilton. I kept my head low and dissolved into more tears every few minutes.

"Todd came by the hospital," Roz said. "He just wanted you to know he was here."

I nodded and turned my head to stare out of the window. It was the middle of the night. And as we drove, I kept getting hit and over and over again with the knowledge that Big was gone.

This morning, I thought. This morning right here he is not going to see.

When I got to my hotel room, it immediately began to fill up with my friends Roz and Toni and Big's friends, most of whom had been with Big when he died. Damion was there, as well as Cease and Gutter. I don't know where Puffy was. I never saw him after we left the hospital. I can only imagine he was probably shocked and terrified. None of us knew where he was.

My room quickly became Command Central. I kept moving, trying to just focus on taking the very next breath and trying to get to the next moment without breaking down. Of course the first thing we all did was try to figure out who did this.

"Is this about Tupac?" Toni asked. "Would niggas really kill Big over that?"

"I don't think this is about Tupac," I said. "People know Big had nothing to do with him getting killed..."

"Well then what the *fuck*," someone said.

"Cease," I said. "You were there. What did you see?"

"I just saw some dude with a close-cropped haircut and a bow tie. He pulled right up next to us."

"Why would they do some shit like this to my man?" someone asked.

"I just don't get it," I said. "It makes no sense."

"That's a big risk to take," said someone else. "They shot my man in front of a crowd of people!"

"Yeah," I said. "And whoever it was knew that Big always sits in the passenger seat. Those bullets were meant for Big."

We continued to talk, cry, and connect for hours, trying to figure out what went wrong. I got a call from Todd. He was in the area and wanted to come by to check on me. I told him to please come through.

The room started to get really crowded. I ended up talking in the bathroom with D-Roc.

"Yo. I got a friend coming through here," I told him.

Damion nodded and passed me the blunt that he'd just finished rolling.

"Look. He's from out here. But he's cool people. He's really been good to me."

"It's all good, Faye."

I started to cry. Damion comforted me.

"Everybody know you had love for Big. Don't even trip over that shit."

There was a knock on the door, and I left the bathroom to let Todd in.

"Hi, Todd," I said. We hugged briefly.

"I just wanted to check on you," he said. "I'm sorry. I am so sorry."

"Thank you," I said.

It was awkward. I had been looking forward to seeing Todd that night. I wanted him to know that I really liked him and was hoping we could see where our feelings might take us. But the timing just kept being off. In Atlanta, he had to walk by and see me hugged up with Big. And now I was completely on another planet. It was good to know that he understood.

"Just let me know if you need anything," he said. "And I mean that."

Todd stuck around as a few people went back to their own hotel rooms. Then he got up and prepared to leave as well.

"Don't go," I told him.

"I know you have a lot going on right now," he said. "I don't want to—"

"Please," I said. "Please don't leave. I can't stay here alone."

Todd stayed with me a little longer. I knew I had a tough time ahead of me. I felt so vulnerable and alone that I needed the comfort of a friend. Later that morning, I had to call Ms. Wallace again. Damion had called and broken the news to her initially. I needed to know if she needed anything from me.

"I'm coming on the first flight out," Ms. Wallace said to me. "And I'm bringing Jan with me."

"I'll have a room ready for you when you get here," I told her.

"Faith? Is this really happening? Is Christopher really dead?"

I tried to answer her but nothing would come out. She cried softly.

"I just can't believe this. Damion called and he was just crying and crying and crying and I *knew*. I knew something was wrong. And there are all these people gathered outside the house. Oh Faith, I can't believe my son is gone."

I wanted out of Los Angeles as fast as possible. But I knew we'd have to make arrangements to have Big's body flown out to New York. I had to find out the steps to take to make that happen. I was a little bit overwhelmed. After making a few calls, I learned that the first thing to do was to identify Big's body at the city morgue in Los Angeles.

I knew I wasn't going to be able to do that on my own. The last time I'd seen Big was out of the corner out of my eye at the club. Just two days before, I'd ducked down to avoid seeing him when his car pulled up to mine. And at that airport, I'd try my best to ignore him when he pulled up.

There was no way I would have my last look at my husband without some support.

When Ms. Wallace arrived at the hotel, we hugged and cried together. Jan was standing right next to her with tears streaming down her face. I reached out and took her hand and squeezed it.

I'd never gotten to know Jan. We very rarely crossed paths, and she'd always kept a low profile. But any differences we may have had melted away as soon as I saw her. I knew what she'd meant to Big. And she was the mother of the daughter he was absolutely crazy about.

And now the three of us were an ad hoc family, the women who would have to take command of this situation and stay strong for everyone.

Most of the people from New York who had come out for the Soul Train Awards were already back home the morning after Big was killed. There was a lot of fear and uneasiness about what was going on. I wanted to run away and just bury my head under a pillow. I wanted someone to comfort me, hold me, and tell me everything was okay. I didn't have that option. I needed to be all those things for Ms. Wallace and Jan, the same way they were for me.

After they got settled into their hotel rooms, I arranged for a car to take us to the morgue to identify Big's body.

I have to say, I was amazed at how calm Ms. Wallace was. Her only child, a son she loved dearly, had been killed violently. And she was stoic and proud. She may have still been in shock. But when she first arrived, after a brief crying jag when I first saw her, she was all business. And she seemed more angry than sad.

"How could this happen, Faith!" she yelled out as we drove. "Where was all the damn security?"

All I could do was shake my head. "They definitely had security with them," I told her. "I'm sure of it."

"So *how* did this happen? In front of all those people?"

"I have no idea." I said.

Ms. Wallace sucked her teeth and rolled her eyes. "Where the hell is Puffy?"

"I'm not sure. I think he went back to New York."

"*Not here?* What do you mean he's not here? My son was killed and he *left*?"

"Ms. Wallace, you gotta understand. Things are really crazy right now."

Ms. Wallace sucked her teeth again. "My son is *gone.* Someone better have some answers for me."

"Do you know if he was in any pain?" Jan asked softly.

"I don't know," I said. I could only imagine that if the bullet ricocheted throughout his body the way the doctor described at the hospital, he must have been in pain. But I couldn't bring myself to tell Jan and Ms. Wallace that.

When we got to the morgue, they led us into a small waiting room. My stomach was doing flip-flops; I felt like I was going to throw up. I took in a sharp breath and steeled myself. I knew I had to be strong. I closed my eyes and prayed that I could see Big without falling apart.

Ms. Wallace stood between Jan and me. We were all tense, waiting to see what the next step would be. I wasn't sure if they were going to bring Big's body into that room with us or if we were going to be led into another room to see him.

Someone came into the room. I'm assuming it was the coroner or someone of that nature.

"Very sorry for your loss," he said. He was holding a few Polaroid pictures in his hand. "We're going to need you to identify the body from these photographs."

The man laid out three pictures of Big. They were horribly graphic, and I took in a sharp gasp when I saw them.

"Oh Jesus," I whispered.

I could describe every detail of how Big looked in that picture. But I will not. It's too painful. Not just for me. But for Ms. Wallace, too. I will say this: He looked like he had been fighting for his life and had just passed away before the pictures were taken.

"I can't identify my son this way!" Ms. Wallace screamed. "How do I know for sure that's my baby? I need to see him! Let. Me. See. My. Son!"

Ms. Wallace began to cry hysterically. Jan and I tried to comfort her. Her cries grew louder and she continued to yell out.

"I don't know for sure. That could be someone else!"

"That's him, Ms. Wallace," Jan whispered. "That's him."

"No," she said, shaking her head vigorously. "How do you know?"

Ms. Wallace looked over at me.

"Faith?" she asked.

I nodded. "It's him," I said. "Ms. Wallace, that's Christopher."

She seemed to deflate. It was as if Big's death didn't really hit her until she saw those photographs. And it was particularly difficult because they wouldn't let us actually see him. As hard as it would have been, we all would have preferred to see him in person. We needed to see him, touch him. That was the only way this could really be real.

"Did you see him?" she asked me. "Did you at least see him when you got to the hospital?"

I shook my head as fresh hot tears streamed down my face. "No. They wouldn't let me…"

We left the morgue and headed back to the hotel.

It was time to make a lot of decisions. And there was no one else left in Los Angeles to make things happen. Ms. Wallace was going to have to trust me, and we were going to have to work together. I wasn't with Big when he died. But I was still his wife. I couldn't be concerned about how I would be perceived or what people were thinking about me. I had to focus, think about what Big would have wanted me to do, and then just get it done.

First, we needed to find a funeral home that could prepare his body and then arrange for him to be flown back to New York City. Later on that afternoon, we went to a nearby funeral home. The associate there talked us into purchasing a fifteen-thousand-dollar solid oak casket. He told us that it was the best one and it would be sturdy enough to support Big.

Jan had to get back home to T'yanna, so we got a car to take her back to the airport. Ms. Wallace and I stayed for one more day to take care of some last-minute details.

"I need to go to where this happened," Ms. Wallace said on our last day.

"Are you sure?" I asked.

"Faith, I never got a chance to say good-bye to my son. I couldn't even touch him. I need to see where he was at that moment. Take me there."

I had our driver take us to the Petersen Automotive Museum. We stopped at a florist and purchased a bouquet of white lilies. When we got to the corner of Wilshire Boulevard, I asked the driver to let us out and wait for us. I walked Ms. Wallace to the front entrance.

"This is where we were that night," I told her, pointing out the museum.

Ms. Wallace looked around. She put her hand to her mouth and closed her eyes. We stood close and placed flowers right next to the building.

After a long moment of silence and reflection, Ms. Wallace and I turned away from that building and all the ghosts surrounding it. We trudged back to the car and prepared to bury the man we both loved.

Ms. Wallace, CJ, and I arrived back in New York on Thursday, March 13. Big's body had been flown out and was at the Frank E. Campbell funeral home in Manhattan. We wanted to have the services right away. But Ms. Wallace's sister was getting married that weekend, so we were going to have to postpone the funeral for a few days. It was a bit unsettling, knowing that Big was not at rest. But it made more sense to celebrate before we grieved.

As soon as I landed, I had to pick up Chyna from my grandparents, who of course had already heard the awful news.

"What happened?" Chyna asked.

"Daddy got hurt," I told her. "He was shot with a gun. And we're not going to see him anymore."

I made a point to tell Chyna the exact truth. I didn't want to sugarcoat anything. But she still didn't seem to understand the finality of what was going on.

We set up camp at a hotel on the Upper East Side in New York City, near the funeral home. By this time I was living in New Jersey, and it was easier for me to just stay in Manhattan rather than driving back and forth every day.

Ms. Wallace and I went to Big's house in Teaneck to begin the process of cleaning up and looking for any necessary paperwork. We decided it would be best for Ms. Wallace to stay there until the house could be sold.

One afternoon we were going through the living room, cleaning up, when the phone rang. I put down a basket of laundry I'd gathered. "Hello?"

"Can I speak to Ms. Wallace?"

"Who is this?" I asked.

"It's Tiffany."

I called out for Ms. Wallace to pick up the phone.

"How are you?" she asked me before I gave the phone to Ms. Wallace.

"I'm all right."

I gave the phone to Ms. Wallace and kept it moving. I knew that Big had been dating Tiffany at the time that he died. But I was his wife and I had responsibilities I had to deal with. There really wasn't any room for me to befriend any of the auxiliary people in Big's life. I wasn't cool with her when Big was alive. There really was no need to try to force a relationship because he'd died.

In addition to cleaning and straightening the house, we had to make sure we knew where all Big's assets were, including his three cars. He had a Mercedes sedan, a Chevy Suburban, and a Land Cruiser. Since he didn't drive, different people would have them, and we wanted to make sure they were all accounted for. Eventually, we figured out who had what. But his Land Cruiser was in Philadelphia at Tiffany's house.

We had the dealership call to confirm Tiffany's address. And then Ms. Wallace told her that it would have to be returned. Someone—I can't remember who—told me she had a fit, crying and saying that Big gave her the car. Whatever. We had the dealership go to her house in Philly in the dead of night and put that truck right on a flatbed and bring it back to Teaneck.

I had no sympathy for Tiffany. That car wasn't paid for. I didn't know what arrangements she had with Big (although I did find a wish list of things she wanted from Big). But we had to secure his property and pay his bills and keep everything organized at the same time we were working out the logistics for his funeral.

I did understand that I wasn't the only woman in Big's life. In all honesty, I never had been. But for whatever reason, he'd married only one of us. And so the responsibilities had fallen on my shoulders. Lisa, the girl who had been a go-between for me and Big in LA, told me that she'd heard Tiffany had tried to commit suicide when she heard about Big being killed. And then Ms. Wallace told me how Kim was crying, telling her that she was coming with her and Jan to Los Angeles.

"What did you tell her?" I asked.

Ms. Wallace rolled her eyes. "I said over my dead body…"

Neither of us had any patience for catering to the feelings of people who probably genuinely loved Big but didn't have an official place during such a sensitive time. I'm sure Tiffany and Kim were both distraught and grieving, as we all were. But I just could not concern myself with their needs.

A representative from the funeral home called to let us know we could come and view the body. Ms. Wallace and I prepared to go over there.

Ms. Wallace sat on his large pine bed and ran her hands across the comforter.

"I don't want to make a spectacle of my son's death," she said softly.

"It won't be," I said. "It will be tasteful."

"Why can't we just have a completely private memorial service?" she asked. "Just close family and friends and that's it."

I shook my head. "We can't do that," I said. "There were so many people whose lives Big touched. It doesn't have to be open to the general public. But there are a lot of people who need closure, too."

Ms. Wallace nodded. "I guess you're right. It's just all…it's just too much. The media, all of these people…"

"It'll be okay," I assured her.

"I know my son," she said with a smile. "He would not have wanted anything small." She smiled softly. "He'd want all of Brooklyn to be there."

"You know that's right," I said.

"I'm going to let Brooklyn say good-bye. After the service, we'll go by St. James Place on the way to the cemetery."

"I think that's a great idea."

The Frank E. Campbell funeral home has held services for foreign dignitaries and celebrities like Frank Sinatra. It's swank and elegant and full of cherrywood furniture. There are several meeting rooms with plush sofas and fireplaces, and they did their best to make the atmosphere less depressing. But even with the luxurious accommodations, when I walked in with Ms. Wallace, I couldn't forget the reality of why we were there. Big's body was there, and we were going to have to view him and make sure he was prepared for the services.

"Right this way," said the director.

We followed him to a viewing room. About ten feet in front of me, I saw the solid wood casket Ms. Wallace and I picked out in Los Angeles. It was completely quiet in that room. It was beyond quiet. The room was carpeted so I couldn't even hear my footsteps.

As I walked up to the casket to see Big, I felt like I could hear his voice in that room. Even before I could see him up close, I could see that he was so very still. I'd never seen him so quiet. His presence was so thick around me that I felt like I could hear him talking.

I saw him flipping through my pictures at that photo shoot...

What's your name?

Then there he was, sitting in the front seat of my Land Cruiser in front of 226 St. James.

I'm gon' marry you...

I could see him putting Chyna in that cardboard box and rolling it around...

Nah, Chyna, you gotta stay in this box forever!

...holding both my hands as we stood in front of the clerk in Rockland County.

I, Christopher George Letore Wallace...do take you Faith Renée Evans...

I got closer to the casket, reached out to touch it, and opened my eyes. I breathed a small sigh of relief. Big looked like Big. Not in pain, like the picture at the morgue. Ms. Wallace and I noticed that at the top of his head was a large scar. It made us uncomfortable.

I felt a sense of peace after finally being able to see Big. But then I was troubled all over again when I saw the scar and noticed that he didn't seem to fit into the casket properly.

Ms. Wallace and I went into an office after viewing Big's body and I asked them if we could replace the casket.

We were so pissed. We'd spent thousands of dollars on that damn casket out in Los Angeles and they didn't even make sure that

Big could fit in it properly. Ms. Wallace and I decided we would have to go ahead and purchase another one.

We picked out a new casket and explained to the director that we were going to need a lot of assistance keeping uninvited guests from attending.

"I'll have car services for people coming from Brooklyn," Ms. Wallace said. "If they are walking in from off the street, they cannot be let in."

The director nodded and jotted down some notes. "We'll do our best to safeguard your privacy."

I felt like I didn't want Big to be overly exposed during the services. There were going to be at least two hundred people there, and I didn't like the idea of people touching him. I'd sung at enough funerals to know that people who were grieving could sometimes go too far and end up defiling the body with too much contact. Sometimes, I noticed that there would be white netting draped loosely over the open half of the coffin. And I told the director I wanted that for Big.

You would still be able to see Big clearly, but random people would not be able to touch him. Something about that made me feel better.

At the hotel, Ms. Wallace and I talked to Mark Pitts about what Big should wear.

"This guy from 5001 Flavors was making him a white suit," Mark said. "He had all his measurements. I think we can have him finish it."

I thought about the scar on the top of his head and shuddered a bit inside. "He needs a hat," I told Mark. "Make sure you get a fedora for him."

I still needed to get some music ready for the funeral. It would not be enough to just have an organist. It has long been a part of our tradition and culture as black folks to infuse farewell services with heartfelt singing. I contacted the members of 112 and asked them to sing "Cry On." I then called my old friend Donovan, the same guy who'd eaten with me at Je's restaurant in Newark every day when I was pregnant with Chyna. I asked him to play the organ and I asked Schon, one of my background singers, to accompany him.

"What about you, Faith?" Donovan asked me. "Are you going to sing?"

I'd thought about it. But I just couldn't envision myself having the strength to do it.

"No," I told Donovan. "I'm not going to sing."

The morning of the service was a bustling commotion of children and people and conversations about the logistics of getting hundreds of guests to the funeral home. Ms. Wallace hired dozens of cars to take people from Brooklyn into Manhattan. The family left from the hotel in a cavalcade of limousines.

CJ, Chyna, and T'yanna were dressed in all white. We all piled into the limousine and headed over for the short ride. The finality of what was happening started to sink in, and I felt like I was shrinking in that seat. While we were preparing for the funeral, I hadn't had to actually think about a time when it would just be over. And that moment was approaching. I had no more business to take care of involving this day. And once the funeral was past, I was going to have to get on with the business of living. With two children, one of whom would never know his father.

Chyna, wearing her usual one ponytail in a little puffed ball on top of her head, looked up at me.

"Mommy," she said. "Daddy's still hurt?"

"Yes. He's still hurt. He's not going to come back. We're not going to see him anymore."

Chyna thought this over. I could practically see the wheels turning in her head.

"So we'll see him tomorrow or another day?"

All I could do was sigh and kiss the top of her head and look out of the window of the car.

When we got to the front entrance, there was a small crowd there. Photographers and reporters lined the street as close to the front doors as they could get. Security guards and police officers kept uninvited guests and random people off the street from getting too close.

My good friend Roz wasn't able to get a ride from Jersey, so when she got there they made her stand outside for the whole service. That always bothered me, especially since she'd been with me the night Big died.

Our limo pulled up directly to the front. We all got out and made our way into the funeral home.

The room was designed to hold up to 250 people. We had at least three hundred packed in, if not more. Ushers walked me, Ms. Wallace, Puff, Mark Pitts, Jan, her siblings, and the kids to the front row. In the second row were my girls Toni, Cheryl, and Misa, my grandmother, my mom and my aunt Hope, my godmother Dorothy, and some of Big's extended family. One row behind them were Damion and Cease, Lil' Kim, and the rest of Junior Mafia.

As we all entered and took our seats, Donovan began playing "I Will Always Love You." And then, as Schon, my background vocalist, began to sing, I heard a voice crying out.

"Yes I will! I will *always* love you..."

It was Lil' Kim. And every time Schon sang a line, she would get a bit louder.

"Oh yes...oh yes...Yes. I love yooooou..."

Ms. Wallace, sitting next to me, had her lips set into one thin line. Without even opening her mouth a full inch, she leaned over and whispered, "Somebody better calm her down or take her out!"

I can't speak on what Kim was feeling. I know people grieve in different ways. But it just seemed extra to me. And no one was setting that tone. This was why Ms. Wallace wanted to have a private service—so that she wouldn't have to deal with this kind of thing. It wasn't that it was disrespectful. I just didn't understand why Kim had to be the loudest person in the building.

Ms. Wallace came to the front and read a verse from the book of Job. Her voice was clean and unwavering, her eyes glassy but not teary. I only glanced at her briefly before putting my head back down. I was having a hard time focusing on who was taking the podium. I kept my head down unless someone spoke to me directly. The members of 112 came to the front, assembled themselves, and then waited for Donovan to start playing "Cry On." Their unique four-part harmony was as crystal clear as I remembered from the first time I'd heard them in Atlanta. While their voices were soothing, it was a raw beauty that felt almost too intense.

I could hear soft moans and cries coming from different parts of the crowd. But I couldn't lift my head to look at anyone directly. I just hummed along, swaying and crying.

I sat there and breathed in deeply, trying to hold on to the presence of Big that I felt all around me in that room. Big and I had not been together when he passed away. But I loved him deeply and was proud to be the mother of his child. I couldn't even fathom not being able to call him and curse him out or cook him my world-famous lasagna or sit in the car and listen to his latest song. I was focusing so hard on feeling his spirit that I felt like he was speaking to me.

You can't sing for me...

I'd sung at many emotional events, from weddings to funerals. But this was different. There were so many people. And some small part was still a bit concerned about how people would perceive me. I just wanted to stay in my seat and keep looking at the floor.

The receiving line began and hundreds of people walked from the back of the room down to Big's casket and then turned left, past the first row, and back to their seats. Our row was led first. I followed Ms. Wallace. Lance "Un" Rivera, Big's good friend, carried

T'yanna in one arm and Chyna in the other. I saw Chyna's face when she looked down at Big, the man she called Daddy. And I think she finally understood the finality of what was happening.

We returned to our seats as the people continued to file down, take their last look at Big, and then walk past our row, offering hugs, squeezing hands, and giving small words of comfort. I barely remember all the people filing past me. But I appreciated every pat on my shoulder or small hug. There was Heavy D, who had told me that Big had been shot. Jay-Z was there, as well as Queen Latifah and Foxy Brown. There was Busta Rhymes, who'd often stopped by me and Big's apartment to say hello.

Tiffany came down, wearing a full-length fur coat, flanked by two of her girls. She stopped at Big's casket, cried for a minute, and then was led away by her friends.

A few minutes later, Lil' Kim walked to the casket. Mary J. Blige was supporting her because she wasn't able to walk without breaking down. She stopped at Big for a moment and cried. And then Mary began to lead her away, past the row where I sat. Kim kept crying while Mary addressed everyone in my row briefly.

When Mary got to where I sat, she didn't say one word. She just held Kim's arm and walked farther down the row. And then she continued offering her condolences to the other people seated next to me.

I was stunned. And I was hurt. I knew she was cool with Kim. But me and Mary went back—way back. And she knew I never had any beef with her—ever. She couldn't comfort Kim and offer her sympathies to me at the same time? I'd made sure that people like her and Kim could be at the service. When Ms. Wallace said she wanted a family-only ceremony, I talked her out of it. And now, we couldn't put aside petty bullshit at Big's funeral?

I felt a stirring of something inside me that I couldn't name. But it was more powerful and emotional than my grief. I could hear Big's voice again...

You can't sing for me? You better get your ass up and sing, girl.

I watched Mary walk to the back of the room, still stung by her dismissal. Big would have not liked it. None of it. And I knew he would have been pissed off that I wasn't singing during his service.

I leaned over to Mark. "I'll go up," I said.

I had spent too many years concerning myself with what other people thought about me. I had to move out of the cloud I'd cocooned myself in. I'd never been the type to really put myself out there and address crowds unless I was performing. But something overtook me, and I composed myself and walked to the front of the room.

Mark addressed the audience: "Big's wife, Mrs. Faith Evans Wallace, is going to sing for her husband."

I stepped up and took the microphone. "This is not for Big," I said to the crowd, my voice soft but clear. "This is for all of us. There's a lot going on here right now. And it's not right. The media is saying that we're fighting with each other." I shook my head. "We cannot sit up here and still fight with one another about petty things. Not after all the grief that we have seen this can cause. We need to pray. I think we need Jesus to walk with us…"

"All right now, Faye," I heard my mom say from her seat.

The energy in the room became prickly with electricity. Before I sang a note of "I Want Jesus to Walk with Me," I felt people leaning into me, preparing to hear the word.

As I sang, I saw hands fly up into the air. Just like when I was a little girl. It seemed like some people had no control of their bodies as they stomped their feet and shook their heads.

The members of 112 began to shout, completely overtaken by the intense spirituality of the song. There are certain times when a gospel song can pierce an audience and take them collectively to another place. I felt like that was happening as I sang. Before I could get to the end, there were many people on their feet, testifying and co-signing.

When I was done, the room erupted in a combination of more tears, hands being raised, and rousing applause.

I floated back to my seat, tingly and spent from the experience. It felt like the exact right thing to do in that moment. I stopped staring at the floor and sat up straight. There was no reason for me to hang my head. Big was gone, and I knew I would grieve for him for the rest of my life. But I also had a responsibility to celebrate his life, to make a joyful noise in remembrance of his time with all of us.

As the service came to an end, I felt a sense of peace. We filed out of the funeral home and into the waiting cars.

It was time to go to Brooklyn.

I could not believe the crowds lining FDR Drive to watch Big's final ride. It was truly a magical moment. We drove down the FDR toward the Brooklyn Bridge and saw throngs of folks standing and cheering. People were hanging out of office windows, waving and yelling.

"Oh my goodness...," Ms. Wallace whispered.

I could only smile. Big would have loved it.

When we got over the bridge and entered Brooklyn, it was complete bedlam. We drove down Fulton Street and there were literally thousands of people pouring out of their homes and stores, standing on top of cars, blaring Big's music, chanting and cheering, pumping fists in the air, crying, laughing, smiling, and waving. My heart flipped over at the sight. Big, who was once called the Mayor of St. James, was really getting back all the love he had for Brooklyn.

The cavalcade made its last stop at a cemetery in Queens where Ms. Wallace was going to have Big's remains cremated. After leaving, we went back to Big's house in Teaneck. Dozens of Big's friends and family members were there, along with enough food for ten times as many people. There were catered dishes from Sylvia's in Harlem. And there were soul food dishes that my grandmother and other family members made as well.

At Big's house, the vibe became more festive. We laughed and joked, sharing funny stories about Big's life and the type of person he was.

"Yo. Y'all gotta watch this," D-Roc said. He walked over to the television in the living room and turned on the DVD player. "Some dude sent this to the offices over at Bad Boy and Big ended up with it..." D-Roc turned it on and we all gathered around.

There was a man, tall and super-skinny, with a long, dripping-wet Jheri curl. He was riding a unicycle in circles in the middle of what looked like a country road.

"Yeah, look at me," the man said. "Look what I can do. You've *gotta* sign me to Bad Boy! I'm the first hip-hop cyclist! Look at me! Y'all can have me onstage at your concerts!"

We all roared with laughter. Not just because it was the silliest thing we'd ever seen—though it was. But because we could see why Big would love it.

"Yo. Big made us watch this tape over and over and *over*," D-Roc said, shaking his head and laughing.

It seems weird, but it was really special to sit there and watch this inane video. Because knowing how much Big loved it said so much about who he was and why we were always crazy about him. In essence, he was a fun-loving man who enjoyed life to the fullest.

And now that would be our job—to live life to the fullest in honor of Big.

CHAPTER TWENTY-FOUR

Every Breath I Take

I disappeared.

After Big's death, it was like I'd never been signed to a record label, like I didn't have an album that was still selling briskly. I was Faith Evans, a single mother of two children living in central New Jersey.

I took Chyna to day care every morning, then came home and took care of CJ. I slept a lot. And I didn't have many visitors. It was all just too much to handle. The phone rang often. Sometimes it was Ms. Wallace, wanting to see her grandson. Sometimes it was my own mom and grandparents, checking in to see if me and the kids were doing okay. I usually let the answering machine take a message.

I spent a lot of nights thinking. I would put the kids to bed, pour a glass of wine, roll a small joint, and sit outside in my backyard, trying to suspend reality momentarily.

It would hit me unexpectedly. One minute, I'd be brushing Chyna's hair. The next moment, I'd be holding back tears. I'd laugh as CJ smiled at me while I changed his diaper. And then I'd look up toward the sky, thinking about how much I wanted Big to see how handsome his little boy was.

I was lucky that I had Todd. He never shied away from everything going on in my life. And CJ especially became close to him very early on. Because he was so young when Big died, he had no memories of him at all. So the first father figure he ever really had was Todd. Chyna still remembered Big, but she was only four so it didn't impact her as deeply as it might have if she were a bit older.

In the immediate aftermath after Big's death, I was in transition with management. Queen Latifah and Shakim Compere's Flavor Unit Management had been getting tour dates for me and were very supportive after Big's death. Many people sent gifts to me and Mrs. Wallace through Flavor Unit and they made sure we received them. We got thoughtful presents from perfect strangers who sent paintings of Big and Coogi blankets in honor of his favorite clothing line. I also received a book on spirituality from Quincy Jones and his daughter, Kidada, who had been dating Tupac at the time of his death. I was really touched that they thought of me and the inscription in the book from both of them was sweet.

For the first time in my entire life, music had taken a backseat. I wasn't writing. I wasn't performing. I didn't even sing around the house anymore. I was in my own world. I wanted to know who was responsible for Big's death. Ms. Wallace was making a lot of calls to the Los Angeles Police Department for that, and I tried to make myself available for any questions she had.

I had so many questions to answer. I wanted to know who'd killed Big and why. I wanted to know if I was going to be strong enough to make it through without him. When was I going to sing again? When would the feelings of despair and loneliness pass? And there was a part of me—a small, silent part that I only listened to when I was slightly tipsy or half asleep. That part of me asked: Will you ever love again?

I was supposed to go on my first official date with Todd on the night that Big was killed. And he'd had to play a backseat again. But he never fully disappeared, which he could have. I think seeing how he handled that made me like him even more.

I took one afternoon to myself and went to his hotel in Midtown Manhattan. For one afternoon, I wanted to just be Faith. I didn't want to be Big's widow or a recording artist or any of the other labels that had begun to define me. I wanted to be a woman with feelings and interests and a mind of her own.

A few weeks later, Whitney Houston reached out to me. Now, of course, Whitney and I are both from Newark and she's always been a legend to me. But I didn't know her well. The first time I met her was at Clive Davis's legendary pre-Grammy party back in 1995. I was performing my first single that night. His pre-Grammy party has always been where he introduces his latest talent. Before I performed, Whitney glided up to me, singing the opening line to one of my songs: *I have the faith/to move any mountain . . .*

I remember being shocked, awed, and so humbled that someone like Whitney Houston was up on my music and singing it back to me! We remained friendly throughout those early years but we hadn't really hung out. So when she reached out to me after Big's death, I was very appreciative. I knew she was trying to make sure that I didn't only wallow in grief.

She took me to a swanky party at the Manhattan townhouse owned by Donatella Versace. I remember seeing people like Madonna and Demi Moore there and I had a great time.

"Us Jersey girls gotta stick together," Whitney told me that night, giving me a hug.

I'm not sure she knows how much that meant to me. But a glamorous evening out on the town was just what I needed at the stressful point of my life.

Although I was starting to go out again, I wasn't ready to record or perform yet. So when Puffy called my house in New Jersey, I took a deep breath and prepared to say no to whatever he wanted.

"You gotta come to the studio," said Puff. "We 'bout to make history."

"Puff, I need more time. I'm just trying to adjust to Big not being here."

"I understand that. But I'm doing this for Big and I have to have you on it."

"I just don't know if I can do it…"

"I know you can," Puff said. "I want it to be you. We gotta make it come together."

"I really don't know if I can…"

"Listen. I want to do a tribute and I want to make it the biggest song we've ever done. All the money is going to Big's kids…"

I sighed. Knowing that this would be a tribute to Big that would ultimately benefit CJ and T'yanna, I couldn't say no.

"When do I need to be there?"

"Come to Daddy's House tomorrow at seven."

When I got to Daddy's House the next day, the mood was sober and somber. Puff was there. Stevie J, one of Puff's longtime producers, was also there. Stevie J was the same guy who was in the studio with Puff the day me and Kim got into it. I couldn't believe that was less than six months before. It felt like worlds away.

I went into the studio to hear what they were working on. Stevie and Puffy were trying to rework the O'Jays' "I Miss You." But it wasn't coming together. "Miss You" is a beautiful song. But it's very slow and just didn't seem to fit what we were trying to do. We ended the session early and tried again the next day.

This time, there was another song playing on repeat in the studio, "Every Breath You Take" by the Police. At first, I wasn't sure how that song would work. When you listen to the lyrics, it's actually a slightly creepy love song about a man who is practically stalking his ex-lover.

"The song is dope," Stevie J said. "We just need to write a new hook."

"I can rework the same hook with different words," I told him.

I listened to the track over and over. The new lyrics came to me very easily. I began to sing along to the track.

As soon as Stevie heard my reworked lyrics, he told me to go into the booth and lay them down. I loved the way it worked with my voice, and I began to sing the lines over and over.

But before I could go into the booth, I found myself gripped by a paralyzing grief and began to cry. The intensity of the song, coupled with the fact that I hadn't sung since Big's funeral, made the tears flow down my face. I had to excuse myself.

Puff came to the studio, and Stevie J played him the track to show him how things were coming along.

I've never known Puffy to be the emotional type—at least not when it comes to grief. He can be emotional and scream on people or get mad and throw stuff around. But I hadn't ever seen Puff this moved by something happening in the studio.

As my voice boomed out of the speaker, tears filled up his eyes and spilled over. I saw him swallow a few times and then close his eyes tight as he collected himself.

"That's it," he said. His voice was barely above a whisper. "You see why I needed you for this song, right?"

I nodded.

It was almost as if there was a memorial service going on in that recording studio. I cried as I recorded my vocals a few more times. The members of 112, all of whom had become good friends of mine, were in the studio, and they were teary-eyed as well as they worked out the harmonies they would add to the backing vocals.

"I need a bridge, Faith...," Puff said. "We gotta come up with something hot."

I listened to the track repeatedly, trying to find something that would go with the beat and the refurbished lyrics. The bridge is what connects the chorus and verse to the climax. It's a onetime break from the song's structure, usually a dramatic interlude.

I thought of that early morning when I headed back to my hotel from the hospital after Big was killed. I thought about how devastated I felt when I realized that I wouldn't see him that morning—or any other morning ever again. I thought about a classic standard gospel hymn called "I'll Fly Away." The song's lyrics reference the idea of flying away one morning. I began to sing the song, changing the words slightly.

Everyone in the studio just started nodding intently with their eyes closed. It was clear that we were in the middle of accomplishing something very special.

Sometimes you just know that you have something monumental on your hands—even before you leave the studio. And this session was definitely one of those times.

I left the studio feeling better than I had in a long time. History would always have this musical tribute to my husband. T'yanna and CJ would always be able to listen to what we were able to contribute to their father's memory.

I still wasn't ready to be a full-time entertainer yet. But I was able to see the future. I wouldn't see Big again until one glad morning when this life was over. Until then, I was going to take baby steps. A few weeks after we recorded "I'll Be Missing You," I went into the studio and started writing songs for my next album. I took things extra-slow, still giving myself time to heal.

By the summer of 1997, Puff released his album *No Way Out*. And "I'll Be Missing You" was released as the second single. The song took off immediately, as I knew it would. It quickly became a number one single. I could not turn on the radio for more than ten minutes without hearing the song. And I could not turn on the television without seeing the video.

I hadn't actually wanted to shoot the video. Recording the song was cathartic. But I wasn't prepared to do all of the other stuff that goes along with promoting a single. I didn't really have a choice but to suck it up and deal with it, though. The song was so huge, there was no way I could beg off appearing in the video.

As the song gained more and more popularity and Puff began to do more publicity to support the record and his album, I fell back. I still wanted to be in the background even though my voice was on what would become the biggest song of 1997.

That summer was a very pivotal one for me. When it came to music, I was dabbling. And when it came to moving on in other ways, I was also trying.

Todd didn't give up on me. And he became a very bright spot during a tough time. As I traveled back and forth to LA for business, we always made time to see each other. And whenever he came to New York City, he always came to see me, Chyna, and CJ.

The fact that Todd and I had been in the same circles since I came into the music industry was comforting. When I recorded "You Used to Love Me" and all those industry folks came through, he was one of them. He'd come to the studio with Michael Bivins and told him how much he loved my voice. When he was looking for writers for 702's first album, which he executive-produced, he knew he wanted to work with me but was told by an executive: "Nah, you don't want Faith. She needs to be in pain to write."

When I performed before thousands at Madison Square Garden for the Urban Aid concert, I was so nervous that I looked for a familiar face in the crowd. I saw Michael Bivins, and Todd was sitting right next to him.

We met and became cool when Missy began staying at my place. And things had just gradually progressed.

But I was still concerned. By the summer of 1997, I saw Todd as my man, plain and simple. As far as I was concerned, we were a couple. He was still tying up the loose ends of his last relationship, but I was fully head over heels for him.

Now, Big had only been gone for four or five months at this time, and I was still considered the hip-hop widow. I didn't want anyone to think I was disrespecting Big's memory by moving on. But the truth was that Big and I were not together when he passed away. History can't be rewritten. I'd already started liking Todd before he passed. Big was dating Tiffany and possibly other women as well. So though it may have looked like I was rushing into something new, we were actually just trying to pick up where we'd left off.

Todd blended into my life with CJ and Chyna seamlessly. After he moved to the East Coast for his job, we began to see more and more of each other until it became clear that we were becoming a family.

But not even the support of my new man could prepare me for Puff's next request. In late summer, while "I'll Be Missing You" was still running the airwaves, Puff was invited to perform the song along with myself and 112 at the MTV Video Music Awards.

I heard through Cheryl that he wanted me there, and I told her it was not going to happen.

"I did the song. I did the video. But I'm not ready for that kind of performance," I told Cheryl.

"You know Puff's not trying to hear that," she said.

"I don't care. I have to put my foot down. Why can't I just take some time?"

I began to avoid Puff at all costs. If I heard he was at the studio, I didn't go. If I got a message that he called, I didn't call back. I hoped he would give up and just use a backing vocal track for my part of the song. I felt like I didn't need to physically be there to sing the song. Puff was promoting his album and I understood that. But I was leery of performing at that point. I was still trying to figure out what my next move would be in the music industry. And in many ways, I was still trying to deal with my own grief. I just needed time to work on my family and myself and adjust to what the next steps would be.

Cheryl was with me at the studio one afternoon when Puff called looking for me. She answered the phone, and I could tell by the look on her face that Puff was cursing her out.

"She's just not ready to perform that song...," I heard her say.

I could hear screams coming from the other end of the phone.

"I understand that but things have been really—"

Cheryl winced and just looked at me, exhaled, and passed me the phone.

"Puff, I'm not ready," I said.

"You not ready?" he yelled. "What the fuck are you talking about!"

"I'm still trying to get my shit together."

"Look. We here. And we gotta live. We have a hit song right now and we need to perform it—together. If you not ready, get ready."

"It's not that simple—"

"Faith, listen to me," Puff said in a low voice. "You want to give up on your career? Fine." His voice began to get louder and louder. "But you WILL NOT fuck up my shit. DO YOU HEAR ME?"

"FINE!" I said. "I'll do the show."

I hung up and collapsed onto the sofa in the studio lounge, sobbing hysterically. Cheryl sat down next to me and tried to comfort me.

"You could have said no," she said.

"I *know* that," I said, still crying. "But he just gets under my skin and I feel like I can't."

Cheryl let me cry for a few minutes. My shoulders rocked up and down, and I began to catch my breath in spasms as the tears began to subside. I was pissed off at Puff for taking me there emotionally.

And I was mad at myself that I allowed him to have this kind of effect on me.

I threw my head back on the sofa and began to massage my temples with my fingers.

I knew in that moment that something was going to have to change.

Chapter Twenty-five

Life After Death

T ime flew by during my first few years in the music industry. From meeting Big to getting married, having CJ, and then losing Big—it all seemed to happen in the blink of an eye. But the next phase of my life, filled with even more life lessons, spun out even faster.

On a cool November afternoon, I was out in Los Angeles with Todd for the weekend. We practically lived together when he was on the East Coast. And we were pretty much a team in every way. I'd come out to Los Angeles with him to meet with some songwriters and producers I was thinking of working with for my second album.

Todd had become my rock. I depended on him quite a bit—especially with all the craziness that was going on in the music industry. I'd given in and performed with Puff at the MTV Awards a few months before. I didn't regret it. The moment was very special. Puff even got Sting to perform with us. And after the show, Sting told me that he loved my voice—which was thrilling.

That day was special for Puff, 112, and me. But I still had some issues with the way Puff had screamed on me to get me to perform.

I was determined to stop allowing him—or anyone else for that matter—to push my buttons. I was angry at Puff for a lot of reasons. Around this time, he began working with Lil' Kim and the rest of Junior M.A.F.I.A. Now, Puff can work with whoever he wants. But they weren't signed to Bad Boy. And I felt like I was having a hard time getting his attention to discuss my album. Again, just like when Bad Boy went on a world tour and I stayed behind, I felt really disconnected from Puff and the label. I wanted the support. But I just didn't feel like it was there. In many ways, I felt like Todd was one of the few people who truly had my back.

In many of my relationships, I've moved a bit quickly. Sometimes too quickly. And my relationship with Todd was no different. In early November, after we'd been dating for several months, I found out I was pregnant.

My first thought was to terminate the pregnancy. It was just too much. I had Chyna and CJ, who was barely one year old. I knew the next time I had a child, that man would have to be my husband. And he would have to be ready to be a father figure to *all* my children. Although I cared deeply for Todd, I wasn't sure if he was ready for that responsibility.

Todd and I had a long heart-to-heart about our options. And we decided not only to keep the baby but to get married as well.

I was starting a whole new life, including a new family. And although it was happening very quickly, it felt right. Todd and I went back to the East Coast and got to work on planning our futures. Todd's years of experience in the music industry made it feel natural for him to be not just my husband but my manager as well, and we started working on the business aspects of that move. At the time, I was being co-managed by two incredible women, my girl Cheryl, who used to be my road manager, and Shirley Bell, an executive with Flavor Unit who resigned and worked with me after I left the management company.

But I would never escape that I was still Big's widow and I needed to deal with that. When Big died, he left no will. When that happens, the entire estate goes directly to his wife and his children. My long-time lawyer, Stuart Levy, had advised me that I would have to come in to talk about how to set up a trust fund for the kids and deal with Big's estate. But for months and months I'd put it off. Now that I was remarried and having a baby, I knew I had to deal with it. I couldn't truly move on knowing that I had to deal with divvying up Big's estate.

I was automatically awarded 50 percent of Big's estate as his wife. Twenty-five percent automatically belonged to CJ, and 25 percent to T'yanna. But I needed to sit down with Stuart to figure out what other payments needed to be made. I also needed to figure out how to take care of Ms. Wallace. Big would have definitely wanted me to make sure she was very well taken care of. She was in the process of buying her first house when Big died, and I knew he'd want to make sure she was able to have everything she needed to make that happen.

I also had to look at Big's royalty structure at Bad Boy. Because he had been a recording artist with records that were still selling, I had to consider how the money that was continually being earned by his estate would be managed and divided. Just thinking about it gave me a headache. But a few months after Todd and I got married, it was time to deal.

I had just started showing but I wasn't ready to make any announcements. So I wore a blousy top and pants under my bulky winter coat when I went to Stuart's Midtown Manhattan office to meet with him.

I'd called Ms. Wallace a few days before to tell her that she should come to the meeting as well. She needed to be there. I could have just made sure she was taken care of and then had my attorney let her attorney know our plans. But I wanted actual input from her on how she wanted things to be handled. And I wanted to have her there just as a way to show her that I was trying to be open and collaborative in the whole process.

As soon as I walked into Stuart's office, I knew something was off. First of all, it was crowded. I'd told Ms. Wallace about the meeting, so I'd expected her to be there with her attorney. But somehow the word had gotten out that I was having this meeting about Big's estate, and people had come out of the woodwork to lay claim.

"What is going on here?" I asked Stuart.

"I don't know why all these people are here. Did you tell them to come?"

"I just told Ms. Wallace to come. I thought we were just going to sign the papers to establish his estate?"

The room filled quickly and there was a very tense vibe. Damion, Big's longtime friend, was there; some of Big's old accountants and old lawyers were sitting across from me. I looked around as they all started filing in and sitting down and felt strange. People were avoiding eye contact with me like I'd already done something wrong.

Now, I knew Big's estate had debts — that was normal and to be expected, and I was sure that Stuart would handle it. I would definitely sign off on whatever payments were necessary. But I didn't understand why the people in that room were looking at me like I was trying to get away with something. I was just signing some papers to establish the estate since I was the only adult beneficiary who could lay claim to it.

It felt like the people gathered had their own reasons for wanting to know what was going on, and it made me uncomfortable. What was supposed to be a simple meeting where I could work out some details and keep Ms. Wallace informed felt like it had turned into some kind of thing with me versus Ms. Wallace. Like we were on opposite sides. And as far as I was concerned, we were *not*.

The problem was that in the months after Big's death, we hadn't spoken much about the estate. We communicated mostly about the kids. I brought CJ to Big's house in Teaneck on the weekends and that was about it. I was in my own world. And then I got pregnant, got married. I was moving on. And I should've talked to Ms. Wallace in detail. Because it seemed obvious that other people had.

The chatter going back and forth in that conference room became a dull roar in my ears. I sat back in my chair and tried to catch my breath, pulling my sweater over my growing belly. All the voices started to meld together in my head, and I felt my breath beginning to come sharply.

I'd thought I was doing the right thing by meeting with the lawyers and making sure Ms. Wallace was involved. But as I looked around the room, I got more and more upset. I could understand if all these people wanted to come there with Ms. Wallace to support her. But ultimately, none of them needed to be in there. I invited Ms. Wallace so that she'd know we were in this together. But I didn't have to answer to anyone else.

"Excuse me please," I said, standing up.

I barely made it out of the room before I burst into tears. Damion quickly got up from the table and followed me out. He led me into a small lounge area.

"Faith, take a deep breath," said Damion.

"D-Roc, I don't need this!" I tried to stop crying but I couldn't. "I'm just trying to do the right thing."

Damion touched my arm and looked me in my eyes. "You *are* doing the right thing. You don't have to answer to anyone."

"Why are all these people here? I just asked Ms. Wallace to come so she would know I want to include her. And all of these people are here like they need to be informed—and they don't!"

"Yeah. You just gotta do what you gotta do. Don't even sweat them."

"I'm out of here," I said.

"Wait," D-Roc said, reaching out to me. "Don't just walk away. Tell them how you feel..."

"I'm not telling them shit. I'm *done*. I'll meet with my lawyer on my own time!"

And with that, I walked out of his office and out of that building. Slowly but surely, I was determined to shed the negativity from my life. I was not trying to allow caustic people and situations to poison my world. I had a child on the way, a husband, and two children who needed to be cared for. I had no time for any of the bullshit.

It turned out that Big's estate was an absolute mess. With all those attorneys and accountants sitting in on that meeting, I couldn't understand how his paperwork could have been so shoddy. Big had several business ventures that should have brought substantial profits. But most of those arrangements turned out to be little more than handshake deals with nothing formal outlined. It was obvious that Big had paid little attention to his money and how it was spent or invested.

A few weeks after that meeting, I spoke to my attorney and told him I wanted to share the administration of the estate with Ms. Wallace.

Even though I tried to not let the business stuff get to me, it still did. I wasn't even sure if I was handling it all properly.

A prime example of this was when I decided it was time for me to move on to a new attorney. To this day, I don't feel like I handled it in the right way. Stuart Levy had been there for me since I sang background vocals as a teenager in high school. But making tough business decisions took a certain skill that didn't come naturally to me back then.

All this affected me as I went into the studio to record my second album. After Big's death, my relationship with Bad Boy really suffered. At the time that he died, I'd already felt like I was on my own. Afterward, I really felt isolated.

I was having a hard time connecting with Puff, literally and figuratively. He was producing tracks for Lil' Kim's album, and I saw that he was hanging out quite a bit with the members of Junior M.A.F.I.A. This was totally fine, but I was actually signed to his label and I felt like my project should take precedence.

I've always been an artist who benefits from being nurtured. Like the relationship Clive Davis has been known to have with his artists. But Clive Davis is not an artist. And as Puff moved closer and closer to performing outright—as opposed to just doing a verse here and there—it became more difficult to get his attention. When we won a Grammy for "I'll Be Missing You," I wasn't at the ceremony.

I retreated more and more into a shell. As my belly continued to grow and I prepared for the birth of my third child, I was in and out of the studio recording. I have to admit, I didn't choose the songs as carefully as I wanted to. I just felt myself being pulled in so many directions. It was nothing like the making of my first album. Big had been taking me through a lot back then, and that emotion came out in the music. But it was nothing like this. It wasn't just a wayward husband now; it was like the whole world was out to get me.

I started thinking about leaving Bad Boy. Maybe I needed a fresh start on a new label. But anytime I breathed a word of this to anyone besides Todd, people looked at me like I was crazy. I was starting to feel like I was in some kind of mafia that you couldn't voluntarily leave. I met with a new attorney, just to float around the idea of possibly shopping for a new deal. Weeks after we met, he ended up taking a job at Bad Boy. It was like I couldn't walk away.

By the time I completed my second album, which I titled *Keep the Faith*, I'd given birth to my third child, a son whom Todd and I named Joshua. I barely had time to breathe and recover from labor and delivery before I had to shoot the video for my first single, "Love Like This." The girls in wardrobe had to get out the duct tape to make sure I could fit into the outfits for that shoot.

Dealing with the media was tough. I have to give Todd credit for helping me. By the time I had to do press for the album, I was remarried with another child. That could have been awkward. But Todd didn't let me wallow in feeling uncomfortable. It was what it was. I'd moved on. And if people had an issue with it, that was their problem, not mine. I reveled in my new family. Chyna was just as smart and sassy as ever. CJ was getting so big, looking more like his father every day, and my baby Josh was a sweet antidote to the stresses of my day-to-day life.

We all relocated to Atlanta for a fresh start and an opportunity to have a larger house for our growing family. *Keep the Faith* became a top ten album, and the first two singles charted in the top ten on Billboard's Hot 100 Singles.

I went on tour with Dru Hill to support the album. I will always be indebted to Chuckii Booker, who served as my musical director on the tour. *Keep the Faith* went on to sell one million copies and was certified platinum, just like my debut album.

I was happy with the way things were moving forward. I had a husband I was crazy about, three healthy children, and a flourishing career. And I was looking forward to recording my next album. But I wanted to make sure that Puff would be able to focus on me. After I'd released my album, Puff released his first solo record, *No Way Out,* and I was worried that he would get farther and farther away from actually taking care of his artists on a day-to-day basis.

Todd and I decided I would start recording on my own, without waiting for Puff to set up my official recording budget and put me in the studio. We flew back and forth from Atlanta to Los Angeles and met with several producers.

It cost us quite a bit of money but we knew if we wanted to get Puff's attention, we'd have to take some risks of our own and not just wait for him to take notice. When I had six or seven songs recorded, we called Puff and met with him at a hotel in Manhattan.

"We've been working," Todd told Puff. "She's ready."

"And I've been working on my look, too," I said.

I had gained a lot of weight when I got pregnant with Joshua, and it had been really tough getting it off. I know how Puff is about having the look right. And it's not just him—it's the entire music industry. So I'd been furiously trying to get back into shape.

"I see. You been working out?" Puff asked.

"Absolutely!" I told him. I'd also had a bit of lipo and a breast lift.

We played him one of the songs I'd recorded in Los Angeles, a joint called "You Gets No Love." It's a simmering kiss-off with a hot club-ready beat. I even did a little rapping. I always rhyme a little bit in the studio as a part of my warm-up for writing or singing. But this was the first time I'd actually rapped with the intention of having it on the song. And it turned out *hot*. I knew without a doubt that Puff was going to love it.

As soon as the song came on, I watched Puff's face intently. I knew he wouldn't flip out and tell me right away that he liked it, even if he did. Todd and I had taken a big risk by going outside the usual Bad Boy family. If he didn't like it, he would be quick to tell me so. And if he did, he still wouldn't really go out of his way to show it.

But I know Puff very well. And as he sat there quietly and listened to the record, I knew he was feeling it. He didn't smile. Didn't say a word. No head nodding, no toe tapping. Just listening quietly like he was a college student in a lecture hall. The song ended, and he finally looked at me.

"It's hot," he said. "I like it."

I knew this meant that Puff was actually *in love* with the song. That's just his way. He's not gonna go all crazy over something. But the next day, he asked me to send him a copy of the song. I knew we had him hooked.

Puff asked me to come down to Miami to start working on the

record. He was in the middle of several different projects but now I was his priority. I'd achieved my goal. I got his attention by bringing him a hot track and showing him that I meant business. We made plans to settle in Miami for a few weeks to work on my third record together.

We recorded several songs at Circle House, a legendary studio owned by veteran reggae artists Inner Circle. We ended up being there on Mother's Day 2001. Puff brought his mother, Todd brought the kids from Atlanta, and we all had a great time together. For the first time in a long time, I felt like Puff and I actually bonded.

For this album, I was determined to have a very relaxed recording atmosphere. My first album I recorded in the middle of a torrid affair. My second album was recorded while I was both still grieving for Big and falling deeply in love with someone new. This time around, I felt centered and settled.

I had dozens of red currant votive candles all over the studio and a bottle of Pinot Grigio on ice at every session. Since I'd started working out more and trying to lose weight I had a personal chef prepare meals for me like grilled fish and fresh salads. Puff saw me lose ten pounds by working out stringently during that first week. He was proud of me and even told me I could fly my trainer down. I did, and Angie and I began to work out twice a day.

I have very fond memories of my time in Miami. In order to really do your best work when you're on a label like Bad Boy, you really have to have a decent relationship with the head of the label. It's not just about paperwork and recording. I had to go that extra mile to bond with Puff, and it was paying off.

I tend to be a loner. Sometimes, I just want to stay in the house and be with my children. Todd urged me to think outside the box. It's not always enough to bang out hot songs. Face time with producers and with Puff was important, too.

I'd gone outside my comfort zone in a lot of ways while I was in Miami, and I felt like I was going to have a lot to show for my efforts. Puff was happy with what I was working on — something that always made me breathe a sigh of relief. I was happy with what I was working on. And I had a good feeling about how this album was going to be received.

"'You Gets No Love' is your first single," Puff said over dinner one night.

"You think so?"

"Absolutely!"

We all made a toast — to the success of my next release. I was very happy about how my first two albums had been received. Between the two of them, I'd sold nearly two million records. But I was ready for a breakthrough to the next level.

Before I even started working on my third album, I'd recorded "Heartbreak Hotel" with Whitney Houston and Kelly Price. The song was the first single from Whitney's new album, *My Love Is Your Love*, and the exposure I received from being on her number one single and featured in the video put me on a slightly different playing field. I was exposed to a pop audience as well as my always loyal R&B listeners, and I was poised to introduce myself to a whole new legion of fans.

But even as we all hung out in Miami together, there were things going on back in New York that I was not privy to — things that would have a huge impact on my future at Bad Boy.

A record label is like a giant machine with thousands of gearshifts needed to get it moving. When a new record is released, it takes dozens of people working on the same exact page to make things come together. The publicity department has to make sure the artist is featured in the media at the right time. The promotions department has to make sure that the right single is playing at the right stations as often as possible. The marketing department has to ensure that any way the artist can be exposed to the record-buying public is happening on a grand scale. If there is any glitch in the matrix, the entire setup of an album can falter. And it is almost impossible to get back on course once that happens.

As I was traveling to support the album, I got some distressing news. Almost as soon as my first single, "You Gets No Love," was released, I was hearing through the grapevine that Puff was moving Bad Boy from Arista to Universal Records.

I had just released a brand-new album and I was very fearful that all of our hard work in Miami was going to go down the drain. If Bad Boy was moving, what did that mean for me? Sometimes, in these situations, the parent label can keep certain artists. For example, when Clive Davis left Arista to start J Records, Whitney Houston had to stay at Arista. So I wasn't sure if Puff was taking me with him or if I was staying at Arista. Todd and I met with LA Reid, but I left that meeting still confused about my status.

As I continued to promote my album, I became more and more discouraged. There didn't seem to be any incentive for people to really push my project—I was caught in the shuffle of Puff's move from one label to another.

I know that Puff had to make his own business decisions, and things couldn't be timed to benefit me. But all I could think about was everything I'd done to show him that I was serious about taking my career to the next level. I worked out, ate right, worked with new producers, stretched my voice in new ways, ventured out more, and became more accessible. I'd worked really hard to strengthen my relationship with Puff. And now I didn't even know if I was still under his wing.

"All of that hard work in Miami," I complained to Todd. "And for *what*?"

Todd shook his head. "Look. You did your job. You delivered a great album."

"But that wasn't enough," I said. "I feel like it never is."

*　　*　　*

When I sang for Puffy at that studio back in 1994, I was barely twenty-one years old. I knew next to nothing about the music business and how I would fit in. All I really knew is that I wanted to sing. Everything else I'd learned had been a baptism by fire.

Working with someone like Puff is like being in a marriage. And sometimes, when you realize the love is just not what it used to be, it may be hard for you to let go and move on. Even if you know it's the right thing to do.

As I toured the country to promote my third album, I realized it would be my last as an artist on Bad Boy. I had very little support due to Bad Boy's transition. And I took that as a sign: It was time for me to transition as well.

This would mean asking Puff for a release from the label. Confronting Puff had never been easy for me. My throat was tight with fear the first time I ever sang for him. I could barely look him in the eye when I asked him for a writer's fee once he had me working for his artists in the studio. I folded and agreed to perform with him after he cursed me out about not wanting to do the MTV Awards. How in the hell was I going to tell him I didn't want to be on the label anymore?

Todd and I had meetings with the heads of just about every black music division of every major record label.

I'd play them the music I was working on in my home studio, and the response was positive. But there seemed to be a sense of wariness. And we didn't hear back from anyone. I think these executives were worried because they still had to work with Puff. They might want him to do a remix or have one of his producers working with their artists. He was a very powerful man at this point, and I think that scared some people off. I knew it was time to have a heart-to-heart with Puff about my future with the label.

I already had a trip to New York planned because I was auditioning for the role of Mimi in the Broadway show *Rent*. While I was in

New York, I was going to talk to Puff and tell him my concerns. I'd never had an easy time talking to him face-to-face about business. But that was going to have to change.

I sat on the plane and thought back to my eight years in the business. I had always had a hard time speaking up for myself. Like many artists, I loved learning about music and creating music. As I added more and more equipment to my home studio in Atlanta, I loved tinkering and making new songs. I didn't necessarily like dealing with the business side. I never had.

For example, after I moved to Atlanta, a friend of Todd's told us about an up-and-coming rapper who was garnering a lot of buzz in Los Angeles. I was asked to contribute to his debut album and I did, for a much lower price than I would normally charge. I didn't even file all of the official paperwork for songwriting credits. I wasn't sure if the album would ever be released. I was just doing a favor for a friend. The album ended up selling ten million copies worldwide. I'd never received a writer's credit or writer's royalties for the song. Once again, I learned how important it was to stay on top of my paperwork.

But those incidents were rare at that point in my life. Now that Todd was my manager, I finally felt like I had someone completely on my side to go to bat for me, and that was great. But talking to Puff was something I would have to do on my own. I had no beef with him. I just needed to let him know where I stood. And he needed to hear it directly from me.

I auditioned for *Rent* the day after I got into New York. I knew I had the songs down perfectly. But the role of Mimi was going to have way more dancing—up and down poles no less—than I was going to be able to handle. So I left that audition knowing it wasn't going to work for me and took a cab to Puffy's four-story brownstone on Park Avenue in Manhattan.

One of his assistants walked me up several staircases. Each floor we passed seemed to have a different theme. We got to one floor that was decorated wall-to-wall and top-to-bottom in white. From there we went up one more flight where there were several offices; assistants were opening boxes of clothing from his new line, Sean John.

There was a quiet hum throughout the well-appointed house. Numerous aides and employees were hard at work, comparing notes, taking calls on cell phones, sending faxes, and whispering orders at each other.

Puff had come a long way from having the entire operation working out of his mother's house in Scarsdale. I thought about when he used to walk me down to the West Village for my weekly tanning session and then wait for me until I was done so we could walk back to the office together. I couldn't imagine he ever had the time to dote on his artists that way anymore.

Finally, we went up another level to a large but cozy kitchen. Puff was sitting at a round kitchen table as his chef stood at the island in the center of the kitchen, preparing his breakfast.

"What up, Faith?" Puff said, standing up from the table and leaning over to give me a hug and a brief kiss on the cheek. "You want some breakfast?"

I shook my head and told him I'd eaten earlier.

Puff poured himself a glass of orange juice from a heavy glass carafe and looked at me.

"So. What's going on?"

"I feel like I'm in limbo right now. And I feel like you've got a lot going on right now."

Puff brought his juice to his lips, took a very small sip, and put his glass back down. He looked at me and waited for me to continue speaking.

"I feel like I've gotten lost in the shuffle..."

Puffy nodded.

"And I feel like I don't have your support. I've been working very hard. I got in the gym. I've been working on the image. Staying in the studio. This last album...I really feel like I did everything you asked of me. And I just do not feel like I got the support back from you that I needed."

Puffy's chef brought him a plate with eggs, turkey bacon, and toast. Puff leaned in and inspected the meal, then picked up his fork and began to eat.

"You sure you don't want anything?" he asked.

I shook my head.

Puff took a long moment to chew and swallow a bite of food. "I understand what you're saying," he said. "I think you just need to be patient and work out some of the—"

"Just let me go, Puff."

Puffy put his fork down.

"Excuse me?"

I sat up straight and looked him in the eye.

"Release me from my contract. Let's work out the money and figure out how to make this work. It's time for me to move on."

I could see that Puff was swirling this around in his mind. He didn't seem to like what I was saying. But for once, I felt like I was doing a good job at making what I wanted clear. He wouldn't be able to deny it.

"I thought we was better than that..."

"We are. So if you can't nurture me the way I need to be, it's best for you to just let me go."

"If that's what you want. It's cool."

"It's the right thing to do," I said. "For all of us. I'm just ready to try something new."

Puff chewed his food thoughtfully as I continued to speak. "I think we did a lot of amazing things together. But I'm ready to branch out."

Puff finished his meal and sighed heavily. "You have to do what you have to do," he finally said.

We changed the subject and talked about old times, about Big and the early days of Bad Boy. We talked about our children and how they would grow up and hear some crazy stories about our wild days. After about an hour, it was time for me to go. Puff walked me downstairs.

"You know that we're bonded for life, don't you?" Puff asked as I stood by the door.

I thought about how nervous I was the day I sang for him; how he encouraged me to work the camera at the video shoot for "One More Chance." I saw his shocked face when Big and I told him we were married. This was the man who pulled me off Kim when I finally got my hands on her in the studio that day. I remembered how he came over to see CJ and marveled over how much he looked like Big. I thought about Big's funeral and how I had never seen him so broken and distraught. We'd performed together countless times. Our children were close in age. There was no doubt that this man was family.

"We're definitely bonded," I said. "For life."

"No matter what happens, I always got love for you."

I smiled and gave him a hug.

"And if you ever need anything," Puff said. "Do not hesitate."

I left Puff's house and got into a taxicab for the ride back to my hotel. As the car sped up Park Avenue, I felt like a heavy weight had been lifted from my shoulders. In the years since Puff had put me on, I'd learned so many valuable lessons. I'd finally figured out how to toughen up and fight for myself when necessary. I'd been talked about like a dog without ever trying to defend myself. I only remained committed to the truth—no matter what others tried to say.

I'd loved—hard and with reckless abandon—and had to pay

the price for it. I'd grieved in a way I would never wish on my worst enemy and somehow found the strength to stay composed. As an entertainer, I'd sold millions of records, racked up kudos and awards and standing ovations. And the crazy part—I was just getting started.

Puff was right. I would always be a part of Bad Boy. I was the First Lady there. I'd met my husband there. I'd lost my husband there. A chapter of my life that was rich with happiness and pain was closing.

I wasn't just leaving Bad Boy. I was starting a whole new journey. The idea of being on my own, no longer in Big's shadow, no longer in Puff's shadow, was both thrilling and frightening. I closed my eyes, clasped my hands together, and prayed for the strength to make it to the next step—wherever it would take me.

Epilogue

a, look. There's Mary."

My daughter Chyna and I were in the mall a few months ago when she spotted Mary J. Blige walking with her husband Kendu Isaacs. I'd just given birth to my fourth child, my son Ryder, and I was picking up a few things.

"Let's go say hello," I said to Chyna.

We walked past them and then turned around abruptly.

"Helllloooo there!" I said. I made my voice really high-pitched and energetic, just the way I used to ten years ago, back when me and Mary were running the streets of Manhattan.

"Oh my goodness! Faith!" Mary said.

We both embraced and shared a warm hug. Then Mary did a double take when she saw Chyna standing next to me. She put her hand to her mouth in surprise.

"This is *not* Chyna. It can't be."

"Yup. That's Chyna," I said. "Can you believe she's fourteen!"

Mary just kept shaking her head back and forth.

"I remember when she was just a little baby."

"Time goes by so fast," I said.

Mary and I caught each other's eyes for a brief but meaningful moment.

"It does, Faith," she said. "It really does."

As you get older, things from the past become less and less important. What really mattered as we stood in that mall together was that Mary and I were both survivors. There were many singers and entertainers we knew from the old days who were no longer recording or performing. We were blessed in many ways. And we had a shared history. We were a part of a golden age in black music. And we'd both survived working with Puffy!

"So what have you been up to?" Mary asked.

I shrugged. "I'll be in the studio soon. But right now I'm just living life. Having babies."

We both laughed out loud. And then Mary's face got serious again. "It's so good to see you, Faith," she said. "Really. It is."

"It's good to see you, too, Mary."

We hugged each other tight once more, and she went on her way.

That's how I get down today. I mind my business. And I don't hang out much. I spend more time at my sons' football games than I do at industry parties and concerts. I always knew I'd want a different kind of lifestyle. At thirty-plus, I'm just not interested in the scene. I get more joy from family than I do anything else.

And I don't have any beef or grudges with anyone. Whatever tiny stuff Mary and I went through is so far in the past today, it barely matters. And even though my friendship with Missy didn't continue to grow, I never held a grudge against her, either. I'm still very proud of what she's accomplished in this business. I even asked her to perform with me on the song "Burnin' Up" from my third album. She came to my trailer on the day we shot the video and we were cutting up and joking just like the old days.

Of course, Missy asked me about Chyna, the little girl she spent so much time with years ago. It's so funny, when I run into a lot of people I toured, performed, or recorded with—whether it's Missy, Busta Rhymes, Monica, Xscape—the first thing they say is always, "How's Chyna!?" before they even ask about me! My daughter really grew up in that world and so many people still care about her and have a lot of love for her.

Just a few weeks ago, I got a call from Misa, Puff's ex-girlfriend and Justin's mom. She was in Los Angeles for work, and we met up to have a few drinks and talk about the good old days. While we were together, Missy called her and said she was nearby as well. We all ended up at an LA bowling alley, drinking and reminiscing. So no matter what, we have a history that transcends our differences.

Lil' Kim has gone on to become an icon—I don't even fault her for all the drama with Big. We were so young back then, and he obviously had feelings for both of us. When I was recording my most recent album, I worked with producer Scott Storch. We met up at a studio in Manhattan and I took my daughter Chyna and my little sister Janeal. At one point, Scott moved me to a writing room on another floor of the studio. Later on, Chyna told me that while I was upstairs, Lil' Kim came into the studio to see Scott Storch and noticed Chyna was there.

"Wow," Kim said, "This little girl is like my goddaughter and my niece all in one!"

I thought that was pretty interesting. And I think it's further proof that we've all moved on.

Ms. Wallace and I get along wonderfully. She loves seeing her grandson. I'm so happy that in a lot of ways she was able to see past a lot of the crap from the people who were trying to get into her ear when we were dealing with Big's estate. We're now a team when it comes to maintaining Big's legacy. I know Big would appreciate that. Jan and I make sure that all the kids get together, especially during the holidays. I'm blessed that she's always been cool and laid-back. Jan ain't never been about the drama. And our kids have a wonderful relationship because of that.

As for Puff? I like him even more today than I did when he was my boss. I called Puffy recently and told him I needed Bad Boy to sponsor my sons' uniforms—and he did it with no questions asked. No matter what we go through on the business side of things, there's a love between me and Puff that goes deep. We will always have Big in common. I don't always like how he handles things as they pertain to maintaining Big's legacy. But I can never front on the history we made together and the bond we share.

Every year, Puff somehow manages to get FedEx to deliver gifts to all my kids on Christmas Day. How he does that I'll never know. But my kids are always excited when their extravagant gifts come from Uncle Puff. And last year, Puff came to LA with his three sons and took all the kids to Michael Jackson's Neverland Ranch for the day. I hope as time goes on, CJ is always able to have a relationship with the man who was such a large part of his father's life.

I've settled down quite a bit. But my life is not all roses. Life never is. A perfect example is what happened to me and Todd a few years ago. We loaned our truck to some friends who were shooting a video and then we drove back to our home on the outskirts of Atlanta, where we were still living at the time. We got pulled over in Hapeville, Georgia.

The officer said our temporary plates were "improperly displayed" and then decided he needed to search the car as well. We explained that we hadn't had the car for the entire day. At any rate, after the search, we were both arrested for drug possession. The officer said that he found a minimal amount of marijuana and cocaine residue in the car.

My first instinct was to fight all the charges, no matter how much time and money it took. I felt like we were being targeted for being black and driving a luxury vehicle and that our car had been improperly searched. Just because I don't have my license plates properly affixed doesn't give cause to have my vehicle searched.

But I let it go. I'm no innocent. I've been very open in this book about my occasional use of marijuana. Like most people, I've experimented here and there with lots of things. And although the picture of me painted in the media after my arrest was that of a drug addict, nothing could be farther from the truth.

That minor setback did not stop me one bit. I continued working on the music I was recording in my home studio. Shortly after that drama went down, I signed to Capitol Records and released my fourth studio album, *The First Lady.* This album debuted at number two on the Billboard charts, the highest first-week appearance of my entire career. The album was very well received. It makes me feel good to know that after over a decade in this business, I am still loved and appreciated.

I am still hard at work trying to bring those who are responsible for Big's death to justice. His memory is as strong in my heart and mind as it was the day Roz led me out of that hospital. And I owe it to him and our son to never give up making sure that whoever was responsible is held accountable—no matter what.

I still have a lot of growing to do. God is not through with me yet. I have more books to write, more music to make. I have four children to raise.

And I have to take care of me. There's only one way I can do it all.

I have to keep the faith.

Acknowledgments

I would like to thank God for keeping me through all of life's up and downs, and for giving me the most beautiful children I could ever have asked for.

To my husband, Todd: I love you. Thanks for your support and love. You always told me that the world needs to hear my story!

To my mom, Helene: I've learned a lot from your strength and wisdom. I love you!

To Mae and Bob: Thank you both for being unselfish in the way you've looked out for others. I love you both!

To all my family: Now, I couldn't possibly list every name if I wanted to, but y'all have definitely inspired this memoir in many ways. Thanks to the entire Evans, Arnold, Strain, Calhoun, Kennedy, Scantling, Addision, and Standifer families—you know who you are. Thanks for being real friends.

To my friends: You know who you are. Thanks for being real friends.

Thanks to Reverend Shamberger and Emanuel Baptist Church and Bishop Simmons (RIP) and St. Paul Sop Church.

Shoutout to Brick City, Hillside, Irvington, and my folks in all surrounding areas.

Shoutout to all my LA folks and all my Cali folks.

Thanks to Kiyamma, Bonita, Wendell, and the Griffin family.

Thanks to the Russaw family.

Thanks to the Henry, Hayes, Shamberger, Therlonge, Moore, Jenkins, Wilson, Rawls, Jackson, McGill, Owens, Boxley, Allen, Malachi, Noble, Terry, Flowers, Coleman, Jones, Melton, Ferguson, Carr, Hart, Rushing, Boxton, Givings, Shoemaker, Exxum, Elmore, Arvin, Harrington, Durant, Mincey, and Arvin families.

Thanks to every teacher and mentor who believed in me.

To Aliya King: You are such a joy to work with. Thanks for hanging in there through delays, pregnancies, etc. I appreciate that you get it…and you're a pretty sharp chick! Thanks to your family for their patience.

Thanks to my mom, Cheryl Briggs, Alex Clarke, Stephanie Williams, Rufus Moore, Nino Brown, and Sharon Carswell for the pictures.

Thanks to Sean Combs and family and the staff and artists at Bad Boy Entertainment, past and present…hey, Mama Combs!

Thanks to Voletta Wallace and the Wallace family: Jan, Jahi, T'yanna (hi, stepdaughter!), Wayne Barrow, and Mark Pitts.

Shoutout to my godkids: Charity, Jlann, Naela, Natalya, Giselle, and Nekhi.

Thanks to Hazel Williams, Louise White, Ms. Jenny, Angie Denkins, Dae Interiors, Marsha Burnett, Victoria Mack, Amber Renick, Enoch Williams, Richard Gross, Richard Glass, and Tina Keshishian.

Thanks to every vocalist, musician, writer, engineer, producer, director, photographer, hair and makeup artist, and businessperson who I've ever worked with or been inspired by.

Shoutout to Axel Niehaus, Tony Maserti, Rob Paustian, Prince Charles Alexander, Ben Briggs, Brad Todd, Jaymz Hardy Martin, Ty Holmes, Big Tone, Big Ken, Big Vern, Rico Perez, Big Jelly, Eric Pratt, Butch Turner, and Big 'Los.

Thanks to Karen Thomas, Latoya Smith, Linda Duggins, Carol

Ross, and everyone at Hachette Book Group USA and the Agency Group.

Thanks to Bert Padell, Trevor Baptiste, and everyone at Padell Nadell Fine & Weinberg.

Thanks to Perry Sanders, Rob Frank, Jill Ramsey, Audrey Matheny, Brad Gage, Sergio Robletto, Chris Brizzalara, Capitol Records, Andrew Shack, Andy Slater, Stewart Levy, L. Londell McMillan, Jess Rosen, Arty Erk, Don Cameron, Vincent Dimmock, Drew Findling, Katherine Brewton and Malik Levy at BMI, Rich Murphy, ICM and Dyana Williams, Yvete Lee Bowser, Robi Reed, and Zola Mashariki.

Thanks to all media outlets, DJs, stores, mom-and-pops, radio stations, TV stations, and magazines that have every shown me love.

Shoutout to my fans across the world! It's amazing how God blessed me to touch so many people and I appreciate the support!

To each and every person I've come to meet, work with, or just passed in the street and given love to: God bless you all!

I have learned so much from so many—please know you're in my heart.

Rest in peace: Grandma Helen, my baby sis Rosalyn, Uncle Dock, Uncle Ch, Uncle Mack, Aunt Leola, Aunt Lillian, Uncle Ruben, Aunt Maggie, Billy Jack, and Cedric.

Rest in peace: Bonney, Rahman Peterson, Corey Stewart, Tonya Mincey, Lamont Ford, Jam Master Jay, Rob Guillery, Calvin Melton, Cathy Malachi, Mr. Moe, Mr. Arvin, Mr. Jimmy, Ann Boxton, Chris Maldonado, Eric Spearman, Tony Thompson, Gerald and Sean Levert, and all our fallen angels.

Rest in peace to Christopher "The Notorious B.I.G." Wallace: The world still feels your presence!

About the Author

Faith Evans is a musical icon in her own right, dropping hit records such as *Faith* (1995), *Keep the Faith* (1998), *Faithfully* (2001), and *The First Lady* (2005).

Born and raised in Newark, New Jersey, Faith Evans started her music career as a songwriter for artists like Hi-Five, Mary J. Blige, Pebbles, Al B. Sure, Usher, Tony Thompson, and Christopher Williams. Faith released four albums, all certified gold or platinum. She has also collaborated with music industry legends, including Whitney Houston, Babyface, and Sting.

In addition to her Grammy Award, Faith has received a Soul Train Music Award, two Lady of Soul Awards, and two MTV Video Music Awards. Faith also made an appearance in *The Fighting Temptations*, costarring Beyoncé Knowles and Oscar winner Cuba Gooding Jr.